D0076928

Michael J. Zimmerman

An Essay on Human Action

PETER LANG
New York · Berne · Frankfort on the Main · Nancy

Library of Congress Cataloging in Publication Data

Zimmerman, Michael J., 1951–
An essay on human action.

(American University Studies. Series V, Philosophy,
ISSN 0739-6392; vol. 5)
Revision of thesis (doctoral) – University of
Massachusetts at Amherst, 1979.
Bibliography: p.
Includes index.
1. Act (Philosophy) I. Title. II. Series: American
University Studies. Series V, Philosophy; v. 5.
B105.A35Z56   1984   128'.4   84-47545
ISBN 0-8204-0122-6

CIP-Kurztitelaufnahme der Deutschen Bibliothek

Zimmerman, Michael J.:
An Essay on human action / Michael J. Zimmerman. –
New York; Berne; Frankfort on the Main; Nancy:
Lang, 1984.
(American University Studies: Ser. 5, Philosophy;
Vol. 5)
ISBN 0-8204-0122-6

NE: American University Studies / 05

© Peter Lang Publishing, Inc., New York 1984

All rights reserved.
Reprint or reproduction, even partially, in all forms such as
microfilm, xerography, microfiche, microcard, offset prohibited.

Printed by Lang Druck, Inc., Liebefeld/Berne (Switzerland)

B
/05
.A3√
256
1984

PREFACE

My main purpose in this book is to present a comprehensive, detailed, enlightening, and original theory of human action. When I say that the theory is designed to be comprehensive, I of course do not mean that it deals with all the major issues of so-called action-theory. That would be too large a task to handle responsibly in one book. Rather, I restrict most of my attention to what may be called the core issues of action-theory, and these are: what acting, in general, is (Chapter 4); how actions are to be individuated (Chapter 5); how long actions last (Chapter 5); what acting intentionally is (Chapter 6); what doing one thing by doing another is (Chapter 7); and what omitting to do something is (Chapter 8). Such a comprehensive treatment of the core issues of action-theory is badly needed. Too often these issues have been treated piecemeal in the literature, without any attempt to ensure that what is said about one issue is consistent with what is to be said about another.

In order to make the theory detailed and enlightening, I have adopted a methodology which permits me to investigate the issues at hand with a degree of precision and (after some work on the part of the reader) clarity that I dare say has not been attained before in the area of action-theory. (This is a bold boast, but I think a careful reading of the text will bear it out.) The degree of detail afforded by this approach is unmatched by any other approach of which I am aware. There is a direct correlation between the degree of detail attained by an author and the degree of "demandingness" imposed on the reader. As a result, this is a pretty demanding book, especially in Chapter 1 where preliminary matters are treated in what is perforce a condensed fashion. There are many formal assumptions, definitions, and theorems presented, and some of these take a fair bit of time and effort to work through. But that is the nature of rigorous philosophy. Still, the occasional difficulty and possible wearisomeness of working through such items can be alleviated by presenting along with them rough, English-prose versions to facilitate their digestion, and so this is what I have done on those occasions where it seems helpful to do this.

It is important that a book as demanding as the present one be original. Now, I claim no great originality in approach or broad outline, but originality in either of these respects is neither so desirable nor so feasible in traditional areas of philosophical inquiry (such as the area of action-theory) as in new areas. What is desirable for traditional areas of inquiry is that some main position be worked out thoroughly – that is, in considerable detail – so that one may assess whether or not it is truly defensible (and not just plausible). This is what I attempt to do here. The main position involved is that of the long-standing (and also long-reviled) volitional theory of action, and it is my concern to develop this theory of action in considerable detail. (Of course, there is in reality not just one volitional theory of action, but rather a common, rough idea concerning volitions that underlies an indefinite number of theories.) The considerable detail that I achieve is wherein the considerable originality of this book lies – or so I contend; and in this regard I refer not just to the details of the theory of action worked out in Chapters 4 through 8 but also to the details of the supplementary material. But these details are far too numerous to list here, and so I must leave it to the reader to discover them in the text itself.

What I have called the supplementary material is that contained in chapters other than Chapters 4 through 8. The material in Chapters 1 through 3 is indispensable preliminary material. It sets the stage for the inquiry that follows. In Chapter 1 I present a theory of events on which the ensuing theory of action is based. Chapter 2 is devoted to a statement of the main problems to be addressed. Chapter 3 contains a detailed discussion of certain concepts which feature prominently in the theory that follows. The material in Chapters 9 through 12 is perhaps not indispensable but it is, I hope, instructive. Chapter 9 contains a discussion of certain concepts related to the concept of volition – one of the concepts discussed in Chapter 3. In Chapter 10 I entertain objections to the theory just presented. Finally, in Chapter 11 I present a detailed account of a libertarian theory of free action based on the theory of action presented in preceding chapters, and in Chapter 12 I tentatively defend this account against certain objections. It would be foolish of me to think that what I say in Chapters 10 and 12, when considering objections to what is presented in other chapters, will succeed in rendering these other chapters beyond criticism. No doubt there is still much that may be criticized in my account. But one of the great merits of the methodology that I adopt is that it permits not only a precise presentation of this account but also, in virtue of this, a precise pin-pointing of where it goes wrong, if it does. That is, not only is an exposition of the account facilitated by this methodology, but so too is its evaluation, and it is this above all else which allows for progress in philosophy.

The methodology that I adopt in this book is one that Roderick Chisholm, above all, has developed and refined. It will be apparent to anyone familiar with Chisholm's work that I am enormously indebted to him, not only for the example he furnishes in his employment of this methodology, but also for much of what he has himself achieved by virtue of this employment. His work has been and continues to be a source of great inspiration to me.

This book is an extensive revision and elaboration of my doctoral dissertation, submitted to the University of Massachusetts at Amherst in 1979. Fred Feldman directed the dissertation. The extent to which he helped and advised me on that project was quite extraordinary. His meticulous approach to philosophy is both exacting and exemplary, and I am very grateful to him for the help he gave me.

Terence Horgan also read the dissertation on which this book is based. I am grateful for the many detailed and penetrating comments that he made.

I have discussed the issues with which this book is concerned with many people, and I have profited greatly from these discussions. It is not possible to list all of these people here by name, but I should like to mention in particular Bruce Aune, Paul Bowen, Douglas Husak, Allen Renear, Tom Ryckman, Ernest Sosa, and Sarah Stebbins.

I am grateful to the editor of the *Southern Journal of Philosophy* for permission to reprint parts of my article "Taking Some of the Mystery out of Omissions," which appeared in Volume XIX, Number 4, pp.541-554 of that journal. Chapter 8 is drawn extensively from that article.

Allen Renear helped a great deal in the preparation of the copy, for which I am grateful.

Finally, I thank my wife, Kathy, for her continued and unwavering support of my study of philosophy, support without which this book would not have been written.

To Kate and Sarah

CONTENTS

PART I
EVENTS

Chapter 1

EVENTS AS ABSTRACT ENTITIES

1.1　*INTRODUCTION*

The adequacy of a philosophical theory is in part a function of the degree of success with which it satisfies its author's original intentions. In this chapter I shall draw up a theory of events, and I must state my purpose in so doing if the theory's adequacy is to be assessed.

A theory of events may be drawn up for a variety of reasons, but my purpose here is strictly limited, my motive ulterior. It is the provision of a comprehensive and enlightening theory of human action that is my main goal, and the theory of events which I shall draw up is intended only to provide a basis for such a theory of action. I take it that actions are events. This assumption has sometimes been denied,[1] but I shall not argue for it; one must start somewhere, and the assumption is surely plausible. It will be seen in subsequent chapters that, when accounting for certain features of human action, I shall rely on the theory of events provided in this chapter for an account, first, of what events are, second, of what it is for them to recur, and third, of how they are to be individuated. Hence I shall, for the most part, restrict my attention to these issues in this chapter.

Philosophers have in the past advocated what may appear at times to be a surfeit of theories of events, and some of these theories differ radically one from the other. For example, some philosophers contend that events are coarsely-grained, concrete entities.[2] Some contend that they are finely-grained, concrete entities.[3] Some contend that they are finely-grained, abstract entities.[4] None, so far as I know, contends that they are coarsely-grained, abstract entities. Some, of course, contend that there are no such things as events at all.[5] This seems to exhaust the main alternatives. Which alternative is one to adopt?

One factor which surely acts as a restraint on any philosophical theory is pre-analytic intuition. That a theory conflicts with such intuition is a strike against it. Unfortunately, it seems to me that *any* theory of events drawn up according to one of the main alternatives just outlined will conflict with pre-analytic intuition to *some* extent. This is a point that I shall not try to demonstrate, but I think it can be confirmed by an investigation of any theory of events yet proposed by philosophers. This fact, if it is a fact, suggests two things: first, pre-analytic intuition with respect to the nature of events is inconsistent; second, a theory of events can seek only to minimize any conflict with such intuition, and not to eliminate such conflict entirely. I shall point out the advantages and disadvantages in this respect of the theory of events to be proposed here as and when this becomes pertinent.

Another factor which acts as a restraint on any philosophical theory is ontological economy. Why such economy should be said to be desirable is an issue that I shall not attempt to resolve, but I shall assume that it *is* desirable. Consequently, "bloated ontologies" (to use the current vernacular) are to be avoided if possible. Now, an ontology can be bloated in either of two ways, first with respect to the number of *entities* it posits, and secondly with respect to the number of *types* of entities it posits. It seems to me that bloatedness of the second sort is a far more serious matter than bloatedness of the first sort, and it is only that of the second sort that I shall seek to avoid. It will be seen that the theory of action that I propose in later chapters will presuppose the existence of entities of the following six sorts: individual things, states of affairs, properties and relations, sets, times, and places. I would like to be able to reduce this number, but I do not know how to do so. Nevertheless, I think an account of events *can* be given which does not require the introduction of any radically new type of entity, and it is such an account that I shall try to give here.

A final factor which acts as a restraint on any philosophical theory is clarity of exposition.[6] Such clarity I take to be of two sorts – methodological and conceptual. In trying to achieve clarity of both sorts I shall unabashedly follow the exacting example furnished by Roderick Chisholm, for I know of none better.

By "methodological clarity" I mean clarity as to what philosophical method is being used and what the purpose of this method is. Now, my aim in this chapter is, first, to provide analyses of the concept of an event and of related concepts in terms of certain other, unanalyzed concepts and, second, by means of these analyses, to highlight certain relations between certain of these concepts. The analyses will have the form "$x =$ df. y," where x is the definiendum (that is, it expresses the concept to be analyzed) and y is the definiens (that is, it expresses those concepts in terms of which the analysis is provided). But a word of caution is in order here. Sometimes a claim of the form "$x =$ df. y" is taken to be equivalent to, or at least to imply, the claim that x means the same as y. This is *not*, in general, the way in which I intend such a claim to be understood. For example – and to anticipate a great deal – the final definition that I shall propose is the following:

D.11.17: S is a person at (time) $T =$ df.
　　　　　 (i) S is an individual thing at T ; and
　　　　　 (ii) there are an event e and times T' and T^* such that it is physically possible that S can at T bring about e actively relative to T' and T^*.

Now, I of course do not think that the sentence (call it *a)* that precedes "$=$ df." in D.11.17 means the same as the sentence (call it *b)* that succeeds "$=$ df." What I do think is that (for *one* common sense of "person") *a* expresses a proposition which is strictly equivalent to the proposition expressed by *b* and, moreover, that this equivalence is especially enlightening in that it affords a certain insight into the nature of persons. In general, then, claims of the form "$x =$ df. y" are to be understood to signify something less than outright synonymy; nevertheless, they are intended to help us understand certain common concepts (such as those of a person, an action, an event, and so on) which are philosophically interesting and important. There is one exception to this general rule, however, and this concerns the uses of "$=$ df." where the concept to be analyzed is not what I have called a common concept but is rather what may be called a technical philosophical concept – a variety of philosopher's artifice. For example, at one point I shall propose the following definition:

D.3.6: S broadly wills e at $T =$ df. either
　　　　 (i) S wills e at T ; or
　　　　 (ii) there is an event f such that S wills f at T for the purpose of e.

Now, the concept of broadly willing something is, in a sense, my own invention.[7] Its invocation is intended, in part, to advance the analysis of the common concept of human action, but it is not itself a concept which we commonly invoke. D.3.6 may thus be regarded as a *stipulative* definition, and, in this case, "=df." may be taken to signify synonymy. Now, it must be admitted that it is on occasion difficult to tell when a concept is "common" and when it is "technical," and thus it is on occasion difficult to tell whether or not "=df." is being used stipulatively. However, this is a matter which I shall not investigate here. To pursue it further would be to become embroiled in the issue of the paradox of analysis; it would also necessitate a discussion of the vexing issue of how best to tread that treacherous path which lies between, on the one hand, mere reporting of how certain common concepts *are* used and, on the other hand, more or less arbitrary stipulation as to how these concepts *ought* to be used. All of this lies beyond the purview of the present enterprise, but it represents a limitation to this enterprise which it is only fitting to acknowledge here.[8]

The method of analysis just outlined is itself intended to promote conceptual clarity. Given the truth of "x =df. y," if y is well understood, then x will be well understood; in addition, if we are also given the truth of "z =df....x...," then not only may one come to understand z, but also the relationships between the concept(s) expressed by z and the concept(s) expressed by y are brought into sharp relief. But it should also be noted that, if y is not well understood, then the truth of "x =df. y" will not provide for the understanding of x. Hence, to attain optimum conceptual clarity – that is, to achieve the clearest account possible of those philosophically interesting and important concepts which constitute the focal point of a proposed theory – those unanalyzed concepts with which one begins one's analysis must be as well understood as possible. This is a difficult goal to achieve, however, partly because it frequently happens that a certain unanalyzed concept is well understood by one person but not by another, and partly because it might well be that a certain unanalyzed concept would itself become clearer on analysis – and yet analysis must start somewhere and its initiation cannot be "pushed back" indefinitely. Thus, just which concepts to allow to remain unanalyzed and which not is an issue fraught with difficulties. One way to try to mitigate these difficulties is to invoke as few unanalyzed concepts as possible. But one must beware of being over-eager in one's pursuit of such simplicity, for one relatively obscure unanalyzed concept, while better than two such concepts, is presumably not as helpful as two relatively clear ones. In addition, one should especially avoid, wherever possible, using technical, as opposed to common, concepts as unanalyzed tools of analysis, since it is far less likely that another person will grasp one's own technical concept than that he will understand a concept common to both him and oneself.[9] Nevertheless, this is a very tricky matter, given that the line between technical and common concepts is not always easily drawn – as already mentioned – and also that many common concepts are not at all well understood by many people. But it is best to be honest about these conceptual difficulties, for they are difficulties which beset any attempt at drawing up a philosophical theory. Indeed, it is a distinct virtue of the method of analysis to be employed here – Chisholm's method – that it allows one to determine precisely where it is that the conceptual difficulties lie. As Chisholm has himself remarked on occasion, by stating at the outset which concepts will be used as unanalyzed tools of analysis and then employing "=df." in the manner described above in order to provide analyses of other concepts, one is "laying one's cards on the table for all to see."

1.2   GROUNDWORK

The theory of events that follows owes a very great deal to the theory of events proposed by Chisholm in Chapter 4 of *Person and Object*.[10] I think Chisholm's theory has several defects, but I shall not undertake a detailed critique of it here, although I shall note *en route* some especially pertinent differences between his theory and mine. But, all in all, the points of agreement between my theory and Chisholm's far outnumber the points of disagreement.

Let me first introduce my theory by giving a brief, informal account of the ontology on which it is based. This ontology shares much with Chisholm's but also differs from his in certain respects. The most outstanding feature of Chisholm's ontology – one which I incorporate wholeheartedly into mine – is that events are said to be proposition-like entities. Chisholm is impressed by the fact of recurrence. It is a datum of pre-analytic intuition concerning events – hence something that it is *prima facie* desirable to include in a philosophical theory of events – that certain events may recur, that is, may occur more than once. For instance, it is certainly true that the sun has shone more than once. Now, it is generally agreed that, if events were particulars, none could recur.[11] If this is so, and if events are particulars, then our pre-analytic intuition misleads us. Several philosophers have asserted that this is indeed the case and that, for example, the sun's shining yesterday is one event and its shining today is another and that the so-called "recurrence" of the sun's shining is to be accounted for simply by pointing out that these two distinct, particular events share a certain special property. But Chisholm takes a different tack. Why not, he asks, simply say that one and the same event, namely, the sun's shining, occurred both yesterday and today? If we are to say this, and if we are to avoid (as Chisholm seems to think desirable) saying that one and the same thing can go out of and then come back into existence, then we must distinguish the occurrence of an event from its existence.[12] That is, we seem obliged to say that, although the sun's shining occurred yesterday, did not occur last night, and recurred today, it existed throughout this period. But there is precedent for this. Ever since Plato's probing of non-being in the *Sophist*, philosophers have pondered how it is possible to think about things which apparently do not exist. At least with respect to propositions, Chisholm proposes to dissolve this puzzle by noting that, by distinguishing the truth of a proposition from its existence and its falsity from its non-existence, there is no need to deny the apparently obvious fact that people entertain false propositions.[13] For, in so doing, people are not related to things which do not exist; rather, they are related to things which exist but which lack the property of truth. Similarly, Chisholm would say, last night the sun's shining existed, but it lacked the property of occurrence.[14] In fact, Chisholm takes this analogy one step further and says that events and propositions are (mutually exclusive) subspecies of the species of states of affairs and that truth just *is* occurrence.[15]

I propose to follow Chisholm's lead here and to provide an analysis of the concept of an event according to which events constitute a subspecies of entities (namely, states of affairs) of which propositions also constitute a subspecies. My primary purpose in so doing is to achieve the sort of ontological economy which I have already said I take to be desirable; it is an added benefit that certain pre-analytic intuitions are thereby accommodated, although it must also be admitted that some such intuitions fail to be satisfied thereby. These matters will be noted in more detail and in due course below.

The other entities which figure irreducibly in the ontology I presuppose are relations (and properties), individual things, sets, times, and places. Now Chisholm's ontology differs here, in that it shuns the last three types of entity just mentioned. In *Person and Object* Chisholm does mention sets, times, and places. But, first, with respect to sets, he claims that these are "reducible" to properties (that is, they may be shown to be a kind of property). He does not seek to prove the truth of this claim, however, and I am not persuaded that it is true. Consequently, though somewhat reluctantly, I shall take the cautious course here of accepting that sets constitute a distinct basic type of existent. As for times and places, nowhere in *Person and Object* does Chisholm claim, let alone seek to show, that they are reducible to existents of any other basic type. Now, I am not at all confident that such a claim can be proven true, and so once again I reluctantly take the cautious course here of accepting that times and places constitute distinct basic types of existents.[1][6]

I turn now to a formal presentation of the theory of events to be presupposed in later chapters. In presenting this theory I shall make use of the following unanalyzed concepts: the concepts of a state of affairs, a relation (a property being a monadic relation), an individual thing, a set, a time, a place, existence, existence-in, occurrence, exemplification-at, membership, metaphysical necessity, physical necessity, consideration, acceptance, and being-earlier-than. I shall also appeal to the "logical" concepts of negation and material implication, in terms of which the concepts of conjunction and disjunction may be conventionally analyzed. This is a fairly long list, but I think it can be made shorter only at considerable expense to conceptual clarity. Nevertheless, the list as it stands is certainly not free from conceptual obscurity, and certain comments on it are in order here.

I assume that: states of affairs, relations (and properties), times, and places exist necessarily; individual things do not exist necessarily; and sets, if they have any members at all, exist if and only if their members exist (for the sake of convenience, we may suppose that the null set exists necessarily). By "necessarily" here I intend to express what I have called metaphysical necessity – that sort of necessity which some call logical necessity and which is often expressed nowadays in terms of "truth in all possible worlds."[17] (In general, I shall drop the "metaphysically" from "metaphysically necessary.") Physical necessity I take to be that which others have recently expressed in terms of "truth in all possible worlds with the same (natural) laws as the actual world." For both types of necessity I shall follow convention and accept that it is possible that a state of affairs occur if and only if it is not necessary that it not occur.

A time may be a period or a moment; a place may be an area or a point. I shall thus use "time" and "place" somewhat liberally. I shall not attempt to reduce periods to moments, or *vice versa*, or areas to points, or *vice versa*. Any such project is, I think, fraught with difficulties, and I shall simply side-step the issue here.

Chisholm talks of exemplification and takes it to be a relation that holds between things and properties. (He uses "thing," as I shall use it, as a generic term which refers to entities of all types.) But I shall talk of exemplification-at and shall take this to be a relation that holds between things, properties, and times. The reason for this is important. It allows me to dispense with complications concerning tense. In *Person and Object* Chisholm at times apparently takes tense seriously, but at times he apparently does not.[18] Briefly, and roughly, one takes tense seriously if and only if one uses and understands phrases in such a manner that the meanings of the phrases are taken to be contingent in part on the tense or tenses in which the phrases are couched. For instance, when tense is taken seriously, the phrase "*s* occurs" means the same as the phrase "*s* occurs now," and its truth does not imply and is not implied by the facts that *s* did occur or will occur. But when tense is not taken seriously, the truth of the phrase "*s* occurs" does *not* imply the fact that *s* occurs now, although it *is* implied by each of the facts that *s* did occur, does occur now, and will occur. There is a marked difference, then, between these two treatments of tense. Note that, when tense is not taken seriously, it seems to be the usual practice to use verbs as if they were in the present tense. Now, all of Chisholm's definitions and assumptions in *Person and Object* are couched in the form of the present tense, and so for each such definition and assumption the question arises as to whether or not tense is treated seriously in it. In *Person and Object* Chisholm makes no explicit comment on this matter, and in fact his treatment of tense in this book, as mentioned, appears inconsistent. Consider, for instance, the following assumption: for every state of affairs *s*, there is a state of affairs *t* which is necessarily such that *s* occurs if and only if *t* does not occur.[1 9] Chisholm says that any such states of affairs *s* and *t* *contradict* one another. Clearly, prime candidates for such contradictory states of affairs are, for example, Socrates's being alive and Socrates's being dead. But notice that, in the absence of any mention of times, these two states of affairs do *not* satisfy Chisholm's formula *unless* tense is taken seriously in that formula. For it may of course be that Socrates's being alive (tenselessly) occurs at some time *T1* and Socrates's being dead (tenselessly) occurs at some other time *T2*. But if tense is taken seriously in the formula and "occurs" is understood to mean the same as "occurs *now*," then this problem does not arise. For it is of course impossible that Socrates's being alive and Socrates's being dead should both occur *now*.[2 0]

But now consider the following definition provided by Chisholm: *p* is a proposition =df. *p* is a state of affairs and it is impossible that there be a time *T* and a time *T'* such that *p* occurs at *T* and does not occur at *T'*.[2 1] Surely tense is *not* taken seriously in this definition. When times are specified as they are in the definiens, it is the usual practice to take those verbs associated with the times to be used tenselessly. Indeed, if tense is used seriously in a phrase of the form "*p* occurs at *T*," especially where "*T*" refers either to a past time or to a future time, then the phrase has no clear sense.[2 2]

This problem concerning how tense is used by Chisholm in *Person and Object* in fact infects many of the definitions and assumptions that he provides. The problem arises, it seems to me, mainly because Chisholm does not wish to commit himself to the existence of times as irreducible entities. Since I assume here that times do exist and that they do constitute a basic type of existent, the problem may be avoided. Throughout this work I shall *not* take tense seriously. Locutions involving the specification of times may be handled first of all by appealing to the concept of exemplification-at. That is, we may start by saying that a state of affairs occurs at a time just in case it exemplifies occurrence at that time. Or, more formally (where "*s*" ranges over states of affairs and "*T*" over times):

D.1.1:   *s* occurs at *T* =df. *s* exemplifies occurrence at *T*.

And we may safely assume that whatever occurs necessarily (with respect to both metaphysical and physical necessity) occurs at all times. (This point does not hold *vice versa*, of course.) Also, we may assume that, if it is metaphysically necessary that a state of affairs *s* occur, then it is physically necessary that *s* occur. (Again, this point does not hold *vice versa*.)

Now, before going on to show how it is that D.1.1 may be used to handle other locutions involving the specification of times, a certain typographic convention that I shall adopt should be explicitly noted. I have already designated one state of affairs by means of the phrase "the sun's shining." In *Person and Object* Chisholm tends to use gerundial nominalizations such as "the sun shining" for the same purpose. Either practice runs into trouble, I think, when designations of states of affairs are embedded within designations, or designations within variables, or variables within variables. For clarity of exposition I shall make use of square brackets surrounding sentences or sentence-variables where Chisholm uses gerundial nominalizations. So, instead of "the sun's shining" or "the sun shining" I shall write "[the sun shines]"; or again, instead of "Socrates's being alive" or "Socrates being alive" I shall write "[Socrates is alive]"; similarly, instead of "*x*'s shining" or "*x* shining" I shall write "[*x* shines]"; and so on. Examples of the sort of embedding just mentioned are: "[Smith considers [the sun shines]]," "[Smith considers [*x* shines]]," or (where "*S*" ranges over persons) "[*S* considers [*x* shines]]," and so on.[2][3] In short, I shall use square brackets to highlight a distinction between use and mention or, as I should prefer to say in the present context, a distinction between expression and designation. Thus, by writing "the sun shines" I mean to express that state of affairs which may be perspicuously designated by means of "[the sun shines]."

Given this use of square brackets, we may now make the following definitions on the basis of D.1.1:

D.1.2:   *x* exists at *T* =df. [*x* exists] occurs at *T* ;

D.1.3:   *S* accepts *p* at *T* =df. [*S* accepts *p*] occurs at *T* ;

and so on for the concepts of consideration at (a time), existing in (a place) at (a time), and being a member at (a time).

I said above that all states of affairs exist necessarily; this is *not* to say that all states of affairs *occur* necessarily. Chisholm sometimes makes this point by saying that all states of affairs are "eternal objects," although only some are "necessary" – *i.e.*, occur necessarily (an example of such a state of affairs is [there are no round squares]); some, indeed, are "impossible" – *i.e.*, necessarily fail to occur (an example of such a state of affairs is [there are round squares]); the rest are "contingent" (one example being [the sun shines]). Analogous remarks may be made concerning properties and relations, which, again, I have said exist necessarily. For instance, where italicizing with respect to phrases expressing properties or relations performs the same function as square brackets do with respect to phrases expressing states of affairs, we may say that the property *being either round or nonround* is necessary, the property *being round and nonround* is impossible, and the property *shining* is contingent.[2][4]

Whatever occurs, then, is a state of affairs, and whatever is exemplified at a time is a relation or property. It should also be pointed out explicitly that: the relata of existence-in are individual things and places; the relata of membership are things and sets; the relata of consideration are persons and things; and being-earlier-than (a relation which I assume to be both transitive and asymmetrical) relates times to times. The concepts of consideration and acceptance deserve some comment.

I take consideration simply to be thinking about something, and I assume that anything may be thought about. Chisholm sometimes uses the term "entertainment" instead of "consideration" and limits the objects of entertainment to states of affairs, but such limitation seems to render the concept unduly technical. However, whereas Chisholm seems to be too conservative with respect to the objects of consideration, he seems at first sight to be too liberal with respect to the objects of acceptance. As Chisholm does, I take accepting something simply to be believing it (or believing it to be true). But Chisholm has taken acceptability to be the mark of states of affairs in general. Indeed, he has proposed: *s* is a state of affairs =df. it

is possible that there be someone who accepts *s*.[25] But while it is
clear that only states of affairs can be accepted, it is not at all clear
that all states of affairs can be.[26] Actually, Chisholm would defend
the definition just cited by pointing out that in it he means to take
tense seriously; in particular, any substitution for *s* would be a designation of a state of affairs in which tense is taken seriously.
Thus, for instance, if [the sun shines] is taken to be the same state
of affairs as [the sun shines now], it seems that it is open to acceptance by someone. On the other hand, if in "[the sun shines]" tense
is *not* taken seriously – and, to repeat, I shall not take tense seriously in this work – it seems not to be a proper candidate for acceptance, given the absence of any specification of a time at which
the sun is believed to shine. But if such a time *is* specified – as time
T1, say – then the state of affairs in question (namely, [the sun
shines at *T1*]) clearly is open to acceptance. But in such a case the
state of affairs seems to be of a particular sort – and I shall call
states of affairs of this sort *propositions* – and not all states of affairs are of this sort.[27] Henceforth, then, I shall adopt the more
traditional view and assume that the objects of acceptance, or belief,
are and can only be propositions.[28] Beyond saying that acceptance
is a propositional attitude, I shall have nothing enlightening to say
concerning the concept *except* that I mean by "acceptance" what has
come to be called, by many, *dispositional* belief and *not* what has
come to be called *occurrent* belief.[29] Occurrent belief, I take it, is a
matter of accepting *and* considering a proposition at the same time;
I assume that, in general, accepting a proposition does not require
considering it.[30]

Some preliminary comments must be made on the conjunction
and negation of states of affairs and properties or relations, and
also on related matters. In addition to the assumptions already
made, and made somewhat informally, above, I shall assume the
following: first, that, for every property or relation, some state of
affairs occurs just in case it is exemplified and some state of affairs
occurs just in case it is not exemplified; second, that every state of
affairs has a negation; third, that every two states of affairs have a
conjunction; fourth, that every property or relation has a negation;
and fifth, that every two properties or relations have a conjunction.
Or more precisely, where times are specified (and it is crucial, for
precision's sake, that they be specified):

A.1.1:   Necessarily, for any property or relation *F*, there are states of affairs *s* and *t* such that, for any time *T*, *s* occurs at *T* if and only if *F* is exemplified at *T* and *t* occurs at *T* if and only if *F* is not exemplified at *T*.[3] [1]

A.1.2:   Necessarily, for any state of affairs *s*, there is a state of affairs *t* such that, for any time *T*, *s* occurs at *T* if and only if *t* does not occur at *T*.[3] [2]

A.1.3:   Necessarily, for any distinct states of affairs *s* and *t*, there is a state of affairs *u* such that, for any times *T* and *T'*, *u* occurs at *T* and *T'* if and only if *s* occurs at *T* and *t* occurs at *T'*.[3] [3]

A.1.4:   Necessarily, for any property or relation *F*, there is a property or relation *G* such that, for any time *T*, *F* is exemplified at *T* if and only if *G* is not exemplified at *T*.

A.1.5:   Necessarily, for any distinct properties or relations *F* and *G*, there is a property or relation *H* such that, for any times *T* and *T'*, *H* is exemplified at *T* and *T'* if and only if *F* is exemplified at *T* and *G* is exemplified at *T'*.

We may say that, in A.1.2, *s* and *t* *contradict* one another, and that, in A.1.4, *F* and *G* *contradict* one another. Similarly, we may say that, in A.1.3, *u* is *a conjunction of s* and *t*, and that, in A.1.5, *H* is *a conjunction of F* and *G*. In the same spirit, assumptions concerning disjunctive and conditional states of affairs and disjunctive and conditional properties or relations may be drawn up, but I shall forgo that task here.

Notice that, while it is correct to say that, in A.1.2, *s* and *t* contradict one another, it would be incorrect to say either that *s* is *the negation of t* or that *t* is *the negation of s.* (This point holds analogously for *F* and *G* in A.1.4.) For [two and two are four] and [two and two are five] contradict one another, but presumably neither is the negation of the other. It would seem that the negation of [two and two are four] is [two and two are not four], and that the former is also the negation of the latter. To capture the concept of negation with respect to states of affairs, we may, I think, say the following:[3] [4]

D.1.4:   *s* involves *t* =df. Necessarily, for any time *T*, whoever considers *s* at *T* also considers *t* at *T*.

D.1.5:   *s* properly involves *t* =df. *s* involves *t* and *t* does not involve *s*.

D.1.6:   *s* explicitly denies *t* =df. *s* contradicts *t* and also properly involves only *t* and what *t* involves.

D.1.7:   *s* is the negation of *t* =df. either *s* explicitly denies *t* or *t* explicitly denies *s*.

Note that, given D.1.7, the relation of being-the-negation-of is symmetrical. Examples of mutual negations are: [two and two are four] and [two and two are not four]; [the sun shines] and [the sun does not shine]; and so on.

Chisholm relies on a very "strong" analysis of the concept of the entailment of one state of affairs by another. He proposes: *s* entails *t* =df. *s* is necessarily such that (i) if it obtains then *t* obtains and (ii) whoever accepts it accepts *t*.[3] [5] I shall again follow Chisholm's lead here. In order to avoid problems concerning tense, and the concomitant problem concerning the possibility of accepting a state of affairs which is not a proposition, I propose to proceed as follows:

D.1.8:   *s* strictly implies *t* =df. Necessarily, for any time *T*, if *s* occurs at *T*, then *t* occurs at *T*.

We may then say that one state of affairs entails another just in case the former strictly implies the latter and the former is such that whoever accepts it accepts the latter. Or more precisely:

D.1.9:   *s* entails *t* =df.
      (i) *s* strictly implies *t* ; and
      (ii) necessarily, for any time *T*, whoever accepts that *s* occurs at *T* accepts that *t* occurs at *T*.

And then, with respect to properties or relations, we may say:

D.1.10:   *F* entails *G* =df. for any thing *x* and any time *T*, [*x* exemplifies *F* at *T*] entails [*x* exemplifies *G* at *T*].

The concepts of entailment analyzed in D.1.9 and D.1.10 can be used to furnish us with identity-criteria for states of affairs and properties or relations. These are based simply on mutual entailment:

A.1.6:   Necessarily, for any state of affairs *s* and any state of affairs *t*, *s* is identical with *t* if and only if *s* entails *t* and *t* entails *s*.[3][6]

A.1.7:   Necessarily, for any property or relation *F* and any property or relation *G*, *F* is identical with *G* if and only if *F* entails *G* and *G* entails *F*.

Notice that these criteria are metaphysical, and not epistemological, in nature, in that they are not primarily intended to facilitate decisions, on particular occasions, as to whether or not a state of affairs *s* is identical with a state of affairs *t* or whether or not a property or relation *F* is identical with a property or relation *G*. While on the subject, we may give identity-criteria for the rest of our basic ontological types. The bases for these are as follows: for individual things, existence in the same place; for sets, identity of membership; for times, identity of objects that exist at these times; and for places, identity of objects that exist in these places. In particular, we may say:

A.1.8:   Necessarily, for any individual thing x and any
            individual thing y, x is identical with y if and only
            if, necessarily, for any place P, x exists in P if
            and only if y exists in P.[3][7]

A.1.9:   Necessarily, for any set X and any set Y, X is
            identical with Y if and only if, necessarily, for
            any thing x, x is a member of X if and only if x is
            a member of Y.

A.1.10:   Necessarily, for any time T and any time T', T is
            identical with T' if and only if, necessarily, for
            any thing x, x exists at T if and only if x exists at
            T'.

A.1.11:   Necessarily, for any place P and any place P', P
            is identical with P' if and only if, necessarily, for
            any thing x, x exists in P if and only if x exists in
            P'.

Just as A.1.2 and A.1.4 do not capture the concept of being-*the*-
negation-of, but only of contradiction, so too A.1.3 and A.1.5 do not
capture the concept of being-*the*-conjunction-of, but only of being-*a*-
conjunction-of. But here D.1.9 can be put to use, for we can say,
roughly, that one state of affairs is *the* conjunction of two others just
in case it is a "minimal" conjunction of them. More precisely:

D.1.11: u is the conjunction of s and t =df.
            (i) u entails s ;
            (ii) u entails t ;
            (iii) s does not entail t ;
            (iv) t does not entail s ; and
            (v) for any state of affairs v, if v entails both s
            and t, then v entails u.

An example of such conjunction is [[John is tall] and [Mary is short]], which is the conjunction of [John is tall] and [Mary is short]. Similar examples may be concocted. (Whenever a state of affairs *u* is the conjunction of states of affairs *s* and *t*, an acceptable and more revealing name for *u* is "[*s* and *t*].") In like manner, the matters of one property or relation being the conjunction of other properties or relations, one state of affairs being the disjunction of other states of affairs, and so on, may be treated.

D.1.4 and D.1.9 have what some may regard as an objectionable aspect in that they both concern a claim of the form "Necessarily, if *S* has mental attitude *m* to *s*, then *S* also has *m* to *t*." For instance, concerning Chisholm's analysis of the concept of entailment, Jaegwon Kim says:

> But the second condition [of Chisholm's definition of "entailment"] gives rise to a host of problems: the main problem is how we are supposed to apply it to particular cases. Is it the case, for example, that whoever accepts 2 and 2 being 4 also accepts 4 being 2 and 2? What about 2 and 2 being 4 and 2 times 2 being 4? How are we supposed to decide? More generally, who are the cognitive beings we should consider here? What cognitive powers, in particular what logical powers, are to be ascribed to them? Should we consider only "rational beings" in some idealized or normative sense of "rational" or should we also consider flesh-and-blood ordinary human beings?[3][8]

But, while I have some sympathy with Kim on this matter, I think his remarks are essentially misguided. It seems clear that the cognitive beings Chisholm has in mind are ordinary human beings, indeed persons. It is not so clear whether Chisholm believes such beings to have a minimal capacity for rational thinking. (I am sure that he would not wish to rule out the possibility that such beings have some inconsistent beliefs; and obviously he thinks such beings are capable of believing a necessarily false proposition.) Now, my treatment of the subjects of the mental attitudes of consideration and acceptance mirrors Chisholm's in this regard. (For instance, I

take such subjects to be capable of holding inconsistent beliefs.)
None of this provides any grist for Kim's mill, however, for it seems
to me that he confuses a metaphysical matter with an epistemological one. That is, for instance, D.1.9 is not intended as a criterion
by which one might *decide* in particular cases whether or not one
state of affairs entails another. (It is for this reason that I called
A.1.6 and A.1.7 metaphysical, and not epistemological, criteria.)
Rather D.1.9 is presented simply as an analysis of the concept of
such entailment, and it seems to me to be satisfactory in this regard. After all, it makes no use of any terms not included in the
original vocabulary or defined therefrom. Of course, with respect to
D.1.9, there is an alternative course that one might follow here if
one thinks that claims of the form "Necessarily, if S has mental attitude m to s, then S also has m to t" are unduly obscure, and that
is simply to take the concept of entailment as primitive along with
the concepts of acceptance, necessity, and material implication
(while noting in an assumption that entailment involves strict implication, as recorded in clause (i) of D.1.9). I have no real quarrel
with taking this course, except to note that it fails to draw the connection between the concepts of entailment and acceptance that I
think it is plausible to draw.[39] On the other hand, it should be noted that no such easy alternative suggests itself with respect to
D.1.4 and the technical concept of involvement, a concept which
features prominently in several of the definitions to follow.

   With this groundwork out of the way, we may now focus our attention more sharply on the particular problems that immediately
concern us here – how to characterize events and how to count
them. These problems will be the subject-matter of the next three
sections.

1.3   *EVENTS AS A SPECIES OF STATES OF AFFAIRS*

   What are we to say about events? Chisholm says that they are
not propositions, and I agree. Accordingly, we require a definition
of "proposition," and I propose that we accept the following:

D.1.12: p is a proposition =df.
            (i) p is a state of affairs; and

(ii) it is impossible that there be a time T and a time T' such that p occurs at T and does not occur at T'.[40]

I also share Chisholm's intuition that such "contrived" states of affairs as [Jones is such that Smith walks], [[John is tall] or [Mary is short]], [John is such that he has walked], and so forth, ought not to be ranked as events. Providing a definition adequate to the ruling out of all such contrived states of affairs but adequate also to the ruling in of all events properly so called is, however, a fairly formidable task. Some preliminary definitions are required.

I think the thing to notice about events – what distinguishes them from other sorts of states of affairs – is that they "directly concern," in some sense, "straightforward" properties of individual things. For instance, [Socrates walks] "directly concerns" the "straightforward" property *walking,* whereas [Socrates is such that Plato walks] does not "directly concern" any such "straightforward" property. It seems to me that the way to capture these two notions of "direct concern" and "straightforwardness" is as follows. First of all we need an analysis of the concept of a simple property, a property which is neither negative, nor conjunctive, nor disjunctive, nor conditional. Unfortunately, we therefore require all of the following:[41]

D.1.13: F involves G = df. for any time T, [F is exemplified at T] involves [G is exemplified at T].

D.1.14: F properly involves G = df. F involves G and G does not involve F.

D.1.15: F is negative = df. there is a property G such that:
(i) F properly involves G; and
(ii) necessarily, for any time T, F is exemplified at T if and only if G is not exemplified at T.

D.1.16:   *F* is conjunctive =df. there are properties *G* and
           H such that:
           (i) *F* properly involves both *G* and *H* ;
           (ii) *G* does not entail *H* ;
           (iii) *H* does not entail *G* ; and
           (iv) necessarily, for any time *T*, *F* is exemplified
           at *T* if and only if both *G* and *H* are exemplified
           at *T*.

D.1.17:   *F* is disjunctive =df. there are properties *G* and *H*
           such that:
           (i) *F* properly involves both *G* and *H* ;
           (ii) *G* does not entail *H* ;
           (iii) *H* does not entail *G* ; and
           (iv) necessarily, for any time *T*, *F* is exemplified
           at *T* if and only if either *G* or *H* is exemplified at
           T.

D.1.18:   *F* is conditional =df. there are properties *G* and
           H such that:
           (i) *F* properly involves both *G* and *H* ;
           (ii) *G* does not entail *H* ;
           (iii) *H* does not entail *G* ; and
           (iv) necessarily, for any time *T*, *F* is exemplified
           at *T* if and only if either
               (a) *G* is exemplified at *T* only if *H* is exem-
           plified at *T*, or
               (b) *H* is exemplified at *T* only if *G* is exem-
           plified at *T*.

We may then say:

D.1.19:   *F* is simple =df. *F* is neither negative, nor con-
           junctive, nor disjunctive, nor conditional.

   Simplicity is not the only mark of "straightforward" properties,
however. Such properties must also not be such that it is possible

that everything may exemplify them. That is, they must not be universalizable, where:

D.1.20: F is universalizable =df. it is possible that, for some time T, everything that exists at T has F at T.

Moreover, such properties must not be had (*i.e.*, exemplified) essentially by whatever has them, where:

D.1.21: F is essential =df. necessarily, for any thing x and any time T, if x exists at T and has F at T, then there is no time T' such that x exists at T' and does not have F at T'.

Finally, "straightforward" properties must not have certain types of implication regarding past or future exemplifications. In order to clarify what types of implication are acceptable in this respect and what types are not, we require the concept of one property being a "reflection" of another, that is, of one property being such that, if it is exemplified, then another has been or will be exemplified. More precisely:

D.1.22: F is a reflection of G =df.
    (i) F is distinct from G ; and
    (ii) necessarily, for any thing x and any time T, if x exemplifies F at T, then there is a time T' distinct from T such that x exemplifies G at T'.

We may also say:

D.1.23: F is reflective =df. there is a property G such that F is a reflection of G.

Now, we cannot simply claim that all "straightforward" properties are not reflective, for there are a few special properties, such as those of *dying, finishing a book,* and so forth, that are intuitively "straightforward" and are also reflective. What can be said about these special properties? It seems to me that any such property is exemplified by a thing, x, if and only if it is necessarily the case that there was a time at which x did not exemplify it. And so I propose:

D.1.24: F is emergent =df. necessarily, for any thing x and any time T, if x exemplifies F at T, then there is a time T' earlier than T such that x does not exemplify F at T'.[4][2]

I think that we now have all the equipment we need to characterize the concept of a "straightforward" property. Such a property is simple, non-universalizable, non-essential, and either reflective or emergent. What of an event's "directly concerning" such a property? Roughly, what this amounts to is, I think, that an event occurs just in case something has a property which entails a straightforward property. More precisely, I believe that the following definition adequately captures the concept of an event:

D.1.25: e is an event =df. e is a state of affairs such that:

(i) e is not a proposition; and

(ii) there is a property F such that

(a) necessarily, for any state of affairs s, s entails e if and only if s entails [there is something which is F],

(b) necessarily, for any thing x and any time T, if x exemplifies F at T, then x is an individual thing,

(c) for any time T, it is possible that nothing exemplifies F at T, and

(d) there is a property G such that

(1) F entails G,

(2) G is simple,

(3) G is not universalizable,

(4) G is not essential, and

(5) either G is not reflective or G is emergent.

Let us run this through a few test cases. Consider, first, the case where e is [two and two are four]. Is this an event? No, it is a proposition, and thus ruled out by clause (i) of D.1.25. What, then, of the case where *e* is [Jones is such that Smith walks]? I believe that there is no candidate for the property *G* in this case. (In particular, any otherwise likely-looking candidate will fail either clause (ii)(d)(3) – as does *being such that Smith walks* – or clause (ii)(d)(4) – as do *being Jones* and *being an individual thing.*) Hence *e*, in this case, is not an event. So too with the case where *e* is [Jones is such that he has walked]. (Any otherwise likely-looking candidate for *G* in this case will fail either clause (ii)(d)(4) – as do *being Jones* and *being an individual thing* – or clause (ii)(d)(5) – as does *being such that he has walked.*)

Some states of affairs, nevertheless, are events, according to D.1.25. Consider the state of affairs [Socrates dies]. One property which satisfies what is required of *F* in this case is *being such that he is Socrates and is dying*. Now, *F* entails *(being such that he is) dying*, which is simple, non-universalizable, non-essential, and emergent; thus what is required of *G* is satisfied. Hence [Socrates dies] is an event.[4][3]

Or consider the state of affairs [Smith washes his car]. One candidate for *F* in this case is *being such that he is Smith and is washing his car*. One candidate for *G* is *(being such that he is) washing his car*, for this property is entailed by *F* and is simple, non-universalizable, non-essential, and non-reflective. Hence [Smith washes his car] is an event.

But D.1.25 also rules out certain states of affairs as events that some may consider to be events and rules in certain states of affairs as events that some may consider not to be events. For instance, the requirement that *G* be non-essential rules out [Jones is Jones] as an event, and this seems right.[4][4] But it also appears to rule out [there are horses] as an event. Is the latter an event? I am not sure that it is. But if it is, D.1.25 could, I think, be modified so that it rules [there are horses] in while still ruling [Jones is Jones] out. But I shall not undertake such modification here.[4][5] D.1.25 also rules in as events such conjunctive states of affairs as [[Smith washes his car] and [two and two are four]]. I am not sure that this is not an event; but if it is not, D.1.25 could, I think, be modified so as to rule it out. Once again, however, I shall not undertake such modification here.[4][6] Moreover, it might be objected that D.1.25 takes no account of the phenomenon of change or transition, and that this is essential to a state of affairs' being an event.

For instance, it may be protested that, according to D.1.25, [Socrates sits] is an event, but that since, to put it very loosely, nothing (much) happens when Socrates is sitting, [Socrates sits] should *not* be said to be an event. I have some sympathy with the intuition underlying this protestation. It is generally recognized that, in some prominent sense of "event," all events involve change. Some insist that this is the only proper use of the term.[47] Others allow for a broader use.[48] I side with the latter, and D.1.25 is testimony to this. However, I think that the concept of an event which essentially involves change is an important one, and I believe that an analysis of this concept could be given in terms of D.1.25. But I shall not undertake this analysis here.[49] For notice that actions need *not* involve change. Think of a guard's standing to attention and maintaining his position for two hours; it is clearly appropriate to say, in some prominent sense of "act," that the guard acts simply by virtue of maintaining his position. Hence it would not be in keeping with my original purpose of providing a theory of events to insist that all events involve change – not if, as assumed, all actions are events.

Finally, it should be noted that events may not only occur but may also *"take place"* in the sense that a particular location is to be associated with them whenever they do occur. It is desirable that this notion of taking place be made more precise. In this connection, I shall again follow Chisholm's lead to some extent.[50] Let us say, first of all, the following, in the spirit of D.1.9 and D.1.10:

D.1.26:   *s* entails *F* =df. necessarily, for any person *S* and
           any times *T* and *T'*:
           (i) if *s* occurs at *T*, then *F* is exemplified at *T* ;
           and
           (ii) if *S* accepts [*s* occurs at *T*] at *T'*, then *S* accepts [*F* is exemplified at *T*] at *T'*.

Let us also say:

D.1.27:   *Y* is a proper subset of *X* =df.
           (i) every member of *Y* is a member of *X* ; and
           (ii) some member of *X* is not a member of *Y*.

Given these definitions, we may move on to an analysis of the concept of concretization and of the concept of taking place. Roughly, we may say that a set concretizes a state of affairs just in case the set is the smallest set which is such that some member of it has every property exemplifiable only by individual things and entailed by the state of affairs in question. And then we may say that a state of affairs takes place just where the members of its concretizing set are. More precisely:

D.1.28: X concretizes s at T = df.
      (i) X is a set;
      (ii) s occurs at T ;
      (iii) for every property F, if s entails F and it is not possible that something other than an individual thing exemplify F, then some member of X has F at T ; and
      (iv) there is no proper subset Y of X such that, for every property F which s entails and which it is not possible for something other than an individual thing to exemplify, some member of Y has F at T.[5][1]

D.1.29: s takes place at T in $P1,...,Pn$ = df. there is a set X such that:
      (i) X concretizes s at T ; and
      (ii) for every place P, if P is identical with $P1$, or..., or P is identical with Pn, then some member of X exists in P at T.[5][2]

It follows from the foregoing definitions that every event is such that, if ever and whenever it occurs, it takes place in some place or places.

1.4   *RECURRENCE*

Assuming that what has just been said succeeds in capturing the identifying characteristics of an event, we may now turn our attention to the second main question that concerns us here, and that has to do with the counting of events. How are we to explicate the concept of recurrence? What is it for an event to occur once, twice, or any number of times? In *Person and Object* Chisholm seems to think that, roughly, an event occurs once at every time and place at which it has been in some sense "completed." If this is Chisholm's insight, it is one with which I am in rough agreement. However, in his analysis of the concept of recurrence,[5][3] Chisholm seems to be committed to the view that *cessation* is the mark of completion. While this does seem to be the case with certain types of events (such as the event [rain falls], which occurs once at every time and place at which it ceases to occur), it is *not* the case with certain other types of events. Consider, for instance, the event [Jones walks around the block]. Such an event may occur several times *in succession*; Jones may walk around the block once and then *continue* to walk around the block. Chisholm's analysis appears to be inadequate to this fact.[5][4] Now, Chisholm is aware of this sort of objection, and his response amounts to this: [Jones walks around the block], in this context, is "better described" as [Jones completes his walking around the block], and this latter event occurs once at every time and place at which it ceases to occur.[5][5] But this response is unsatisfactory. First of all, it is false that [Jones walks around the block] is better described, in any context, as [Jones completes his walking around the block]. For this latter event, it seems to me, is the same event as [Jones walks around the block once], and this is certainly distinct from the event [Jones walks around the block].[5][6] Secondly, while it may be true that [Jones walks around the block] occurs once at every time and place at which [Jones walks around the block once] occurs, and that this latter event itself occurs once at every time and place at which it ceases to occur, pointing this out is hardly helpful to us in our attempt to come to understand the expression "Jones walked once around the block."

Cessation, then, is sometimes, but not always, the mark of completion. It fails to be the mark of completion with respect to events like [Jones walks around the block], [Smith swims a lap], and so forth, for these events may occur more than once in succession. Now, it seems to me that every event which can happen more than once in succession involves a "measure" of some sort; the measure may be a block, a lap, a mile, or whatever. Moreover, measures may be divided into fractions; one can walk halfway around the block, swim half a lap, run half a mile, and so forth. And it seems to me that the distinguishing mark concerning the completion of measure-events is that such events are completed when and only when all their fractions have occurred.

But what is it for one event to be a fraction of another? In a sense, an event which involves a measure – a "measure-event" – has its fractions as its "parts," and these parts, when "added," "yield" the whole. In this context, what this amounts to is, I think, that the occurrence of a measure-event implies and is implied by the occurrence of its fractions. But note that the question of *time* of occurrence is a tricky one. I think that it is correct to say both that a measure-event occurs at all the times at which its fractions occur, but also that a measure-event occurs only if all its fractions occur. Thus, if I swim a lap, my doing so occurs from the moment that I begin to the moment that I finish; but if I embark on a lap and give up half way through, my swimming a lap has not occurred at all. This perhaps sounds paradoxical – for it requires us to admit that whether or not an event has begun to occur may depend on whether or not some other event occurs later – but I think that it is accurate. We should note, too, that a measure-event may be divided into fractions in an indefinite number of ways, and that there is thus an indefinite number of combinations of fractions which "yield" the measure-event. But any such combination is such that (if minimal, that is, given no "overlap" of the fractions that it contains) the fractions occur in sequence. Let us call such fractions "combination-fractions." We may then say:

D.1.30: $f1,...,fn$ are combination-fractions of e =df. $f1,...,fn$ and e are distinct events such that:
   (i) necessarily, for any times $T1,...,Tn$, if $f1,...,fn$ occur at $T1,...Tn$, then e occurs at $T1,...,Tn$; and

(ii) if X is the set whose members are $f1,...,fn$, then

    (a) there is no proper subset of X whose members are such that, necessarily, for any times $T'1,...,T'm$, if these members occur at $T'1,...,T'm$, then e occurs at $T'1,...,T'm$,

    (b) necessarily, for any time T, if e occurs at T, then some member of X occurs at T, and

    (c) necessarily, if $f1$ is distinct from fn, then for any event fi that is a member of X and is distinct from fn, fi occurs at a time earlier than that at which $fi+1$ occurs.

D.1.31: e is a measure-event $=$df. there are events $f1,...,fn$ that are combination-fractions of e.

An example of a measure-event is, as already said, [Smith swims a lap]. Examples of combination-fractions of this event are [Smith swims the first half of a lap], and [Smith swims the second half of a lap]; [Smith swims the first third of a lap], [Smith swims the second third of a lap], and [Smith swims the third third of a lap]; and so on. And now the two types of completion may now be accounted for in one formula:

D.1.32: e is completed at T $=$df. e is an event and T a time such that: either

    (i) (a) e is not a measure-event, and

        (b) there is a time T' such that

            (1) T is just prior to T',[5][7]

            (2) e occurs at T, and

            (3) e does not occur at T'; or

    (ii) (a) e is a measure-event, and

        (b) for any events $f1,...,fn$, if $f1,...,fn$ are combination-fractions of e, then, for any fi, if fi is identical with $f1$ or...or fi is identical with fn, there is a time T' such that

            (1) T' is earlier than or identical with T, and

            (2) fi occurs at T'.

Before applying this analysis of the concept of completion to the analysis of the concept of recurrence, one further distinction must be drawn up, and this concerns the fact that some events may be said to be more *determinate* than others. In fact, restricting the term "determinate" to those events which may be said to be *fully* determinate, let us say:

D.1.33: d is a determinate event = df.
     (i) there are no events e and f such that d is the conjunction of e and f; and
     (ii) for all events e distinct from d, either
       (a) there is some event f such that e is the conjunction of d and f, or
       (b) e does not entail d.

(See D.1.11 above.) In other, rougher words: a determinate event is one which is not itself conjunctive and which is entailed only by itself and conjunctions.[5][8] Given this definition, every event so far mentioned in this chapter is an event which is *not* determinate. Consider, for instance, [Smith washes his car]. This is not a determinate event since there is a non-conjunctive event f ([Smith washes his car vigorously], for example) which is distinct from it and which entails it. Indeed, it is evident that it is highly unlikely that any revealing designation of any determinate event (*i.e.*, a designation which reveals the "content" of the event) can be given, since any such designation would be indefinitely long. Nevertheless, this does not alter the fact that some events are in fact determinate. Now, events which are not determinate fail to be so for at least one of two reasons: either they are the conjunction of other events or they are non-conjunctive events entailed by other non-conjunctive events (or both, of course). What is significant about these events is the following: if they occur, they occur *"in virtue of "* other events. That is: a conjunction occurs in virtue of its conjuncts' occurring; and a non-conjunctive, non-determinate event occurs in virtue of some determinate event's occurring. This should guide us in our account of recurrence.

Notice that among those events that may recur are some determinate events. But no determinate event, I think, can occur more than once *at a time*. For an event can occur more than once at a time, it seems, only if there is something "indeterminate" about it.

For example, [Smith raises a hand] can occur more than once at a time only because the property *raising a hand* is indeterminate with respect to the number of hands at issue. Hence, if Smith raises two hands at $T1$ (his left and his right, say), then [Smith raises a hand] occurs twice at $T1$, once in virtue of [Smith raises his right hand] occurring then and once in virtue of [Smith raises his left hand] occurring then. Notice, in this connection, that some non-determinate events may even occur more than once *at exactly the same time and place*. While [Smith raises a hand] does *not* seem to be such an event – for (given D.1.29) [Smith raises his right hand] will take place in part where Smith's right hand is located, and [Smith raises his left hand] will take place in part where Smith's left hand is located, and these locations are distinct – [Smith becomes emotional] *does* seem to be such an event. For example, [Smith becomes emotional] may occur twice at $T1$ – in virtue, say, of [Smith becomes sad] and [Smith becomes angry][5][9] – and yet at only one location, namely, where Smith is. Given these observations, I think that we may say the following, where *e* is a *determinate* event:

D.1.34:   *e* occurs exactly *n* times =df. there are exactly *n* times $T1,...,Tn$ such that *e* is completed at $T1$ and, ..., and *e* is completed at Tn.

Now, if we call those events which are neither determinate nor conjunctive *derivative* events (since their occurrence necessarily *"derives"* from the occurrence of determinate events), we can say: necessarily, a derivative event occurs once if and only if some determinate event which entails it occurs once. And, finally, with respect to conjunctive events, we may say: necessarily, a conjunctive event occurs once if and only if all its conjuncts occur once.

1.5   *THE INDIVIDUATION OF EVENTS*

According to the theory of events just outlined, events are, in the vernacular of the current literature, finely-grained abstract entities. The contention that events are finely-grained is controversial, as is the contention that they are abstract. I think that there are definite advantages to be gained from asserting the truth of both these contentions, but this is a matter that I shall leave aside here.[60] There have of course been rival theories proposed in the literature, as I mentioned in Section 1.1. But, again, I shall not investigate the rival theories here.

There is one point, however, concerning the finely-grained nature of events that should be taken into account here.[61] I would imagine that, if we have any pre-analytic intuitions at all concerning the individuation of events, we would favor a theory according to which events are coarsely-grained rather than finely-grained. And perhaps it does appear, at first glance, that a theory where events are finely-grained multiplies the number of events unacceptably. For instance, suppose Jones slanders Smith viciously and with venom. How many events occur here? According to the theory, several events occur, among which are [someone is slandered], [Jones slanders Smith], [Jones slanders Smith viciously], [Jones slanders Smith with venom], [Jones slanders Smith viciously and with venom], and so forth. (These are all distinct events, given A.1.6 above.) Some may object that only one event is involved here. I disagree, however, and I know of no argument which successfully refutes my contention. But, it may be urged, surely it is obvious that, when Jones slanders Smith (whether it be viciously and with venom or not) just *one slandering* occurs; yet the present theory has it otherwise. But, in fact, the present theory does *not* have it otherwise; and, although I contend that several events occur when Jones slanders Smith, I agree that only one slandering occurs (at that time and place). After all, what is a slandering? It is reasonable to say that a slandering simply is the event [someone is slandered]. And, according to the account of recurrence given in the last section, *this* event occurs exactly once at the time and place at which Jones slanders Smith. It seems to me that the principle implicit in this response may be extended to all similar cases (*e.g.*, a murder is the event [someone is murdered], a theft is the event [something is stolen], and so on), and hence it seems to me that the theory of events presented here is not counterintuitive after all, at least in the respect just discussed. It might of course be retorted that this strategy for counting slanderings (and murders and thefts and the like) just will not do, in that it is just implausible to say that [Jones slanders Smith], [Jones slanders Smith viciously], and so on, are not each of them slanderings. I find this retort unpersuasive.

It is of course true that, whenever one of these events occurs, a slandering occurs, but that is not something I deny. If one *is* intent upon calling each of these events a slandering, then one must adopt some other strategy for counting slanderings, for otherwise too much of our pre-analytic intuition is sacrificed. For instance, there is surely good reason to say that it was reasonable to accuse Lee Harvey Oswald of at most one murder when President Kennedy was assassinated; it would have been a travesty of justice if Oswald had been accused of an indefinite, perhaps infinite, number of murders simply because the prosecutor subscribed to a theory of events according to which events are finely-grained entities.

With this my presentation of the theory of events that I shall presuppose in my theory of action is complete. I turn now to this theory of action.

Notes

1   Perhaps most recently by Kent Bach in Bach (1980).

2   *E.g.*, Davidson (1969, 1970).

3   *E.g.*, Goldman (1970); Kim (1973; 1976; 1977); Brand (1976); Thomson (1977).

4   *E.g.*, Chisholm (1970a; 1971b; 1976, Chapter 4).

5   *E.g.*, Horgan (1978).

6   This is not to suggest that the three factors mentioned here are the only factors which act as a restraint on philosophical theories, but only that these are the three factors that I take to be most important for present purposes.

7   Perhaps it is better to say that I discovered it.

8   What has been said in this paragraph concerning the proposed

use of "=df." accords, I think, with Chisholm's own use of "=df."

9 Sometimes, it seems, Chisholm has been guilty of errors of the sorts just mentioned. See especially A.Baier's comments on Chisholm (1970b) in Baier (1970) p.651. See also Chisholm (1971a) and Bruce Aune's comments in Aune (1971), p.70ff.

10 Chisholm (1976).

11 Presumably, it is claimed that particular events could not recur because, first, it is assumed that, if events were particular, they would occur when and only when they existed and, secondly, nothing may pass out of and then back into existence. As for the first point: I am not clear as to why one should make such an assumption, although it is true that it seems to be one implicit in most of the particularist theories of events that have been proposed. As for the second point: I am not sure what to make of the contention that nothing can pass out of and then back into existence. Chisholm apparently subscribes to it, however, and I shall not dispute the matter here.

12 Hacker (1982), p.479, claims that it is senseless to talk of events as existing or as not existing, especially when their existence is distinguished from their occurrence. He does not argue for this claim, however, and what I say here seems to make sense to me.

13 See Chisholm (1976) pp.117-8 and (1977) Chapter 5. This treatment of truth and falsity accords with certain passages in Chapter 3 of G.E.Moore (1953) but offended Bertrand Russell's "robust sense of reality" in Chapter 12 of Russell (1959).

14 Of course, this is not quite correct, since the sun continues to shine even after night has fallen. This is easily accommodated, however, by talking, with respect to some place P, of the event of the sun's shining on P, and then by noting that, after night has fallen on P, the sun's shining on P has certainly ceased to occur.

15   Chisholm (1976), p.122ff.; Chisholm (1977), definition D5.3.

16   On the reducibility of sets to properties, see Chisholm (1976),
      p.217, n.21. Although Chisholm presents no explicit account in
      Person and Object as to how sets are to be reduced to proper-
      ties, on p.8 of *The First Person* (Chisholm, 1981) he does say
      explicitly that he will understand "the class [*i.e.*, set] of things
      that are *F* is *G* " to mean the same as "for every property *H*, if
      H is exemplified by all and only those things that exemplify the
      property of being *F*, then *H* has the property of being *G*." My
      concern is that it appears that, for some sets, the only property
      that will satisfy what is said of *F* in this formula will be one
      which is identifiable *only* by reference to the set in question.
      As for times and places, it should be noted that, since writ-
      ing *Person and Object*, Chisholm has attempted to analyze the
      concept of a time in such a fashion that times turn out to be a
      type of states of affairs. (See Chisholm (1979), pp.357-9.)
      However, it should also be noted that he has not yet attempted
      any such reduction with respect to the concept of a place.

17   I shall leave entirely to one side any question as to whether or
      not a wedge may be driven between logical necessity and me-
      taphysical necessity. *Cf.* Farrell (1981).

18   I am grateful to Tom Ryckman for first pointing out to me,
      both in conversation and in Ryckman (1978), just how impor-
      tant Chisholm's use of tense is in *Person and Object*.

19   Chisholm (1976), p.119, slightly modified.

20   *Cf.* Chisholm (1979), p.345.

21   Chisholm (1976), p.123.

22   But it must be acknowledged that sense *can* be given to sen-
      tences of the form "*p* occurred at *T*" (where *T* is past) and "*p*
      will occur at *T*" (where *T* is future). See Chisholm (1979),
      p.358.

23   This notation is not without problems of its own, however. In

particular, it rides roughshod over the issue of referential opacity. For such opacity arises in contexts where variables are embedded within square brackets. Let us suppose that the thing denoted by "x" is identical with the thing denoted by "y"; we cannot without further qualification immediately infer that the state of affairs denoted by " [x exists]" is thus identical with the state of affairs denoted by " [y exists]." For "x" and "y" may be nonequivalent expressions which happen to be satisfied by one and the same individual. (For example, let "x" be "Jones" and "y" be "the tallest man in the room.") One way to try to avoid this problem is to assume that all things have unique essences and then stipulate that variables used within square brackets are to be replaced only by expressions which express the *essences* of those things over which the variables range. The notation would thus be understood to employ objectual quantification on one level combined with substitutional quantification on another level. It is in this way that I propose that the notation be understood here. Of course, such "mixed quantification" faces problems of its own and certainly the assumption concerning essences on the basis of which this move is made is itself most problematic. (*Cf.* Chisholm (1979), p.317ff.) But I cannot pursue these matters here. Still, for purposes of illustration, consider the formula "S accepts [S' s hand rises]." Let S be Smith; then [S' s hand rises] will be the state of affairs [Smith's hand rises], where the "Smith" within the brackets is understood to express Smith's unique essence.

Of course, there are other ways to try to avoid the present problem. One way is to resort to the use of certain *de re* locutions. (Chisholm (1981) is a good example of this.) But I shall resist this move here, for two reasons. First, it is not itself unproblematic; second, it would render the present treatment of action even more complicated than it already is.

I am indebted to Allen Renear for bringing this issue to my attention.

24 The analogy is not perfect, however. One complication with contingent properties, as I have called them, is that some things may necessarily fail to have, or exemplify, them. For instance, no abstract entity can have the property *shining*. Also, there is a distinction to be made between necessary prop-

erties and essential properties, and between impossible properties and properties which things essentially lack. But I shall
not pursue this here.

25   Chisholm (1976), p.117. This definition is in fact rejected in
     Chisholm (1979), p.342.

26   *Cf.* Kim (1979), p.155.

27   I am here glossing over the problem as to whether [the sun
     shines now] (call this *s*) and [the sun shines at *T*] (call this *t*) –
     where *T* is now – are identical or distinct states of affairs. The
     problem is a very difficult one. Chisholm would say that *s* is
     distinct from *t* and that, while the latter is (perhaps) a proposi-
     tion, the former is an event. But it is not clear to me that this
     is correct. (*Cf.* Chisholm (1979), pp.348-9.) The resolution of
     this issue (and I am not in a position to provide such resolution)
     requires a full treatment of exactly what it is to take tense se-
     riously. One aspect of the problem is whether, when designat-
     ing *s* as [the sun shines now], it is possible to understand tense
     not to be taken seriously in this designation and, when desig-
     nating *t* as [the sun shines at *T*], it is possible to understand
     tense *to* be taken seriously in this designation. If neither is
     possible, how are these designations to be compared with one
     another? Another aspect of the problem is the apparent
     reflexivity inherent in "now" (which is not inherent in "at *T*").
     Does such reflexivity affect the issue at hand? I am not sure.
     (For a related problem concerning reflexivity, see the first two
     paragraphs of Chapter 3, Section 3.2.) For more on the matter
     of tense, see Wolterstorff (1979), p.183ff., and Chisholm
     (1979), p.344ff. For more on the matter of reflexivity, see
     Chisholm (1981), Chapters 3 through 5.

28   Since writing *Person and Object* Chisholm has changed his view
     and declared the primary objects of belief to be what he calls
     properties *de se*. (See, *e.g.*, Chisholm (1979), pp.325-6; Chis-
     holm (1981), Chapter 4.) I shall not follow his lead here.

29   *Cf.* Braithwaite (1932), pp.30-1.

30 For instance, I take it that many people currently accept – and yet are not thinking about – the fact that there are at least one thousand people on earth. Can they believe this without *ever* having considered it? Yes, I think so. That is, not only does [*S* accepts *p* at *T*] not imply [*S* considers *p* at *T*], but it also does not imply [there is a time *T'* such that *S* considers *p* at *T'*]. But perhaps it is true that [*S* accepts *p* at *T*] does imply [there are a time *T'* not later than *T* and a proposition *q* such that *S* considers *q* at *T'*]. For instance, can anyone believe that there are at least one thousand people on earth without ever having considered some fact to the effect that there are at least *n* people on earth (where *n* is greater than or equal to one thousand)? I am not sure.

31 *Cf.* Chisholm (1976), p.119, assumption (2).

32 *Cf.* Chisholm (1976), p.119, assumption (3).

33 It seems that Chisholm (1976, p.120, assumption (4)) is willing to say that there is a conjunction *u* for a pair of distinct states of affairs *s* and *t* only if *s* and *t* co-occur. (I say "seems", because it is not absolutely clear that Chisholm intends tense to be taken seriously in his assumption.) But I have allowed *u* to "span" distinct times, thus allowing conjunctions to have conjuncts which do not co-occur. This is crucial, given that I shall later claim that an action is just such a conjunction.

34 What follows is very close to proposals made by Chisholm (1979), pp.343-4.

35 Chisholm (1976), p.118.

36 *Cf.* Chisholm (1976), p.118.

37 In giving this criterion I ignore possible problems with high-velocity, subatomic particles. It should be remembered that, as I use the term "individual thing," no set is an individual thing and also that, as I use the term "exist in," only individual things may exist in a place.

38   Kim (1979), p. 151.

39   Allen Renear has pointed out to me, however, that it also seems plausible to say that some propositions are such that they cannot be believed and that there are "paradoxes" of "doxastic implication" which mirror the "paradoxes" of strict implication. If this is correct – and it may well be – then A.1.6 and, likewise, A.1.7 are to be rejected – *unless* D.1.9 is rejected. Under such circumstances, I would again have no quarrel with taking the concept of entailment as primitive, thus preserving A.1.6 and A.1.7 at the expense of D.1.9.

40   This is essentially the same definition as that provided in Chisholm (1976), p.123. This puts me in the camp of "eternalists," to use Mark Richard's term (Richard (1981)), at least with respect to propositions. But with respect to events I am closer to what he calls a "temporalist."

41   *Cf.* Chisholm (1979), pp.350-1.

42   *Cf.* Chisholm (1979), pp.352-3.

43   It is worth noting that Chisholm's analysis of the concept of an event in Chisholm (1976, p.128) is defective in that, in its reliance on the technical notion of a property's not being such that it may be rooted outside times at which it is had, it rules out such states of affairs as [Socrates dies] as an event. *Cf.* Kim (1979), pp.157-8. Chisholm (1979, pp.352-3) acknowledges this and proposes an alternative definition.

44   Note that if [Jones is Jones] were not ruled out as an event, then other states of affairs such as [Jones is such that Smith walks] would qualify as events.

45   Such modification could be made in the following manner. First, a definition of "s implies F with respect to x " would be given. Then clause (ii)(d)(4) of D.1.25 would be altered to read: "there is no thing x such that, with respect to it, e implies G and G is essential."

46 Such modification could be made in the following manner. D.1.25 would be restricted to an analysis of the concept of a non-conjunctive event. Then it would be stipulated that a conjunctive event is a conjunctive state of affairs all of whose conjuncts are themselves either conjunctive events or non-conjunctive events. And then it would be said that an event is either a non-conjunctive event or a conjunctive event.

47 *E.g.*, Chisholm (1970a); Thomson (1977).

48 *E.g.*, Chisholm (1976); Kim (1973; 1976; 1977).

49 The analysis could be made in the following manner. An analysis of the concept of a state of affairs' entailing change in terms of a property would be given; and then a subclause (6) would be added to clause (ii)(d) of D.1.25 to the effect that *e* entails change in terms of *G*. Notice that even this would not be adequate to a distinction between an event which involves change and a *process*. I am not sure that such a distinction is defensible, but, if it is, I do not know how to defend it. None of this affects the main thrust of the present account, however.

50 Chisholm (1976), pp.124-6.

51 Problems regarding Chisholm's use of tense in *his* definition of "concretization" (1976, p.125) are avoided in this definition. Note that Chisholm has since (1979, p.354) discarded the concept of concretization; but he does so for reasons which, though good, do not, I think, affect the propriety of its use in the present context.

52 Perhaps this definition should be restricted to cases where *X* is a finite set (*cf.* Pollock (1979), p.165), but I shall not go into this matter here.

53 Chisholm (1976), pp.128-130.

54 *Cf.* Pollock (1979), pp.167-8.

55 Chisholm (1976), p.218, n.24.

56   *Cf.* Wolterstorff (1979), p.198, n.24.

57   The notion of one time's being just prior to another does not
     figure in our list of unanalyzed concepts and has not yet been
     analyzed in terms of them. If time is an infinitely dense con-
     tinuum, as I suspect it is, then I am unable to give an analysis
     of this notion, and so it must be added to our list of unanalyzed
     concepts. This is regrettable but, under the circumstances,
     something that I cannot avoid. On the other hand, if time is
     not infinitely dense but is made up of discrete entities, then the
     following definition should suffice:
     T is just prior to T' =df. (i) T is earlier than T';
     and (ii) there is no time T^* such that T is earlier
     than T^* and T^* is earlier than T'.

58   By "conjunctive" and "conjunction" I here mean to characterize
     events which satisfy not only A.1.3 but also D.1.11. This re-
     striction on the use of these terms applies throughout the rest
     of this section.

59   That is, "Smith becomes emotional" is here understood to ex-
     press an event which is entailed both by [Smith becomes sad]
     and by [Smith becomes angry].

60   An adequate discussion of this issue would require the exposi-
     tion and evaluation of alternative theories of events, a project
     which would be inappropriate in the present context. However,
     I can list here what I take to be the three major advantages of
     the present theory of events. The first advantage is that the
     assertion that events are finely-grained does away with the
     need to employ the cumbersome apparatus that is involved
     with talking about events as being "under a description." (For
     contemporary discussions of this issue, see Davidson (1963;
     1967; 1969; 1970); Chisholm (1971b), p.188; Goldman (1970),
     pp.1-10; Wierenga (1974), pp.85-103; Aune (1977), pp.12-19;
     Dretske (1977).) The second advantage is that the assertion
     that events are abstract entities promotes ontological simplici-
     ty; at least, this is so with the theory just presented. The third
     advantage is that, events being abstract entities, the concept of
     recurrence may be interpreted literally. (For a discussion of

this issue see Davidson (1970) and Chisholm (1971b).) But it must be acknowledged that each of these alleged advantages is controversial. Indeed, I know of no *conclusive* argument for or against any of the following claims: (i) events are finely-grained entities; (ii) events are coarsely-grained entities; (iii) events are abstract entities; (iv) events are concrete entities.

61 The objection that follows, and my response to it, are drawn from Chisholm (1976), p.129.

PART II
HUMAN ACTION

Chapter 2

PROBLEMS TO BE RESOLVED

The history of philosophy is rife with accounts of human action, some of greater merit than others. In *Person and Object* Chisholm gives a detailed account of human action. [1] The account that I shall provide in later chapters, while continuing to borrow a great deal from Chisholm's account in terms of *methodology*, shares very little of the *content* of Chisholm's account – except in so far as both Chisholm and I of course treat events as abstract entities. Where it is appropriate to do so, I shall comment on the main reasons for this contrast between Chisholm's account and my own. I shall comment, too, on certain less pressing points of interest in Chisholm's account, but for the most part I shall forgo detailed criticism of his account for fear of unduly impeding presentation of my own account. I shall also forgo detailed criticism of the accounts of human action provided by philosophers other than Chisholm for the same reason, but also partly because no such account that I know of both matches Chisholm's for detail and treats events as abstract entities. [2]

Any adequate theory of human action (henceforth I shall generally dispense with such use of the word "human") must provide acceptable resolutions of certain prominent puzzles in so-called action-theory. I have in mind eighteen problems in particular, and the main purpose of the theory that I shall propose (and, indeed, the underlying motivation for all the twists and turns that the theory will take, some of which will inevitably appear baffling at first) is the resolution of these problems. The problems may profitably be divided into various groups, and the manner in which I shall designate them will reflect this fact.

The first group of problems concerns the concept of acting in general, and the first problem (A1) may be posed by means of the following illustration. In *Singing in the Rain* there is a splendid scene in which Donald O'Connor dances with a dummy. The dummy complements his every move: as O'Connor twirls, so does the dummy; sitting on a couch, the dummy repeatedly puts her hand on O'Connor's knee, and every time he removes it, she replaces it; behind the couch, O'Connor chucks the dummy into the air, then the dummy O'Connor, and when he attempts to extricate himself she pulls him back down. Almost the only thing the dummy does not do that O'Connor does is sing "Make 'Em Laugh" (perhaps because she is headless) – except, of course, that the dummy does not, strictly speaking, do anything at all. But, then, what is it that distinguishes O'Connor from the dummy, in so far as the former does things and the latter does not?

Another related problem (A2) is this. We may safely assume that, while playing this scene with the dummy, O'Connor has been breathing – and breathing hard, most of the time. Is this breathing an action of his? It seems odd to say so. But surely it is not something that just happens *while* O'Connor is doing things, for it is intimately related to his doing these things. What is the nature of this relation?

The second group of problems concerns the individuation of actions. First (B1), consider this case. Late one evening Jones returns home. He opens the front-door and flips the light-switch. The light goes on. The room is illuminated. Moreover, a prowler is alerted to the fact that Jones is home.[3] How many actions did Jones perform after he opened his front door? Some say one; others say at least four. Is Jones's flipping the switch the same action as his turning on the light? Is this in turn the same action as his illuminating the room? And is this, finally, the same action as his alerting the prowler?

A related problem (B2) concerns what may be called the divisibility of actions. Suppose that Jones is a new army recruit. The sergeant-major calls the troops to attention and orders all those who have just joined up to take one step forward. Jones does so. But, in taking one step forward, Jones also takes half a step forward, a quarter of a step forward, an eighth of a step forward, and so on *ad infinitum*. Has he then performed an infinite number of actions?

In similar fashion there is a problem (B3) concerning what may be called the accumulability of actions. Suppose that Jones is out for a walk in the park. During the walk he does many things: he takes many strides; he swings his arms; he whistles a tune; he contemplates the absurdity of existence. But he takes just one walk. Is the entire walk, then, a single action of his?

Another problem (B4) concerning the individuation of actions (and having connection with problem A2) has to do with the distinction between actions and their consequences. What is this distinction? The problem may be put in a particularly striking manner by means of this puzzle. Jones, bent on revenge, shoots Smith. Smith clings to life but succumbs some hours after the shooting takes place. Jones, then, has killed Smith. Is Smith's death a part of Jones's action or a consequence of it? If a consequence, then, following Hume, it is logically possible that Jones kill Smith and Smith yet live. But this is not logically possible. Therefore Smith's death is part of Jones's action. But how can it be part of Jones's action when what Jones did took place hours before Smith died? Intimately tied to this question is the question of how long actions last. This matter, too, must be looked into in detail.

Finally, there is a problem (B5) concerning the distinction between actions and circumstances. Suppose that Jones is partial to nocturnal snacks in weird places. He makes some toast and then butters it. Not only that, he butters it in the bathroom. Moreover, he butters it in the bathroom with a knife. Indeed, he butters it in the bathroom with a knife at midnight.[4] We may safely assume that the buttering is an action. But are the manner (with a knife), the place (in the bathroom), and the time (at midnight) parts or circumstances of Jones's action?

The third group of problems concerns the concept of intentional action. There are three problems in particular that should be raised here. The first (C1) is simply this. How may intentional action be distinguished from action which is not intentional? An acceptable analysis of the concept of intentional action is desirable for many reasons, but in attempting to give it we shall find that we must beware falling into the trap of thinking that to act intentionally is simply to act in such a way that one satisfies certain intentions that one has.

The second problem (C2) may be posed by means of this perplexing puzzle.[5] Hamlet killed and, indeed, intentionally killed the man behind the arras, and the man behind the arras was in fact Polonius. So Hamlet killed Polonius. But Hamlet did not *intentionally* kill Polonius. Surely, however, just one killing occurred at the time and place at which Hamlet killed Polonius. How can this killing have been both intentional and not intentional?

The third problem (C3) has to do with the fact that it is commonly said that all actions, in the "true" or "precise" sense of the term "action," are intentional. Is this so? If so, problem C1 seems to have been mis-stated. But surely the statement of that problem seems innocuous. Is there, nevertheless, *some* respectable sense to be given to the claim that all actions are intentional?

The fourth group of problems concerns the "by"-relation. There are three main problems in this group. The first (D1) is simply that of accounting for the fact that some actions are such that we perform them by performing others, and other actions appear to be such that we "just perform" them. For instance, if we consider again the case of Jones's returning home and alerting the prowler, we find that Jones alerted the prowler by illuminating the room, he illuminated the room by turning on the light, he turned on the light by flipping the switch, and (let us suppose) he flipped the switch by raising his hand. But it seems probable that he did not raise his hand by doing anything else. In particular, it seems that he did not raise his hand by flexing his muscles, that he did not flex his muscles by causing certain neurons in them to fire, and that he did not cause certain neurons in his muscles to fire by sending any physiological "messages" from his brain. He "just raised" his hand, it seems, and this apparent fact needs to be accounted for.

Another problem (D2) is closely related to the first. Whereas, in the case just mentioned, Jones apparently did *not* raise his hand by causing certain neurons to fire, it seems that such a "by"-relation can obtain at times between a hand-raising and a neuron-firing. Suppose that Jones wants to cause his neurons to fire and, in order to do so, raises his hand. It seems legitimate to say that, in such a case, Jones causes his neurons to fire *by* raising his hand (or, equivalently, that Jones raises his hand, *thereby* causing his neurons to fire). This apparent fact must also be accounted for.

The third problem (D3) in this group concerns accounting for instances of the "by"-relation when it holds between events which do not occur simultaneously. In problem D1, there is an element of simultaneity involved in all of Jones's actions (if, indeed, he did more than one thing), but such simultaneity is not necessary for the "by"-relation to hold. Consider the case where Jones drives around the corner by first signalling, then braking, then changing gear, then turning the steering-wheel, and then accelerating out of the corner. An adequate treatment of the "by"-relation must also be able to account for such a case.

The fifth group of problems concerns the concept of omission. There are three basic problems in this group. The first (E1) has to do with the distinction between omitting to do something and merely not doing it. For instance, at the moment there are very many things that I am not doing. (I am not eating, I am not drinking, I am not walking on Fifth Avenue, I am not sunbathing in the Bahamas, I am not propounding a disproof of Goldbach's conjecture, and so on.) Are any of these failures to act omissions of mine? Which ones? What is their distinguishing characteristic?

The second problem (E2) is simply that of distinguishing unintentional omissions from intentional ones. What is this distinction precisely?

The third problem (E3) complements the first. What is the distinction between omitting to do something and doing something? Many philosophers have claimed that omissions are "committed." Is this so? If so, how may the "active" and "inactive" aspects of omissions be reconciled?

The sixth and final group of problems concerns the concepts of decision and choice. In the present context these problems are perhaps not so pressing as those just mentioned; but the fact that their resolution will prove to follow fairly easily from the theory of action shortly to be presented both warrants their inclusion here and adds to the attractiveness of the theory. This theory, as will soon be seen, is in the tradition of "the" volitional theory of action and relies heavily on the concepts of intending and willing, but in so doing allows for an account of the phenomena of deciding, choosing, and trying. The main problems in this area are two in number.

The first problem (F1) concerns the phenomena of willing, deciding, choosing, and trying. How are these phenomena related to one another, and how are they to be distinguished one from another?

The second problem (F2) is that of distinguishing between "short-range" decisions (or choices) and "long-range" decisions (or choices). Is there, indeed, any essential distinction to be determined, for instance, between Smith's deciding to stand up now (and *consequently*, not just subsequently, doing so) and his idly deciding to watch a show on television later (and, perhaps, doing nothing as a consequence of this decision)?

There are, of course, more problems that might be posed here. But eighteen suffice. Moreover, the eighteen that have been posed appear to me to be those most deserving of attention. Before any attempt is undertaken to resolve these problems, however, some new, unanalyzed concepts must be introduced and discussed. This will be the task of Chapter 3. I shall then undertake to resolve these problems in turn, cleaving to the groups distinguished. Hence, I shall treat problems A1 and A2 in Chapter 4, B1 through B5 in Chapter 5, C1 through C3 in Chapter 6, D1 through D3 in Chapter 7, E1 through E3 in Chapter 8, and F1 and F2 in Chapter 9. What emerges from this will be, I hope, a comprehensive, penetrating, enlightening, and accurate theory of human action. This theory will of course appear objectionable in certain respects, and I shall undertake in Chapter 10 to rebut what I take to be the objections most likely to be levelled against it.

Notes

1   Chisholm (1976), Chapter 2.

2   Perhaps the most detailed, sustained accounts of human action provided to date in the literature are those of Goldman (1970), Chisholm (1976), Thomson (1977), Davis (1979), and Hornsby (1980). But, among these, only Chisholm treats events as abstract entities.

3   The example is taken from Davidson (1963), p.4.

4   The example is taken from Davidson (1967), p.105.

5   The example is taken from Davidson (1971), p.46.

Chapter 3
NEW CONCEPTS

The concepts introduced in Chapter 1, both analyzed and unanalyzed, will figure in the theory that is to follow. But, on their own, they are not sufficient for the presentation of this theory. Three new, unanalyzed concepts must be introduced. These are the concepts of causal contribution, intention, and volition. I shall discuss them in turn.

3.1   *CAUSAL CONTRIBUTION*

The concept of causal contribution is one with which most of us are quite familiar. As is customary, I take the primary relata of causal contribution to be events, but I should immediately point out a *caveat.*[1] The term "causal contribution" has been used at times by Chisholm to refer to a relation, one of whose relata is always a person. This relation, which may for the sake of convenience and for the moment be called the relation of *agent*-causation (of a particular, "irreducible" sort), is *not* the relation I am concerned with here. (I shall have more to say on this shortly.) Rather, the relation I am concerned with may be called the relation of *event*-causation or, better, *event*-causal contribution. But since such nomenclature is ponderous, I shall henceforth simply call that relation with which I am here concerned the relation of causal contribution.

A distinction should be drawn between the relation of causal contribution and that of being-the-cause-of.[2] Whatever is *the* cause of an event contributes causally to that event, though not necessarily *vice versa.* As I use the term "causal contribution," a match's being struck may contribute causally to its lighting, but so may the presence of oxygen, the dryness of the match, and so on. Presumably only one of these (probably the match's being struck) ranks as *the* cause of the match's lighting. It is the relation of causal contribution, not the relation of being-the-cause-of, with which I shall be concerned in what follows. How to characterize the latter relation is a matter that I shall not pursue here.

While what has just been said concerning the distinction between the relation of causal contribution and that of being-the-cause-of ought to be intelligible to some degree, it in fact contains a crucial ambiguity which must now be eliminated. Consider again the claim that a match's being struck contributes causally to its lighting. This was not supposed to be understood as a general claim about what always or, better, usually happens to matches when they are struck. Rather, I had a particular match in mind. Call this match *m.* The claim, then, may be put as follows: [*m* is struck] contributes causally to [*m* lights]. But this is ambiguous, because, to put it loosely (and I do mean loosely, since what immediately follows *appears* to reify occurrences in a manner which I tried hard to shun in Chapter 1), given that both [*m* is struck] and [*m* lights] may occur more than once, to say simply that the former contributes causally to the latter is to fail to specify which occurrence of the former contributes causally to which occurrence of the latter.[3] Now this problem may be solved simply by relativizing causal contribution to times (and doing this also obviates the need to reify occurrences as particulars). As an illustration, suppose that [*m* is struck] occurs on two occasions, *T1* and *T2*, and that [*m* lights] also occurs on two occasions, *T3* and *T4*. Now, suppose that *m* lights at *T3* because *m* is struck at *T1*, but also that *m* is struck at *T2* without *m*'s lighting as a result and that *m* lights at *T4* but not as a result of having been struck (we may suppose that *m* is thrown into a fire at *T4*). Given this fragment of *m*'s history, it should be clear why it is inadequate merely to say that [*m* is struck] contributes causally to [*m* lights]. For this is true of *T1* and *T3* but not of *T2* or *T4*. What we should say, I think, is simply this: [*m* is struck] contributes causally relative to *T1* and *T3* to [*m* lights]. This succeeds in completely disambiguating the earlier sentence without recourse to the reification of occurrences as particulars.

But while this is all that needs to be done to disambiguate sentences such as "[*m* is struck] contributes causally to [*m* lights]," there are certain sentences for which this sort of treatment would not suffice for disambiguation. The reason for this is that, while such events as [*m* is struck] and [*m* lights] are apparently capable of occurring at most once at a time, there are (as we saw in Chapter 1) certain events which can occur more than once at a time. Examples of events of the latter sort are: [snow falls], [it rains], [someone sings], [some match is struck], [some match lights], [Jones raises an arm], and so on and so forth. All such events are derivative events, in the sense of "derivative" introduced at the end of Section 1.4 of Chapter 1. Derivative events, it was noted, occur *"in virtue of "* certain determinate event's occurring. And I think that it suffices, to disambiguate sentences concerning the causal contribution by and to derivative events, to relativize such contribution not only to times but also to the determinate events involved. Suppose, for instance, that there are two matches, $m1$ and $m2$, which light at $T2$, and suppose that $m1$ lights at $T2$ in virtue of Smith's striking it at $T1$ but that $m2$ does not light at $T2$ for this reason. Now, our earlier treatment of such a case would allow us to say that [Smith strikes $m1$] contributes causally relative to $T1$ and $T2$ to [$m1$ lights] and not to [$m2$ lights], and this is fine as far as it goes. But it does not go far enough. For it seems clear to me that [Smith strikes $m1$] contributes causally relative to $T1$ and $T2$ not just to [$m1$ lights] but also to [some match lights]; but to say just this is to rest content with an ambiguity, for [some match lights] occurs at $T2$ not just in virtue of [$m1$ lights]'s occurring at $T2$ but also in virtue of [$m2$ lights]'s occurring then, and since [Smith strikes $m1$] does not contribute causally relative to $T1$ and $T2$ to [$m2$ lights], merely relativizing causal contribution to times is insufficient for a complete disambiguation of sentences of the sort that concerns us here. But all that I think we need do here is specify the *determinate* events in virtue of which [some match lights] occurs at $T2$. Suppose that $m1$ and $m2$ are the only matches which light then. Then there will be just two determinate events in virtue of which [some match lights] occurs at $T2$. (Hence, [some match lights] occurs exactly twice at $T2$. See Chapter 1, Section 1.4.) Let us call these determinate events d' and d^*, with $m1$ a "constituent" of the former and $m2$ a "constituent" of the latter. Notice too that [Smith lights $m1$], being a derivative event, also occurs at $T1$ in virtue of some determinate event, and let us call this event d. Then I think that it suffices for purposes of complete disambiguation to say of the present case simply that [Smith lights $m1$] contributes causally relative to $T1$ and $T2$ and to d and d' (but *not* d^*) to [some match lights].

The canonical sentence-schema for the concept of causal contribution is therefore as follows: e contributes causally relative to T and T' and to d and d' to f. (Notice that, in the limiting case where either *e* or *f* is itself a determinate event, either *e* and *d* will be identical or *f* and *d'* will be identical.) Now, I take the following to be implications of sentences of this sort: first, *e*, *d*, *d'*, and *f* are events; second, *T* and *T'* are times; third, *e* and *d* occur at *T* and *f* and *d'* occur at *T'*; and finally, *T* is earlier than or identical with *T'*. I think that all of these assumptions concerning the implications of the canonical sentence-schema are uncontroversial except perhaps for the last assumption, in so far as, first, this assumption does not rule out the possibility that a cause be contemporaneous with its effect and, second, it does rule out the possibility that a cause succeed its effect. Each of these stipulations has been disputed by philosophers, but I shall stick to them. That a cause may be contemporaneous with some of its effects is, I believe, amply (although roughly) demonstrated by the following examples:[4] when a locomotive pulls a caboose, the motion of the former contributes causally to the motion of the latter, even though they move simultaneously; so too when a hand moves a pencil, when a gust of wind causes a leaf to flutter, and so on. Of course, there are innumerable examples also of a cause preceding some of its effects, as when my pressing the brake-pedal contributes causally to the car's stopping, when a child's eating contributes to his having tooth-decay, and so on. And perhaps there are cases of causal contribution where it is difficult to determine whether or not a cause precedes its effects. But there are and can be, I believe, no instances of a cause succeeding some of its effects. I shall not seek to defend this point here, however; I shall simply assume it to be true.

Causal contribution, then, is a fairly complex relation with six relata. We may still say, however, in a fairly straightforward manner (but in a manner that I shall not seek to elucidate further) that, when *e* contributes causally relative to *T* and *T'* and to *d* and *d'* to *f*, *e* and *f* are the "primary relata" involved. But while the present account of causal contribution is thus much in keeping with tradition in that it stipulates that events are the (primary) relata of causal contribution, there is nevertheless a problem with stipulating that only events are the (primary) relata of causal contribution that should be acknowledged here, and that concerns what some philosophers have called "negative events." (Henceforth, I shall dispense with such use of the term "primary," although it will be implicit in what I say.) For, given D.1.7 and D.1.25, it turns out that the negation of an event is not itself an event, and this is because the negation of an event could occur, and in fact would occur, even if there were no individual things in the universe. For instance, [Smith walks] occurs only if Smith exists, but [Smith does not walk] occurs if either Smith exists but does not walk or Smith does not exist. Hence, if by "negative event" is meant the negation of an event, then the name appears a misnomer. But it seems nevertheless that the negations of events can figure in certain causal relations. For instance, it seems perfectly proper to say that it is because Smith is and has been a conscientious user of dental floss that he does not now suffer from gingivitis, and it seems that we may infer from this that [Smith flosses] contributes causally (on some occasion) to [Smith does not suffer from gingivitis]. But [Smith does not suffer from gingivitis] is not an event, and it has been stipulated that only events can be caused. How, then, can the apparent causation of "negative events" be accommodated?

There seem to me to be three main ways to try to accommodate the apparent causation of "negative events." The first way is to accept that the negations of events are *bona fide* relata of causal contribution and then say that, given that the only possible relata of causal contribution are events, we must admit that the negations of events are themselves events. This solution would necessitate a revision of D.1.25, the definition of "event." I am not prepared to accept this solution, and that is because to do so would seem to require us to stretch the application of the term "event" beyond its intuitive bounds. This point is obviously debatable, but I do not propose to debate it here, since there are other solutions to the puzzle that are available.

The second main way to try to solve the puzzle is, again, to accept that the negations of events are *bona fide* relata of causal contribution and then to say that, because the negations of events are not themselves events, we must admit that it is not only events, but also their negations, which may be among the relata of causal contribution. I have no real quarrel with this proposal, except that it tends to obscure the fact that the causation of the negation of an event has a certain characteristic which the causation of an event lacks. Hence, if there is a solution to the puzzle which highlights this difference, it seems to me preferable to the present solution.

There is a solution which highlights this difference and this constitutes the third main way to try to accommodate the apparent causation of "negative events." According to the proposal – and it is the proposal that I shall adopt here – what we should recognize is that there is a relation akin to the relation of causal contribution and which may be analyzed in terms of the latter. We may call this relation causal* contribution and say that an event *e* contributes causally* to a state of affairs *s* just in case *e* contributes causally to some event *f* which causally necessitates *s*. Or more precisely:

D.3.1: *e* contributes causally* relative to *T* and *T'* and to *d* and *d'* to *s* =df.
   (i) *e* is an event;
   (ii) *s* is a state of affairs which is not a proposition; and
   (iii) there is an event *f* distinct from *s* such that
      (a) *e* contributes causally relative to *T* and *T'* and to *d* and *d'* to *f*, and
      (b) it is causally necessary, given that *f* occurs at *T'*, that *s* occur at *T'*.

The concept of causal necessity has not yet been analyzed, and I shall remedy this shortly (see D.3.3 and D.3.4 below). But clause (iii)(b) of D.3.1 is fairly readily understood, I think, in the absence of such analysis. D.3.1 is designed to accommodate the so-called causation of so-called negative events in the following way. Consider again the relation between [Smith flosses] and [Smith does not suffer from gingivitis]. We may say that the former contributes causally* (relative to certain times and certain determinate events) to the latter in virtue of the fact that the former contributes causally (relative to the same times and determinate events) to a *bona fide* event (call it *f*) and it is causally impossible both that *f* should occur at *T'* and that Smith suffer from gingivitis at *T'*. *What* event is *f*? That depends on the circumstances of the case, but it is likely to be some such event as [Smith has healthy gums]. The most prominent distinction between causal contribution and causal* contribution is brought out by noting, first, that it is necessarily the case that, whenever an event *e* contributes causally* to some state of affairs *s*, *e* contributes causally to some event *f* distinct from *s*, but, second, it is not necessarily the case that, whenever an event *e* contributes causally to some event *f*, there is some event distinct from *f* to which *e* also contributes causally. That is:

T.3.1:   Necessarily, if *e* contributes causally* relative to
          T and *T'* and to *d* and *d'* to *s*, then there is an
          event *f* distinct from *s* such that *e* contributes
          causally relative to *T* and *T'* and to *d* and *d'* to *f.*

A.3.1:   It is not necessarily the case that, if *e* contributes
          causally relative to *T* and *T'* and to *d* and *d'* to *s*,
          then there is an event *f* distinct from *s* such that *e*
          contributes causally relative to *T* and *T'* and to *d*
          and *d'* to *f.*

T.3.1 follows directly, of course, from D.3.1. Also, A.3.1 seems
very plausible; at least its denial does not seem at all plausible,
given that it requires that, whenever an event *e* contributes causally
to some event, *e* contributes causally to an infinity of events. Now
the moral to be gleaned from all this is, of course, that a "negative
event" may be "caused" (relative to some times and determinate
events) in the sense that some event may contribute causally* to it
(relative to those times and determinate events), even though no
event may contribute causally to it,-and – given T.3.1 – it is notable
that, whenever a "negative event" is "caused," this is *"in virtue of "*
a (regular) event's being (regularly) caused.

We shall meet up again briefly with causal* contribution in
Chapter 8, where omissions are discussed, but there is more that
can and should be said concerning causal contribution *simpliciter.*
There is one more significant assumption that I wish to make in this
regard, and its presentation requires a definition of "sufficient causal condition." Roughly, we may say that one state of affairs is a
sufficient causal condition of another just in case it is physically
necessary that, if the former occurs, the latter does also. More
precisely:

D.3.2:   *s* is a sufficient causal condition relative to *T* and
          T' and to *d* and *d'* of *t* =df. *s* and *t* are states of
          affairs which are not propositions and are such
          that:
          (i) *s* occurs at *T* ;
          (ii) *T* is not later than *T'*; and

(iii) it is physically necessary, but not metaphysically necessary, that, if s occurs at T, then t occurs at T'.[5]

(We may also say:

D.3.3:   It is causally necessary that t occur at T' =df. there are a state of affairs s, a time T, and determinate events d and d' such that s is a sufficient causal condition relative to T and T' and to d and d' of t.

In addition:

D.3.4:   It is causally necessary, given that s occurs at T, that t occur at T' =df. either
(i) there are determinate events d and d' such that s is a sufficient causal condition relative to T and T' and to d and d' of t; or
(ii) there are a state of affairs u, a time T^*, and determinate events d^*, d, and d' such that:
(a) u is a sufficient causal condition relative to T^* and T and to d^* and d of s; and
(b) u is a sufficient causal condition relative to T^* and T' and to d^* and d' of t.

This definition should now render clause (iii)(b) of D.3.1 intelligible.) Now, the assumption concerning causal contribution that I wish to base on this is the following:

A.3.2:   Necessarily, if e contributes causally relative to T and T' and to d and d' to f, then there are an event g, a time T^*, and a determinate event d^* such that
(i) T is not later than T^*, and
(ii) g is a sufficient causal condition relative to T^* and T' and to d^* and d' of f.

This assumption bears some discussion.

Roughly, what A.3.2 says is that, if on some occasion *e* contributes causally to *f*, then there is a sufficient causal condition of *f*'s occurrence then. But it is important to note that A.3.2 does *not* stipulate that *T* (the time of *e*'s occurrence) be identical with *T** (the time of *g*'s occurrence). It is often claimed that, if *e* causes *f*, then *e* is "part" of some event or condition *g* which is sufficient for *f*'s occurrence.[6] Now, how this claim is to be understood depends on one's interpretation of the term "part," and how this term is to be interpreted depends in part on one's ontology. Given the ontology laid out in Chapter 1, and given the treatment there of events as finely-grained, abstract entities, it seems natural to think of an event *e*'s being a "part" of an event *g* just in case *g* entails *e* (see D.1.9). The claim, then, on the present ontology, would seem to be that *e* contributes causally to *f* on some occasion only if *e* is a conjunct of some conjunctive event *g* which is, on that occasion, a sufficient causal condition of *f*'s occurrence. And it should be noted that, given A.1.3, this requires that *g* occur when (even if not only when) *e* occurs. Now all this is, so far, in accordance with A.3.2. But if, when it is claimed that *e* must be a "part of" such a *g* it is implied that *g* not just occur but *also* be *causally sufficient* for *f*'s occurrence *by or at the time at which e occurs*, then the claim is *false*.[7] For consider this case. Suppose that *e* is [Smith throws a baseball] and *f* is [a window breaks], and suppose that *e* contributed causally relative to times *T1* and *T3* (and to certain determinate events) to *f*. But suppose also that Jones was standing next to the window in question and had it within his power to intercept the ball at *T2* in its flight toward the window, but that he simply chose not to do so. Then, even though *e* contributed causally relative to *T1* and *T3* (and to certain determinate events) to *f*, it is not the case that there occurred an event *g*, of which *e* and certain other events are parts and which therefore occurred at *T1*, such that *g* was a sufficient causal condition *relative to T1 and T3* (and to certain determinate events) of *f*. For Jones could have intercepted the ball at *T2*, in which case the window would not have broken at *T3*. This surely implies that it was physically possible, even given *e*'s occurrence at *T1*, that Jones should intercept the ball at *T2* and hence that the window should *not* break at *T3*. Yet, to repeat, since Jones did not intercept the ball at *T2*, Smith's throwing the ball *did* contribute causally to the window's breaking. This case does not undermine A.3.2, however, which does not stipulate that *e* must be a part of *g* but requires only that there be an event *g* and a time *T** not earlier than *T1* (in fact, *T** must not be earlier than *T2*) such that *g* is a sufficient causal condition relative to *T** and *T3* (and to certain determinate events) of *f.*

At one point in *Person and Object* Chisholm makes a claim inconsistent with A.3.2. He says that an event *e* may contribute causally to an event *f* even if there occurs no sufficient causal condition of *f*, provided that *e* contributes causally to an event *g* which is a *necessary* causal condition of *f.*[8] Without spelling out in detail what Chisholm means by "necessary causal condition," we can see what he is driving at by considering the following case. It might be that on some occasion *e*, [Smith buys some balls], contributes causally to a necessary causal condition *g*, [there are balls available], of *f*, [Jones hits a backhand]; and yet, if *f* occurs *freely*, then (according to Chisholm, for he is an incompatibilist), there occurs on that occasion no sufficient causal condition of *f.* Nevertheless, Chisholm says, in such a case *e* does contribute causally to *f.* Even though I am inclined to accept that incompatibilism is true, I am inclined to deny Chisholm's contention here. Perhaps this is merely a terminological dispute, but I would rather say that on this occasion *e* "provides an opportunity" for *f*'s occurrence rather than that *e* "contributes causally" to *f.* For, whatever terminology one adopts, there seem to me to be two distinct concepts at issue here, and it is just as well to make sure that they are distinguished. I shall not say any more here about the concept of provision of opportunity, although I shall discuss it later in Chapter 11.

With this my characterization of the concept of causal contribution is almost complete, but I think that it would be helpful to round it out, first, by comparing it with certain claims made about causal contribution where events are taken to be concrete particulars and, second, by comparing it with certain claims made about so-called object-causation.

It is commonly claimed (where events are taken to be concrete particulars) that causal contribution is irreflexive, asymmetrical, and transitive.[9] Now, given the present ontology, if this claim is to be seen to hold at all, great care must be taken in its formulation. First, it is clear that an event *e* may contribute causally to itself, if by this is meant the following: it is possible that, for some event *e*, some times T and T', and some determinate events d and d', e contributes causally relative to T and T' and to d and d' to e. One *(roughly* worded) example of such "self-causing" *(loosely* so called) is where there are three levers *l1, l2,* and *l3* such that *l1* drops at *T1,* which causes *l2* to rise at *T2,* which causes *l3* to drop at *T3,* which causes *l1* to rise at *T4,* which causes *l2* to drop at *T5,* which causes *l3* to rise at *T6,* which causes *l1* to drop at *T7.* In such a case it will be true to say that [*l1* drops] contributes causally relative to *T1* and *T7* (and to certain determinate events) to [*l1* drops]. This example shows causal contribution *not* to be irreflexive and, by implication, *not* to be asymmetrical − in *one* sense of these terms. But I am inclined to go along with the claim that causal contribution *is* irreflexive and asymmetric (as well as transitive) in *another* sense of these terms. More precisely, I accept the following assumptions:

A.3.3: It is not possible that, for some event e, some time T, and some determinate event d, e contribute causally relative to T and T and to d and d to e.

A.3.4: It is not possible that, for some events e and f, some times T and T', and some determinate events d and d', both e contribute causally relative to T and T' and to d and d' to f and f contribute causally relative to T' and T and to d' and d to e.

A.3.5: Necessarily, for any events e, f, and g, any times T, T', and T^*, and any determinate events d, d', and d^*, if e contributes causally relative to T and T' and to d and d' to f and f contributes causally relative to T' and T^* and to d' and d^* to g, then e contributes causally relative to T and T^* and to d and d^* to g.

In fact, it will prove useful later on (in Chapter 6) to be able to say (roughly) of e, f, and g in A.3.5 that e contributes causally to g via f, where this is to be understood in terms of:

D.3.5:   *e* contributes causally relative to *T* and *T** and to
           d and *d** to *g* via *f* =df. there are a time *T'* and a
           determinate event *d'* such that:
           (i) *e* contributes causally relative to *T* and *T'*
           and to *d* and *d'* to *f*; and
           (ii) *f* contributes causally relative to *T'* and *T**
           and to *d'* and *d** to *g*.

Given A.3.5, it is of course superfluous to add to the definiens of
D.3.5 a clause to the effect that *e* contributes causally relative to *T*
and *T** and to *d* and *d*.* to *g*.
    Another common claim with respect to causal contribution is one
perhaps originally attributable to Hume, according to whom it is
impossible for an event *e* to cause an event *f* if *e* implies *f*. The
spirit of this claim is preserved in the following assumption:

A.3.6:   Necessarily, for any events *e* and *f*, any times *T*
           and *T'*, and any determinate events *d* and *d'*, if *e*
           contributes causally relative to *T* and *T'* and to *d*
           and *d'* to *f*, then [*e* occurs at *T*] does not strictly
           imply [*f* occurs at T'].

(This assumption is in keeping with clause (iii) of D.3.2 and with
A.3.2, where a certain metaphysically necessary connection between the events involved is proscribed.)
    Finally, the issue of the causation of events by objects needs to
be addressed. ("Objects" is here used to refer to individual things.)
Sometimes we utter such sentences as "the frayed wire caused the
fire," "the poison caused Jim's death," "John caused a mild sensation," and so on, where it seems that a causal relation between an
individual thing and an event is being cited. But such sentences as
these seem easily "reducible" in theory to sentences involving
straightforward causal contribution.[10] It would seem that such reduction may be achieved by conforming to the following schema
(where mention of times and determinate events to which the causation in question is relative is suppressed for simplicity's sake): for
any object *x* and event *f*, if *x* causes *f*, then there is an event *e* of
which *x* is a constituent and which contributes causally to *f*. Just
what event *e* is will depend upon the particular case, but we may

illustrate this schema's use by applying it to the foregoing examples. Thus, the frayed wire (*x*) caused the fire (*f*) only if some event *e* of which the frayed wire is a constituent caused the fire (perhaps *e* in this case was the wire's coming into contact with combustible material). So too, the poison (*x*) caused Jim's death (*f*) only if some event *e* of which the poison is a constituent caused his death (perhaps *e* in this case was Jim's ingesting the poison). Finally, John (*x*) caused a mild sensation (*f*) only if some event *e* of which John is a constituent caused the sensation (perhaps *e* in this case was John's streaking at a formal cocktail party). The pattern should be clear, although just what it is for an object to be a constituent of an event is something that I shall not investigate here.

It is important to mention two points with respect to the foregoing brief discussion of object-causation. First, to say simply that an object *x* causes an event *f* is in a sense incomplete in the absence of any specification of that event *e* of which *x* is a constituent and which causes *f*. Indeed, *x*'s causing *f* is (in part) *explained* by *e*'s occurring. That is, we may say that it is (in part) *because e* occurred that *x* caused *f*. (For instance, we may say that it was *because* the frayed wire came into contact with combustible material that it caused the fire.) Second, very many philosophers have claimed that (human) action essentially involves the causation of events by (human) agents. I believe this contention to be correct. But it should be made clear that it is a particular *sort* of causation-by-agents that is at issue here. For instance, the example was just given of the truth of "John caused a mild sensation" in terms of the truth of "John's streaking at a formal cocktail party caused a mild sensation," and it certainly seems that John's streaking was an action and that, because of this, his causing a mild sensation was also an action. But it might have been that John caused a mild sensation because he fell asleep during an important meeting, in which case the truth of "John caused a mild sensation" would have been parasitic on the truth of "John's falling asleep during an important meeting caused a mild sensation." If such had been the case, John's causing a mild sensation would *not* have been an action precisely because his falling asleep would not have been an action. Hence it is not just any sort of causation-by-agents which is involved in action, but agent-causation of a *particular* sort, namely, one where the agent is "active." But what this stipulation really amounts to – just *what* sort of agent-causation is essentially involved in action – is a source of strong disagreement amongst philosophers. Many claim that the sort of agent-causation at issue in human action is a *bona fide* species of object-causation (and hence reducible to event-causation, that is, analyzable in terms of what I have called causal contribution), and they claim that this species may be demarcated by placing restrictions on the *sort* of event *e* of which the object (in this case the agent) *x* is a constituent. A few claim that the sort of agent-causation at issue in human action is *not* a species of object-causation, and hence *not* reducible to event-causation, but something quite different; or at least they claim that, in addition to there being a type of agent-causation at issue in human action which *is* reducible to event-causation, there is a type of agent-causation at issue which is *not* so reducible.[1] [1] In the theory of action that is to follow, I shall adopt the former approach. That is, I shall treat human action as essentially involving a special sort of causation which *is* a species of object-causation and hence *is* reducible to causal contribution. I shall argue in Chapter 10 that it is a mistake to adopt the second approach and to insist that all human action essentially involves a sort of agent-causation which is not a species of object-causation and is not reducible to causal contribution. But, as will be seen in Chapter 11, there is still a role that agent-causation of the irreducible variety may play in an account of *free* human action.

3.2   *INTENTION*

The concept of intention, like the concept of causal contribution, is a concept with which most of us are quite familiar. Examples of intention abound in everyday life: Brown intends to have a bite to eat, Smith intends that Jones should be happy, and so on. Now, I take intention, strictly speaking, to be a propositional attitude; that is, it relates persons to propositions. And so, for example, when Brown intends to have a bite to eat, what is really involved is: Brown intends at some time T [there is a time T' not earlier than T such that [Brown has a bite to eat] occurs at T'].[1] [2]

Hector-Neri Castañeda would diagnose two major errors in the foregoing paragraph. He claims, first, that propositions are not the objects of intention, but that what he calls *practitions* are. And he claims, second, that intentions expressible in terms of "*S* intends to (do) *a* " are equivalent to intentions expressible in terms of "*S* intends that *he* (*himself*) (do) *a* " and not equivalent to intentions expressible in terms of "*S* intends that *S* (do) *a.*"[13] One argument for the first claim is that propositions are either true or false but that the objects of intention are neither. One argument for the second claim is that Brown may intend to have a bite to eat but, not knowing that he is Brown, not intend that Brown have a bite to eat. Now, each of these arguments has some force, but neither is unproblematic.[14] To try to evaluate them here, however, would take me too far afield, and so I shall rest content with the following observation. If Castañeda is correct on either score, my account of intention (and of volition, and in fact of action in general) is defective. But I am confident that the account could be modified to accommodate Castañeda's claims, and I am also confident that the account does not suffer to any significant degree in the absence of such modification. However, it also seems to me that such modification would complicate the account considerably, and it is partly for this reason that I shall not undertake to accommodate the claims here.

All intention, I think, involves intending that an event should occur. (It might also seem that all intention involves intending that some *action* occur and hence that an account of action based in part on the concept of intention – which is something that I shall shortly try to provide – is in grave danger of conceptual circularity. I shall address this issue more fully in Chapters 9 and 10.) Given this fact, it is convenient to adopt the following abbreviation. I shall say that a person *S* intends an *event e* at a time *T* just in case *S* intends at *T* the *proposition* [there is a time *T'* not earlier than T such that *e* occurs at *T'*]. For it is just such intending of events which features essentially in human action.

Despite its familiarity, the concept of intention is difficult to characterize in any positive way. In fact, it is far easier to say what is not true of the concept than to say what is true of it. But some of the non-implications that may be attributed to it are of significance and should be recorded here. Accordingly, we should note that *none* of the following statements is true:

(1)   Necessarily, if S intends e at T, then, for some
        time T', S considers e at T'.

(2)   Necessarily, if S considers e at T, then, for some
        time T', S intends e at T'.

(3)   Necessarily, if S intends e at T, then, for some
        time T', S accepts [there is a time T^* such that e
        occurs at T^*] at T'.

(4)   Necessarily, if S accepts [there is a time T^* such
        that e occurs at T^*] at T, then, for some time T',
        S intends e at T'.

(5)   Necessarily, if S intends e at T, then, for some
        time T', e occurs at T'.

(6)   Necessarily, if S intends e at T, then it is physi-
        cally possible that, for some time T', e occur at T'.

(7)   Necessarily, if S intends e at T, then it is meta-
        physically possible that, for some time T', e occur
        at T'.

(8)   Necessarily, if S intends e at T, then, for some
        time T', S accepts [it is physically possible that,
        for some time T^*, e occur at T^*] at T'.

(9)   Necessarily, if S intends e at T, then, for some
        time T', S accepts [it is metaphysically possible
        that, for some time T^*, e occur at T^*] at T'.

Other non-implications concerning the concept of intention could of course be cited, but the foregoing are perhaps the most significant.[15] Nevertheless, some fairly uncontroversial implications may also be attributed to this concept, of which the following are perhaps the most significant:

A.3.7:   Necessarily, if S intends e at T and S is rational, then S accepts [there is a time T' not earlier than T such that e may well occur at T'] at T.

A.3.8:   Necessarily, if S intends e at T and S is rational, then it is physically possible that, for some time T' not earlier than T, e occur at T'.

But these assumptions are few in number and present, besides, two obvious problems. The first problem is that they invoke the concept of rationality, an obscure concept that I shall not seek to clarify here. The second problem is that in A.3.7 the locution "may well" is employed. How are we to interpret this? Again, I shall not venture a response here – beyond noting that "may well" does *not* connote "at least a fifty-fifty chance" of occurrence – although I think that the locution has some intuitive appeal.[16]

It would be advantageous to be able to determine the truth-value of such interesting statements as the following:

(10)   Necessarily, if S intends e at T, then S desires [there is a time T' such that e occurs at T'] at T.

(11)   Necessarily, if S intends e at T, then S accepts [S intends e at T] at T.

(12)   Necessarily, if S intends e at T and e entails f and S accepts [e entails f] at T and S is rational, then S intends f at T.

And so on. Several philosophers endorse (10), or something close to it, at least with respect to what they call a broad sense of "want" or "desire."[17] Other philosophers have rejected (10).[18] I am inclined to reject it, although this inclination is tempered with the acknowledgement that the terms "want" and "desire" can indeed be construed very broadly, and that it is certainly arguable that it is in keeping with common usage to construe "desire" so broadly that (10) may be seen to be true on such a construal. (Indeed, we often seem to use "I want to do such-and-such" as a mere stylistic variant of "I intend to do such-and-such." But the question arises whether, in this context, "want" really does express a desire.) And with respect to (11) and (12), I am inclined to accept the former and to reject the latter.[19] But my inclinations with respect to (10), (11), (12), and suchlike are not all that firm, and, rather than plump for or against any of them, it seems to me that the best thing to do is to back off and to acknowledge the fact that the concept of intention, despite its familiarity (to me and to others), is not crystal-clear (at least to me). I shall not force the issue, for, in the absence of an analysis of the concept of intention, there will always be statements of the sort we have been considering and whose truth-value is problematic. After all, there is, I think, no philosophical theory, concerning any topic, which can boast complete clarity with respect to all those unanalyzed concepts employed in its foundation. In the present case, the concept of intention is, I believe, unusually well-suited for the role it is to play in the theory that is to follow; for it is a common concept and is readily, even if a little roughly, understood.[20]

3.3   VOLITION

The third and final concept to be introduced here is that of volition.[21] This concept is neither as common nor as familiar as the concepts of causal contribution and intention; moreover, my use of this concept may differ a little from that use to which one is perhaps intuitively moved to put it. Some philosophers regard volition as a species of desire or desire-*cum*-belief.[22] I do not so regard it (unless, perhaps, "desire" is taken in an extremely broad sense −

see the discussion of statement (10) above). Rather, I regard volition as a species of practical decision. (In general, there is a distinction to be drawn between two broad categories of decision-making, the practical and the theoretical. If I decide to turn in early, I make a practical decision. If I decide that capital punishment is unjustifiable, I make a theoretical decision. It is with the former only that volition is to be allied.) Moreover, although I take every volition to be a practical decision, the reverse is not something that I take to be true. Roughly, it is only when I intend that my decision should be causally effective in bringing about that state of affairs that I have decided should occur, that my decision is a volition. (See A.3.10 below. This point has to do with the distinction between "short-range" and "long-range" decisions mentioned in problem F2 in Chapter 2 and to be discussed more fully in Chapter 9 below.)

Volition, like intention, is strictly a propositional attitude. In fact, I assume the following:

A.3.9:   Necessarily, if S wills p at T, then S intends p at T,

where "p" ranges over propositions and "wills" is the verb whose noun is "volition."[2][3] Like intention, all volition involves intending that an event should occur. Indeed, all volition involves willing that an event should occur. And so, it is again convenient to employ an abbreviation. I shall say that a person S wills an *event e* at a time T just in case S wills at T the *proposition* [there is a time T' not earlier than T such that e occurs at T']. For it is just such willing of events which features essentially in human action.

I do not presume that there is any necessary restriction on the type of event which may be the object of volition; but there is certainly such a restriction operative under normal circumstances, where an agent has a reasonable understanding and expectation of what it is he can and cannot do. (Of course, the terms "do" and "can" are in need of definition – and such definition will be supplied in Chapter 4 and Chapter 11, respectively – but perhaps their use in this context is nevertheless helpful.) Under normal circumstances (where the sort of volition at issue is volition of events rather than propositions), objects of volition are restricted to those events which the agent believes he can bring about. (Under normal circumstances, then, what an agent wills is a guide to or a measure of the confidence he has in his own ability.) Furthermore, as I use the term "volition," objects of volition are restricted, under normal circumstances, to those events which the agent believes he can bring about without having to bring about any other events. Examples are: Smith wills that his arm should rise (*i.e.*, Smith wills [Smith's arm rises]); Jones wills that his right knee should bend (*i.e.*, Jones wills [Jones's right knee bends]); Brown wills that his eyes should move (*i.e.*, Brown wills [Brown's eyes move]); and so on.

There is a sense of "will" which may be analyzed in terms of that sense of "will" that I am using unanalyzed here, and which is perhaps a slightly more intuitive sense of that term than the restrictive sense that I employ here. There are some things that we will just for their own sake; but very often we will things not just for their own sake but also in order that other events may come about. For instance, Jones may will that his arm should rise so that Smith will recognize him and walk over to his side of the street. Now, there is a sense of "will" in which Jones in this case not only wills [Jones's arm rises], but also wills [Smith recognizes Jones], and even wills [Smith walks over to Jones's side of the street]. Let us call this willing in the "broad" sense. Perhaps this sense of "will" is more intuitive than that restrictive sense to which I have appealed; still, it is easily seen that the former is simply an extension of the latter. That is, we may say:

D.3.6:   *S* broadly wills *e* at *T* =df. either
          (i) *S* wills *e* at *T* ; or
          (ii) there is an event *f* such that *S* wills *f* at *T* for
          the purpose of *e*.

It would be helpful if a definition of the locution "*S* wills *f* at *T* for the purpose of *e* " were provided here, but unfortunately I am not in a position to provide such a definition. For this definition would require an account of the concept of the provision of opportunity, and I am not yet in a position to give such an account. (See D.11.16 below.) Nevertheless, there is a limited use of the notion of willing for a purpose which may be accounted for here, and indeed accounting for it here will prove useful later on. I propose that we say, roughly, that a person wills an event *e* in order that an event *f* may occur just in case he wills *e* and has a "second-order" intention to the effect that his so willing contribute causally to *f.* More precisely:

D.3.7:   *S* wills *e* at *T* in order that *f* may occur =df.
      (i) *S* wills *e* at *T* ; and
      (ii) *S* intends at *T* that, for some time *T'* and
some determinate events *d* and *d'*, [*S* wills *e*]
should contribute causally relative to *T* and *T'*
and to *d* and *d'* to *f.*

It should be stressed that this is a purely stipulative definition. The definiens is *not* intended to account for every type of willing for a purpose, but only for one type of such willing. We may also say, in light of D.3.7, the following:

D.3.8:   *S* directly wills *e* at *T* =df. *S* wills *e* at *T.*

D.3.9:   *S* indirectly wills *e* at *T* =df. there is an event *f*
distinct from *e* such that *S* wills *f* at *T* in order
that *e* may occur.[2 4]

Some additional remarks may be made to characterize the concept of volition further. As with the concept of intention, there are many non-implications that may be attributed to the concept of volition, foremost among which are analogues to statements (2) through (9) above where "wills" replaces "intends." But there are also some significant implications and some problematic claims that should be emphasized in this context. Foremost among the former are A.3.9 and also:

A.3.10:   Necessarily, if *S* wills *e* at *T*, then *S* intends at *T*
that, for some time *T'* very close to *T* and some
determinate events *d* and *d'*, [*S* wills *e*] should
contribute causally relative to *T* and *T'* and to *d*
and *d'* to *e.*[2 5]

Roughly, what A.3.10 says is that a person wills an event *e* only if he has a "second-order" intention to the effect that his so willing contribute causally to *e*. The locution "very close to" in A.3.10 is unfortunately vague, but it is difficult to see how it can be improved upon. It is, moreover, accurate. (If I will my arm's rising, I mean for this to happen *now*.) A.3.10 serves to distinguish willing from certain other types of practical decision-making. For instance, if Smith now decides that Jones should be seen by a doctor, it is unlikely that he means for this to happen now and it is even more unlikely that he regards his decision as causally effective in bringing this about now.

Foremost among the problematic claims about volition are the following analogues to statements (1) and (10):

(14)   Necessarily, if *S* wills *e* at *T*, then, for some time *T'*, *S* considers *e* at *T'*.

(15)   Necessarily, if *S* wills *e* at *T*, then *S* desires [there is a time *T'* such that *e* occurs at *T'*] at *T*.

(15) is problematic in just the same way that (10) is, and I shall not discuss it further. But (14) differs from (1) in the following respect. (1), I said, is clearly false, and so it is; but (14)'s truth-value is far from obvious. I am inclined to say that (14) is true for the reason that, when we act, we are commonly aware of what it is we will, and thereby intend, to take place. But to insist on the truth of (14) would seem to be to rule out as actions (in the sense of "action" at issue) so-called "habitual" actions, which differ from "straightforward" actions (as far as I can see) only in so far as they are performed with a certain degree of regularity and, especially, performed without our being (fully) aware of what it is we intend to take place. (Notice that, when we do perform habitual actions, we commonly do so intentionally.) Since I do not wish automatically to rule out habitual actions as actions (in the sense of "action" at issue), I am inclined also to say that (14) is false. And so I have conflicting inclinations with respect to the truth of (14). Perhaps the truth of the matter is that there are *degrees* of awareness, and hence that consideration is not an all-or-nothing affair. (In fact, I am sure that this is true, although I did not go into this in Chapter 1, where the concept of consideration was introduced; and I did not

go into this for the reason that I really have nothing enlightening to say about it.) And it *may* be – although I would not insist on this – that "straightforward" action involves a high degree of awareness of what one intends to do, whereas "habitual" action involves a low degree of such awareness. But it may also be that some "habitual" action involves *no* degree of such awareness – I am just not sure. The hesitant conclusion of this brief discussion is, then: I am inclined on balance to think of "habitual" action as action (in the sense of "action" at issue – and what sense that is will be discussed further in the next chapter); if all such action involves some degree of awareness of the sort mentioned, then I am inclined on balance to accept (14); if not, then I am inclined on balance to reject (14).²⁶

D.3.7 and A.3.10 yield the following theorem:

T.3.2:   Necessarily, S wills e at T if and only if S wills e at T in order that e may occur.

And D.3.7 and A.3.9 yield the following theorem:

T.3.3:   Necessarily, if S wills e at T in order that f may occur, then S intends e at T.

But neither of the following is a theorem, although I think it proper to assume the truth of each:

A.3.11:   Necessarily, if S wills e at T in order that f may occur, then S intends f at T.

A.3.12:   Necessarily, if S wills e at T in order that f may occur, then S intends at T that, for some time T' and some determinate events d and d', [S wills e in order that f may occur] should contribute causally relative to T and T' and to d and d' to f.

Analogues to A.3.7 and A.3.8 (where "wills" replaces "intends") may also, I think, be properly asserted.

With the foregoing as background, I shall now turn to a statement of that theory of human action that I accept and that I propose should be accepted. This statement will be the subject-matter of Chapters 4 through 9. I shall start, in Chapter 4, with an account of what acting in general is.

Notes

1   The reason for the qualifier "primary" will be given shortly.

2   Instead of saying (i) that *e* contributes causally to *f*, I shall sometimes say (ii) that *e* is a cause of *f* and even (iii) that *e* causes *f*. I shall use each of these three expressions interchangeably, although the last of these is perhaps misleading, in so far as it can also legitimately be used to express the relation of being-the-cause-of.

3   *Cf.* Kim (1979), pp.159-160.

4   The examples are taken from Taylor (1966, pp.55-6; 1967, p.65). Although I take it as obvious that simultaneous causation is possible, I do not think it *obvious* that "backward" or "reverse" causation is impossible. Nevertheless, I do believe that "reverse" causation *is* impossible, and A.3.2 (below) reflects this belief.

5   *Cf.* Chisholm (1976), p.58. I use the locution "not later than" to mean the same as "earlier than or identical with."

6   See, *e.g.*, J.L.Mackie's well-known discussion of causes as "INUS" conditions in Mackie (1965).

7   At times – but only at times – Chisholm seems to subscribe to this requirement concerning causal contribution. (See Chisholm (1976), p.205, n.9.) The remarks to follow, then, are pertinent to his treatment of the topic.

8   Chisholm (1976), p.68. Notice that this treatment of causal

contribution is *inconsistent* with the treatment mentioned in the last note.

9   The relation of being-*the*-cause-of is commonly thought to be irreflexive, asymmetrical, and *non*transitive.

10   This is not an original claim. Many philosophers have made it. See, *e.g.*, Goldman (1970), pp.80-5; Aune (1977), pp.7-8; Thomson (1977), Chapter 3; Davis (1979), pp.10-12.

11   Chisholm seems recently to have changed his mind on this point. In his early writings (*e.g.*, 1966) he invokes the concept of agent-causation unanalyzed, but in later writings (1976, pp.69-70; 1979, pp.363-4) he says that it is analyzable, indeed, analyzable in terms of the concept of event-causation. But the matter is complicated. See note 58 to Chapter 10 and note 14 to Chapter 11 below.

12   In general, by "*S* intends *p* at *T* " is meant: [*S* intends *p*] occurs at *T*. Compare D.1.3.

13   See Castañeda (1975), Chapter 6, for one recent statement of these points. Castañeda has made these same points in numerous other places. Note that Chisholm now would also diagnose the same errors (Chisholm, 1981), although he would prescribe different remedies from those prescribed by Castañeda.

14   For instance, with respect to the first argument, some have claimed that the meanings of certain assertoric sentences are propositions, and yet it is certainly odd to say that a meaning may be true or false. Does this oddity clearly show that meanings are not propositions? No; it might be taken merely to show that what it is odd to say may nevertheless, on occasion, be true. With respect to the second claim, it seems to me that whether or not "*S* intends that he (himself) (do) *a* " and "*S* intends that *S* (do) *a* " mean the same depends on what we allow to be a substituend of "*S*." Clearly, Castañeda's point holds if we allow a definite description to be such a substituend; but I have already ruled such substitution out. (See note 23 to Chapter 1.) Still, someone might seek to press the point even

when "*S*" is replaced by a term expressing an individual essence. This is an area into which I cannot venture here. It should be noted, though, that while many philosophers apparently accept Castañeda's claim that "reflexive" statements of the form "*S* intends that he (himself) (do) *a* " are irreducible to statements of the form "*S* intends that...*S*..." (where no mention of the reflexive "he (himself)" is made), not all philosophers agree with this irreducibility thesis. See, for instance, Boër and Lycan (1980).

15 For many other such non-implications, see Davidson (1978), p.83.

16 Something like A.3.7 is proposed by many philosophers, including: Kenny (1966), p.648; Audi (1973), pp.395-6; Davis (1979), p.75. Some have gone so far as to propose something like (3), which I have rejected. (See, *e.g.*, Grice (1971), p.264; Harman (1976), p.432). Others have rejected A.3.7. (See, *e.g.*, Thalberg (1962), p.50ff.) I shall not argue the merits of my acceptance of A.3.7 and my rejection of (3); I shall simply assume that what I say in this regard is true. It should be acknowledged, however, that the issue is not only controversial but difficult to resolve. For instance, I reject (3) because I reject the claim that intention requires the belief that the event intended will certainly occur. But it might be argued that this claim is not implied by (3); indeed, it might be argued further that (3) *is* implied by A.3.7 and hence that acceptance of the latter requires acceptance of the former. I owe this point to Paul Bowen. See Section 6.3 of Chapter 6 for further discussion of this issue as it pertains to "Butler's problem."

17 See, *e.g.*, Kenny (1966), p.647; Audi (1973), pp.395-6; Davidson (1978), p.101.

18 See, *e.g.*, Davis (1979), pp.73-4.

19 Compare my rejection of (12) with Chisholm's principle concerning what he calls the nondivisiveness of intention in Chisholm (1976) p.74.

20   *Cf.* Chapter 1, note 30. What I have said here concerning the concept of intention both accords with and conflicts with what others have said concerning it in ways not yet acknowledged. For instance, some philosophers have attempted to analyze the concept of intention and related concepts *(e.g.,* Baier (1970); Grice (1971); Audi (1973); Bratman (1979)), but they have proceeded in a manner which, for reasons that I shall not enter into here, seem to me objectionable. Others have characterized the concept in ways that I have not mentioned here *(e.g.,* Sellars (1976), p.126; Aune (1967b), p.199; Harman (1976), pp.440-1, 432; Danto (1973), p.21). These are ways with which I cannot express unreserved agreement, either because I think them actually to be erroneous or because I am not convinced of their accuracy.

21   I do not claim that the concept of volition is unanalyzable, as some do *(e.g.,* Prichard (1949)). I only claim not to be able to analyze it.

22   *E.g.,* Goldman (1970; 1976).

23   By "*S* wills *p* at *T* " is meant: [*S* wills *p*] occurs at *T*.

24   D.3.8 and D.3.9 are somewhat inelegant, in that it would seem more natural to make willing the basic notion in such a way that direct willing and indirect willing would *both* be types of willing. The reason why I have not adopted this approach is simply that I shall henceforth confine my attention almost exclusively to direct willing, and, since it is easier to write – and read – "wills" rather than "directly wills," I have stipulated in D.3.8 that the two be synonymous.

25   Harman (1976, p.439) notes that on occasion a person regards his intention itself as a means to what he intends. I think that it would be more accurate to say what is said here by means of A.3.10 and A.3.12 below.

26   Hence the unanalyzed concept of volition remains to some extent obscure, as do all the other concepts invoked unanalyzed in this work.

Chapter 4
ACTING IN GENERAL

4.1   INTRODUCTION

A lot of things fall under the rubric "acting in general," for actions come in many shapes and sizes. Smith may perform an action by (a) raising his hand, bending his knee, extending his arm, signalling, saluting, kicking himself, cursing, concentrating on a problem, reaching a conclusion; or he may perform an action by (b) shooting Jones, killing Jones, frightening Jones, pleasing Jones, even by scaring himself; or he may perform an action by (c) crossing the road, hitting a forehand, singing a song, playing a piano solo, cooking a dinner, multiplying 928 by 254, giving a speech, or saying a prayer. Of course, Smith may perform an action by doing all sorts of other things as well, but this list should give a good idea of the variety of things that he may do. The reason for dividing these examples into three separate groups will be discussed later.

It is best to point out right at the start, however, certain limitations to the current project. While I shall attempt in this chapter to give an account of "acting in general" (that is, of what it is to act – *simpliciter* – rather than, say, of what it is to act intentionally, what it is to do one thing by doing another, and so on, which are issues that I shall address in later chapters), there are certain events which are commonly called actions and yet which will not be discussed here. For instance, while the account is designed to accommodate certain so-called "reflex actions" (such as stepping on the car-brake when a dog darts out into the street), it is not designed to accommodate certain other so-called "reflex actions" (such as when one's knee jerks upon being tapped). Or again, some philosophers have recently turned their attention to so-called "collective actions" (such as the actions that governments, or societies, or corporations, and so on, perform or take); I shall not attempt to provide an account of any such action as this, either, although an account may perhaps be based on what I shall provide here.[1] But these limitations to the present enterprise are in keeping with approaches adopted by other philosophers to the topic, and they are applied for the simple reason that, along with others, I take the sort of action, of which I shall attempt to give an account in this chapter, to be philosophically so important and so significantly different from any other sorts of action that a separate account of it is not only justified but desirable.[2]

I said in the last chapter that I take volition to be essential to action. Now, H.A.Prichard contends that acting consists *simply* in willing something.[3] That is, in the present vernacular, Prichard's claim is:

D.4.1: S acts at T =df. there is an event e such that S wills e at T.

(Perhaps "broadly wills," as defined in D.3.6, should replace "wills" in the definiens of D.4.1, but this is a minor point that need not be pursued here.) I reject this definition, for a reason that I think is good, although I recognize that it is not conclusive. The reason is this: the definition does not seem to conform with the intuition, which I share with many others and which I mentioned in the last chapter, that human action essentially involves an agent's causing an event to occur. That is, it is presumably possible for a volition to be inefficacious, as is perhaps the case where a totally paralyzed person, ignorant of his paralysis, tries to raise his arm. It seems to me plausible to say that, if ever a volition occurs which has no effect, then no action takes place, precisely because nothing has been caused by the agent to happen. But this reasoning is not conclusive, of course, for it rests on a·claim (that all action involves an agent's causing an event to occur) for which I have not argued and for which I do not propose to argue. Moreover, a case might be made in favor of D.4.1 by appealing to the fact that, in attacking it, I have made use of a term which is commonly associated with action, namely, the term "tries." That is, it might be claimed that, whenever one tries to do something, one does something, and if one can be said to try to do something simply by virtue of willing something, then to will something *is* to do something.

My response to this is twofold. First, while I accept that whenever one wills something one attempts something, and while I accept that some attempts are actions, I do not accept that all attempts are actions. Attempts may be divided into two broad categories: those which involve effort, and those which do not. It is the former that are actions; the latter, I think, are not. Now, all of this is very rough, but I shall not try to make it more precise here; for to do so would require an account of what *effort* is, and I am not in a position to provide such an account.[4] Secondly, and perhaps more importantly, it is tidier to have an account of acting which is exceptionless. Now, some acting certainly does consist in the causing of events by agents, so why not say that all acting does? This, at any rate, is what I choose to say, and so I reject D.4.1. If I am wrong in this, my error is easily remedied; the analysis of the concept of action that I shall provide (see D.4.3.c) need only be modified by tacking on to the analysans the clause "or there is an event e such that S wills e at T."

I have said that all acting involves an agent's causing an event to occur, but in the last chapter I pointed out that not just *any* agent-causing may be said to be acting. What I do think is true is that all acting involves an agent's *volition* having some effect e and that the *agent* may be said to cause e because of this. In order to minimize confusion, I shall henceforth talk of an agent's *bringing about* a certain event (rather than of an agent's *causing* a certain event) when he acts; I shall reserve the term "cause" to express a relation between an *event* and an event. At this point, then, I am prepared to commit myself to two assumptions, which may be stated with precision as follows:

A.4.1:   Necessarily, S brings about e relative to T and T' and to d and d' only if there is an event f such that:
    (i) S wills f at T; and
    (ii) [S wills f] contributes causally relative to T and T' and to d and d' to e.[5]

A.4.2:   Necessarily, S acts relative to T and T' and to d and d' only if there is an event e such that S brings about e relative to T and T' and to d and d'.

(Note that the times and determinate events to which the bringing about and acting are relative in these assumptions are the times and determinate events to which the causal contribution at issue is relative. Henceforth, I shall omit any *explicit* mention of the determinate events to which an instance of causal contribution (or bringing about, or acting) is relative. Such mention will of course remain implicit in what I say, but since I shall have no occasion to comment further upon determinate events, omission of any explicit mention of them will simplify the discussion that follows without any serious loss in precision). The question that now confronts us is whether or not all we need do to capture the concept of action is to elevate the two foregoing assumptions to the status of definitions by deleting "Necessarily" and replacing "only if" with " = df." in each case.

4.2   ACTIONS AND ISSUES

In order to answer this question we must draw up a three-fold distinction between actions, issues, and consequences. The distinction between actions and consequences, while at times problematic (see problem B4 in Chapter 2), is familiar enough. But "issue" is here a technical term. I use it in the same way – or close to the same way – as Georg von Wright uses the term "result."[6] I use "issue" instead of "result" simply because the term "result" is commonly used interchangeably with the terms "consequence" and "effect," and there is a sharp distinction to be drawn between a consequence or effect of an action and that which I call the issue of an action. What is the issue of an action? I have said that acting involves the bringing about of an event; an issue is simply an event which is brought about in a certain way. We may introduce here a piece of suggestive terminology and say that to every action there is an issue "internal" to it.[7] That is, in general: an agent S brings about an event e in such a way that the bringing about is an instance of genuine acting on S's part if and only if S's bringing about e is an action of S's and e is the event internal to this action, that is, e is the issue of the action. Examples of this relation of internality abound. For instance, if Smith raises his arm, then he brings about his arm's rising; and so, the issue [Smith's arm rises] is internal to the action [Smith raises his arm]. Similarly, [Smith's knee bends] is internal to [Smith bends his knee], and so on. Five points in particular should be noted here. First, the issue of an action is, to speak loosely, "everything" that is brought about, and not just the "end-state" of that which is brought about. For instance, the issue internal to Smith's raising his arm is, as has been said, Smith's arm's rising (or, as I have put it, [Smith's arm rises]); it is not Smith's arm's having or being risen (or, as it may be put, [Smith's arm is risen]).[8] Secondly, it must immediately be acknowledged that consequences as well as issues can be brought about, and this is because an event may at one and the same time be the issue of one action and a consequence of another.[9] This will be cleared up shortly. Thirdly, an action strictly implies the issue internal to it but commonly implies none of its consequences.[10] Fourthly, it is not being contended that an event which is an issue on one occasion is an issue *whenever* it occurs; it is an issue only when it is brought about by a person – otherwise it is an event which is not an issue. In other words, *being an issue* is a property which an event may have at some times and not others. On the other hand, an action is always – indeed, necessarily – an action.[11] Fifthly, it happens that in English there is often a phrase available to express an action when none is available to express the issue internal to the action. Donald Davidson, for instance, worries about finding phrases to express those issues internal to the actions expressed by "He walked to the corner," "He carved a roast," and "He fell down." He says:

> My problem isn't that I can't imagine that there
> is some bodily movement that the agent might be
> said to make happen, but that I see no way *auto-*
> *matically* to produce the right description from the
> original sentence. No doubt each time a man
> walks to the corner there is some way he makes
> his body move; but of course it does not follow
> that there is some one way he makes his body
> move every time he walks to the corner.[12]

I sympathize with Davidson's worries,[13] but it should be noted that his final remark is irrelevant. True, there is no one way in which a person's body moves every time he walks to the corner, but there is also no one way in which a person's arm moves every time he raises his arm. This point, then, is independent of the question concerning the availability or unavailability of appropriate phrases in English to express issues internal to actions. The main point to be made here, of course, is that the availability or unavailability of such phrases is a purely contingent linguistic fact which itself has no bearing on the ontological structure of an action. An action, such as the carving of a roast, is in fact the bringing about of an event in a certain way, even if there is no phrase available in English to express that event.[14]

It appears that philosophers sometimes confuse actions and issues, although the evidence of such confusion is often equivocal. For instance, those who favor an ontology of events as concrete particulars often say that actions just are bodily movements.[15] Now, [Smith's arm rises] appears to be a bodily movement (or, at least, a movement when it occurs), and yet, while it may on occasion be an issue, it surely is not an action. However, perhaps it may be said that [Smith raises his arm] is also a movement, for we may note that the verb "move" may be used both transitively and intransitively and, on this basis, may distinguish between what may be called "transitive movements" and "intransitive movements."[16] We may then say that [Smith's arm rises] is an intransitive movement, while [Smith raises his arm] is a transitive movement. And, if what is meant by "all actions are bodily movements" is that all actions are transitive bodily movements, then there would seem here to be no confusion of actions and issues after all.[17] But the matter becomes somewhat complicated, even when the conceptual distinction between transitive movements and intransitive movements is drawn, by those who think of actions as concrete particulars. For then they will often say that *one and the same event* is both a transitive movement (under one "description") and an intransitive movement (under another "description"). This complication may be avoided when actions are taken to be finely-grained, abstract entities. Even when actions are so understood, however, there is evidence that actions and issues are sometimes confused.[18] Be that as it may, it suffices to say here that the two ought not to be confused and that I shall make sure not to confuse them in what follows.[19]

4.3   *BRINGING ABOUT AN EVENT DIRECTLY*

I shall give a precise analysis of the concepts of an action and an issue in the next chapter, but perhaps the distinction between these concepts may be adequately understood for present purposes from the foregoing remarks. The point of this brief digression has been to put us in a position to evaluate the suggestion that A.4.1 and A.4.2 be elevated to the status of definitions. Such elevation results in the following (when explicit mention of determinate events is suppressed):

D.4.2:   *S* brings about *e* unrestrictedly relative to *T* and
          T' =df. there is an event *f* such that:
          (i) *S* wills *f* at *T* ; and
          (ii) [*S* wills *f*] contributes causally relative to *T*
          and *T'* to *e*.

D.4.3.a: *S* acts relative to *T* and *T'* =df. there is an event
            e such that *S* brings about *e* unrestrictedly rela-
            tive to *T* and *T'*.

There can be no quarrel with D.4.2, for it is a purely stipulative definition. (I use the term "unrestrictedly" to differentiate that type of bringing about analyzed in D.4.2 from other types discussed below.) But D.4.3.a constitutes an attempt to capture as precisely as possible our common concept of what it is to act, and it surely fails. For it is much too liberal.[20] Suppose that *S* wills some event *f* and that his so willing causes some totally "unrelated" event *e* to occur and no "related" event to occur. For instance, suppose that Jones wills his arm's rising and that his so willing, by some misfortune, causes a blood vessel to burst in his brain and that this in turn causes him to keel over (his arm remaining at his side) and thereupon expire. Although we may acknowledge that, in some sense of "bring about" (namely, that sense given in D.4.2), Jones has brought about his own death, we are surely reluctant to say that he has *acted* in this case. We would rather say that in this case, as in the case regarding D.4.1, Jones has failed to act, despite his attempt. Or suppose that Smith wills that his right knee should bend and that his so willing causes a certain nervous impulse to emanate from his brain, but that this impulse for some reason fades before any muscular activity is produced. Once again, although we may acknowledge that, in some sense of "bring about," Jones has brought about the nervous impulse, we are surely reluctant to say that he has *acted* in this case.[2][1]

It seems that some connection between a person's volition and what this volition causes to happen, other than merely that of causal contribution, is required, if we are properly to say of the person that he has acted. The most natural move in a first attempt to forge such a connection is, I think, to make explicit mention of the event caused by the volition in the description of the volition itself. This may be done in either of two ways. We might try first of all replacing D.4.2. with the following:

D.4.4: S brings about e restrictedly relative to T and T'
= df.
   (i) S wills e at T ; and
   (ii) [S wills e] contributes causally relative to T and T' to e.

And we might then say that a person acts just in case he brings about some event restrictedly. But this would not do. D.4.4 takes only direct willing into account (see D.3.8), and an adequate, enlightening account of action must take into consideration the matter of indirect willing also (see D.3.9). For instance, let e be [Jones's arm rises] and f be the event internal to [Jones summons the nurse], and suppose that Jones wills e but that he wills it in order that f may occur. What if Jones is successful? That is, what if Jones's willing e in order that f may occur contributes causally to f? Surely we should say in such a case that Jones's summoning the nurse is an action and that f is (therefore) the issue of this action. But analyzing the concept of action purely in terms of D.4.4 would leave us none the wiser in such a case.[2][2]

If we introduce the concept of indirect willing into our account, which is the second way to attempt to accommodate the insight that explicit mention should be made of the event caused by the volition in the description of the volition itself, we get the following:

D.4.5:   *S* accomplishes *e* relative to *T* and *T'* =df. there
            is an event *f* such that:
            (i) *S* wills *f* at *T* in order that *e* may occur; and
            (ii) [*S* wills *f* in order that *e* may occur] contrib-
            utes causally relative to *T* and *T'* to *e*.

And then we might say that a person acts just in case he accomplishes some event. But this would not do either; this account of
acting is too restrictive. Sometimes people act unintentionally, and
when they do it may well be that no event (other than that which is
directly willed) is accomplished thereby; nevertheless, they act. For
instance, suppose that Smith wills that his hand should move in order that the event internal to his signalling Jones may occur, but
suppose that he fails to signal Jones and that all he succeeds in doing (other than to move his hand) is to knock over Brown's Ming
vase. [Jones knocks over Brown's Ming vase] is an action of
Jones's, but the account of action just proposed does not allow for
this.

There are innumerable paths that one could take at this point in
order to try to forge a middle way between the overly liberal account of action based on D.4.2 and the overly restrictive account of
action based on D.4.5. But at this stage I shall content myself with
describing just one of these paths – that which I believe preferable
to all others. Just why this path is taken and not some other path
is a matter that I shall not discuss further; my handling of this issue must be judged according to the comprehensiveness, explanatory power, and intuitive appeal of the theory to which it gives rise.

First I require a technical concept. Let us say that an event *e*
constitutes an event *f* just in case whatever causes *e* also causes *f*.
Or more precisely:[2] [3]

D.4.6:   *e* constitutes *f* at *T* =df.
            (i) *e* occurs at *T* ;
            (ii) *f* occurs at *T* ;
            (iii) there are an event *g* and a time *T'* such that
            g contributes causally relative to *T'* and *T* to *e* ;
            and
            (iv) for any event *g* and any time *T'*, if *g* contrib-
            utes causally relative to *T'* and *T* to *e*, then *g*
            contributes causally relative to *T'* and *T* to *f*.

This definition is supposed to accommodate, at least in part, the following sort of intuition. When Jones insults Smith by calling him names, there is a tendency to say that his calling Smith names "just is" his insulting Smith in this case. Or when Jones apologizes to Smith by sending him flowers, there is a tendency to say that his sending Smith flowers "just is" his apologizing to him. Now, as is to be expected and as will be seen in the next chapter, I advocate a criterion for the individuation of actions according to which actions are finely-grained; and so it is false, on my view, that Jones's calling Smith names is *identical* with his insulting Smith or that his sending Smith flowers is *identical* with his apologizing to him. Nevertheless, it is true that on these occasions his calling Smith names *constitutes* his insulting Smith and that his sending Smith flowers *constitutes* his apologizing to Smith, and so we have here at least a partial account of the "just is" intuition.[2 4] Not only is D.4.6 useful in this regard (more will be said in this respect when the "by"-relation is discussed in Chapter 7 below), but also I believe that it is this relation of constitution that will allow us to provide the link that we are looking for, that is, that non-causal link between the volition and what the volition causes to happen whenever a person acts. But, first of all, let us note this theorem:

T.4.1: Necessarily, if *e* occurs at *T* and there are an event *f* and a time *T'* such that *f* contributes causally relative to *T'* and *T* to *e*, then *e* constitutes *e* at *T*.

That is, roughly: every event which is caused constitutes itself. Let us then say that a person brings about an event directly just in case the object of his direct volition both is caused by that volition and constitutes the event in question. More precisely:

D.4.7: *S* brings about *e* directly relative to *T* and *T'* =df. there are events *f* and *g* such that:
(i) *S* wills *f* at *T* in order that *g* may occur;
(ii) [*S* wills *f* in order that *g* may occur] contributes causally relative to *T* and *T'* to *f*; and
(iii) *f* constitutes *e* at *T'*.

And let us now consider the following claim:

D.4.3.b: *S* acts relative to *T* and *T'* =df. there is an event
e such that *S* brings about *e* directly relative to *T*
and *T'*.

D.4.3.b has a lot going for it. Note that the fact that *f* in D.4.7
is both an object and an effect of *S* 's volition rules out the possibility that a person acts when his volition happens only to cause some
totally "unrelated" event to occur. D.4.3.b is therefore an improvement on D.4.3.a. But note too that D.4.7 allows for the possibility
that *e* be distinct from *g*. D.4.3.b is therefore also an improvement
on the suggestion that a person acts just in case he accomplishes
some event. Let us see how D.4.3.b fares in a few test cases.

The simplest case is where "*e*," "*f*," and "*g* " in D.4.7 designate
the same event. For instance, suppose that Smith directly wills
that his arm should rise and that his arm rises as a consequence of
this volition. Has he acted? It would seem so. Does D.4.3.b, via
D.4.7, confirm this? Yes. Let *e* be [Smith's arm rises]. Now, we
know that Smith wills *e* and that his so willing contributes causally
to *e*. We want to able to say that he has thereby acted; specifically,
we want to be able to say that he has raised his arm. That D.4.7
says that, in this case, Smith brings about his arm's rising directly
may be seen as follows. We know, given T.3.2, that, if Smith wills
e, then he wills *e* in order that *e* may occur. Since Smith does will *e*
(at *T*, say), clause (i) of D.4.7 is satisfied; that is, there are an event
f (namely, *e*) and an event *g* (namely, *e*) such that Smith wills *f* at *T*
in order that *g* may occur. Clause (ii) is also satisfied, since we are
given that Smith's willing *e* contributes causally relative to *T* and
some time *T'* to *e*. Moreover, given T.4.1, clause (iii) is trivially
satisfied. Hence, Smith brings about *e* directly relative to *T* and *T'*
and hence, according to D.4.3.b, Smith acts.

Of course, "*e*," "*f*," and "*g* " in D.4.7 need not designate the
same event, and this is part of the strength of that definition. In
general, if *g* is distinct from *e* in D.4.7, then *S* acts unsuccessfully,
and hence unintentionally. (Although this will be discussed in more
detail in Chapter 6, we may note now that whenever one acts intentionally, one acts successfully, though not *vice versa* ; hence all
unsuccessful actions are unintentional, though not *vice versa*.) As
an illustration let *e* be the event internal to [Smith knocks over
Brown's Ming vase], *f* be the event internal to [Smith moves his

hand] (*i.e.*, *f* is [Smith's hand moves]), and *g* be the event internal to [Smith signals Jones]. Now, if Smith wills *f* at *T* in order that *g* may occur, if his so willing contributes causally relative to *T* and *T'* to *f* but not to *g*, and if *f* happens in fact to constitute *e* at *T'*, then, according to D.4.7, we may say that Smith brings about *e* directly relative to *T* and *T'* and, according to D.4.3.b, we may say that Smith acts relative to *T* and *T'*. And this seems absolutely right. But let it be noted that D.4.7, unlike D.4.2, is sufficiently restrictive so that not just any effect of a volition is ruled in as an issue. For example, let *f* and *g* be as before, but let *e* now be the event internal to [Smith turns a somersault]. If it turns out that [Smith wills *f* in order that *g* may occur] contributes causally relative to *T* and *T'* to *e* (which, obviously, would be a very strange, yet presumably possible, turn of events), probably it does not also contribute causally to *f*, and hence clause (ii) of D.4.7 is not satisfied and *e*, appropriately, turns out not to be an issue of any action of Smith's. Or even if Smith's volition does contribute causally relative to *T* and *T'* to *f* in this case, it is highly unlikely that *f* constitutes *e* at *T'*; and, if this is so, clause (iii) of D.4.7 is not satisfied and *e* turns out once again not to be an issue of any action of Smith's.

4.4   BRINGING ABOUT AN EVENT INDIRECTLY

But D.4.3.b, despite its promise, is in fact defective. Let us consider again the case where Smith attempts to signal Jones but succeeds merely in knocking over Brown's Ming vase, and let us now elaborate on this and suppose that Smith thereby breaks the vase, causing Brown to jump up in horror, dance around in a fit of rage, trip, fall over, bump his head on the nearby andirons, and lose consciousness. There is a sense in which Smith brings about not just that event internal to his knocking over the Ming vase, but also all of the following: [the vase breaks], [Brown jumps up in horror], [Brown dances around in a fit of rage], [Brown trips], [Brown falls over], [Brown bumps his head on the nearby andirons], and [Brown loses consciousness]. Now, none of these events is brought about by Smith directly; rather, they are consequences of events that are brought about by him directly. Let us say, therefore, that they are brought about indirectly by Smith. In precise terms:

D.4.8: S brings about e indirectly relative to T and T'
           =df. there are an event f and a time T^* such
           that:
               (i) S brings about f directly relative to T and T^*;
           and
               (ii) f contributes causally relative to T^* and T' to
           e.[2][5]

The question now arises: does our acknowledgement that D.4.8 captures a legitimate sense of "bring about" necessitate a revision of D.4.3.b? I think that it does, although this is debatable. For instance, it might be argued that, although it is true that Smith brings about (indirectly) all of those events mentioned, there is no need to say that they are issues of any actions of his; they are merely consequences of an action of his, namely, his knocking over Brown's Ming vase. Hence, it might be argued, there is also no need to say that the individual, indirect bringings about of these events are actions of his. Moreover, it might be said, we are always able to admit that, in bringing about the vase's breaking, Brown's jumping up, Brown's dancing around, *etc.*, Smith has acted, for it is a theorem that, whenever there is an indirect bringing about, there is a direct bringing about. That is:

T.4.2:   Necessarily, if S brings about e indirectly relative
           to T and T', then there are an event f and a time
           T^* such that S brings about f directly relative to
           T and T^*.

But, although the foregoing line of reasoning has its attractions, I think that we ought nevertheless to say that indirect bringings about are genuine actions and that events indirectly brought about are genuine issues. Granted, many events are thereby admitted as actions and issues which one is perhaps at first inclined to rule out as such (for instance, if I now bring about my hand's rising directly and it turns out that this contributes causally to an atom's being displaced on Mars a million years hence, it is at least questionable whether the atom's being displaced should rank as an issue of some action of mine); but if we do not allow indirect bringings about to be actions and those events indirectly brought about to be issues, many events that appear to be cases of genuine actions or genuine issues are ruled out as such. For instance, I think that Smith's breaking the Ming vase is a genuine action of his, and yet it is not a direct bringing about, but only an indirect bringing about. Let us, for the sake of completeness, assume that Smith knocks over the vase relative to T and T^*. It is hardly likely that the vase breaks at T^*; indeed, let us assume that the vase breaks at T', some moments after T^*. It is then not true that Smith brings about the vase's breaking directly relative to T and T'. For the event that, in this example, Smith wills at T is that of his hand's rising, and this event occurs at T^*, not T', and hence cannot be said to constitute the vase's breaking at T'. It follows that Smith's breaking the vase is not a direct action of Smith's. Yet we are surely inclined to say that Smith's breaking the vase *is* an action of *some* sort.

There is a pattern that may be distilled from this case. What is the breaking of a vase? It is the direct bringing about of some event which itself causes a vase to break; that is, it is the indirect bringing about of a vase's breaking. Similarly, what is the turning on of a light? It is the direct bringing about of some event which itself causes a light to go on; that is, it is the indirect bringing about of a light's going on. Or again, what is the killing of a person? It is the direct bringing about (perhaps in some manner requiring specification) of some event which itself causes (perhaps in some manner requiring specification) a person's death; that is, it is the indirect bringing about (perhaps in some manner requiring specification) of a person's death. Such examples may be multiplied indefinitely. Now, it seems intuitively obvious that these indirect bringings about are genuine actions; hence, D.4.3.b requires modification.

Several points ought to be made here. First, it must of course be acknowledged that there is a third alternative that could be investigated here, other than those of ruling in all indirect bringings about as actions and of ruling out all indirect bringings about as actions, and that is to rule in some indirect bringings about as actions while ruling out others. But I know of no plausible criterion that may be employed for this purpose, and so I have bitten the bullet and concluded that we ought to rule in all indirect bringings about as actions. Secondly, ruling in all indirect bringings about as actions does not alter the fact that those events indirectly brought about are consequences of certain actions, even if they are now themselves to be called issues of certain other actions. For every indirect issue is a consequence of a direct issue, and many indirect issues are themselves consequences of indirect issues. Finally, it might be thought that the implications of admitting indirect bringings about into the class of actions, if persistently and consistently investigated, would result in the following thesis: all issues are either events directly brought about or consequences of events directly brought about. Even if this were true, note that this thesis is quite distinct from the following: any event to which a volition contributes causally is an issue of some action. For this thesis (where the scopes of its quantifiers are read in the most natural manner) has already been dismissed in our discussion of D.4.2. Note also that the related thesis, that all issues are either events directly brought about or consequences of events directly brought about but not both, seems to be false. For when Jones raises his hand and thereby flips the switch, it seems that he brings about both the event internal to his raising his hand and that internal to his flipping the switch directly, indeed that the former constitutes the latter, and yet also that the former contributes causally to the latter (this being a case of simultaneous causation). Moreover, the related thesis that all issues are either events directly brought about, and not constituted by other events directly brought about, or consequences of events directly brought about, is false. Let us suppose that Jones raises his hand quickly. Then he brings about both [Jones's hand rises] and [Jones's hand rises quickly], the former constitutes the latter, both are direct issues, and neither is an indirect issue. But I think that the thesis that all issues are either events directly brought about or consequences of events directly brought about is false anyway, as I shall now explain.[2][6]

4.5   *BRINGING ABOUT AN EVENT SYNTHETICALLY*

Consider this case. Jones is learning how to play tennis. His instructor says that, in order to hit a forehand, Jones must first swing his racket backward, then step across on to his left foot, and then swing his racket forward, making contact with the ball just in front of his left foot. Suppose that Jones does all this and that, lo and behold, he hits a forehand. Is it not clear that Jones's hitting the forehand is an action of his? If it is, then D.4.3.b is again seen to be inadequate. For consider. Suppose that Jones brings about the event internal to his swinging his racket backward (e, say) relative to $T1$ and $T2$, that he brings about the event internal to his stepping across on to his left foot (f, say) relative to $T3$ and $T4$, and that he brings about the event internal to his swinging his racket forward (g, say) relative to $T5$ and $T6$. Now Jones brings about that event internal to his hitting a forehand (h, say) relative to $T1$ and $T6$ and, most importantly, it is not an event that, given D.4.7, he brings about directly. Nor is it an event that he brings about indirectly. It is, rather, an event *composed* of events that he has brought about, some directly, some perhaps indirectly. And yet we have said that it seems that Jones's hitting a forehand is an action of his, or, in other words, that in bringing about h relative to $T1$ and $T6$ Jones *acts* relative to $T1$ and $T6$. But D.4.3.b cannot account for this.

In order to come to grips with this case we must seek to discern the relation between Jones's bringing about e, f, and g on the one hand and his bringing about h on the other. The key word here is one that has already been used: "composed." Jones's bringing about h is *composed* of his bringing about e, his bringing about f, and his bringing about g. Conversely, his bringing about e, his bringing about f, and his bringing about g are all *parts* of his bringing about h. How are we to account for these relations of being-composed-of and being-a-part-of? It is important to note that Jones's bringing about e, his bringing about f, and his bringing about g are neither individually necessary nor jointly sufficient for his bringing about h. It is possible for Jones to hit a forehand without taking a step across on to his left foot; moreover, Jones may bring about e, f, and g on some other occasion and fail to hit a forehand. The proper account is, I believe, the following. We should note that Jones's swinging his racket backward at $T1$ and $T2$ "just is" his hitting a forehand at $T1$ and $T2$, that his stepping across on to his left foot at $T3$ and $T4$ "just is" his hitting a forehand at $T3$ and $T4$, and that his swinging his racket forward at $T5$ and $T6$ "just is" his hitting a forehand at $T5$ and $T6$. And so I believe that, in general, we may say the following:

D.4.9: e is composed relative to $T1$ and Tn of $f1,...,fn$
=df.
    (i) e and $f1,...,fn$ are events; and
    (ii) $f1$ constitutes e at $T1$ and,...,and fn constitutes e at Tn.[27]

We may then say that a person brings about an event synthetically just in case he brings about, either directly or indirectly, the events of which it is composed. More precisely:

D.4.10: S brings about e synthetically relative to T and T'
=df. there are events $f1,...,fn$ and a time T'' such that:
    (i) e is composed relative to T''' and T' of $f1,...,fn$; and
    (ii) for any event f, if f is identical with $f1$ or...or f is identical with fn, then there are times T^* and T^{**} such that:
        (a) T is not later than T^*, T^* is not later than T^{**}, and T^{**} is not earlier than T''' and not later than T', and
        (b) either
            (1) S brings about f directly relative to T^* and T^{**}, or
            (2) S brings about f indirectly relative to T^* and T^{**}.[28]

Now, if it is true in the foregoing example, as it seems to be, that, by bringing about h synthetically relative to $T1$ and $T6$, Jones *acts* relative to $T1$ and $T6$, we must again modify D.4.3.b. In fact, given the foregoing considerations concerning indirect and synthetic bringings about, I suggest that we say first of all:

D.4.11: S brings about e actively relative to T and T' =df. either
    (i) S brings about e directly relative to T and T'; or
    (ii) S brings about e indirectly relative to T and T'; or

(iii) *S* brings about *e* synthetically relative to *T* and *T'*.

We may then say:

D.4.3.c: *S* acts relative to *T* and *T'* =df. there is an event *e* such that *S* brings about *e* actively relative to *T* and *T'*.

There may on occasion be some problem in *applying* D.4.7, D.4.8, and D.4.10 (and hence in applying D.4.11 and D.4.12) despite their accuracy (if they are accurate), but I shall postpone discussion of this until D.5.5 through D.5.8 are provided in the next chapter. At this point I propose that we return to that list of actions provided at the beginning of this chapter. The reason for their being divided into three separate groups should now be obvious. Those actions in group (a) will normally be such that the issues internal to them are brought about *directly* ; those in group (b) will of necessity be such that those issues internal to them will be brought about *indirectly* and those in group (c) will normally be such that those issues internal to them will be brought about *synthetically*. I say "normally" with respect to groups (a) and (c), for there is, I think, no *necessity* that those actions in group (a) be direct and that those in group (c) be (nontrivially) synthetic. Suppose, to take an example from group (a), that Smith has been paralyzed and that he is only beginning to re-learn the use of his leg. In such a case his kicking himself may be synthetic. In order to do it, he may have first to draw his foot backward – this being one direct action – and then bring his foot downward into contact with some other part of his anatomy (presumably his other leg) – this being another direct action. Or suppose, to take an example from group (c), that Smith is a wizard at mental arithmetic. In such a case, he may bring about the issue internal to his multiplying 928 by 254 directly. Most people, of course, must perform all manner of preliminary calculation before arriving at the correct answer.

This case concerning mental arithmetic highlights a desirable feature of both D.4.3.b and D.4.3.c: neither definition rules out the possibility that action may be purely mental. I think that it is obvious that action may be purely mental, although this is a point which, curiously, is often overlooked in the current literature.[29] In this connection mention should also be made of what may be called "abnormal" action. I have in mind in particular both psychokinesis (whose issue must be physical) and telepathy (whose issue must be mental). Suppose that Smith wills an event f in order that a certain lightbulb explode (perhaps f just is [the lightbulb explodes]), and suppose that his so willing contributes causally, by means of alpha-waves emanating from his brain, to f and f constitutes the light-bulb's exploding. Then, in this case, Smith brings about the light-bulb's exploding directly (by psychokinesis). Or again, suppose that Smith wills an event f in order that the image of the ace of spades occur to Jones (perhaps f just is [the image of the ace of spades occurs to Jones]), and suppose that his so willing contributes causally, by means of alpha-waves emanating from his brain, to f and f constitutes the image's occurring to Jones. Then, in this case, Smith brings about the image's occurring to Jones directly (by telepathy). Both cases may seem odd, but this oddness, I would contend, is merely a function of the abnormality of the conditions that are said to obtain. I am sure that it is correct to count the lightbulb's exploding and the image's occurring to Jones as issues of actions of Smith's, given the conditions stipulated in each case.

Not only may some action be purely mental, there is a sense in which some action may be propositional. So far I have stipulated that what is brought about is always an event. But there is a sense in which what is brought about is a proposition.[30] This topic is too large to be properly treated here, but we may note that there is a large variety of ways in which a proposition may be said to be brought about, all of which conform to the following roughly stated schema (where "p" ranges over propositions): S brings about p if and only if there is an event e such that (i) S brings about e and (ii) e's occurring is sufficient for p's occurring. The varieties of propositional bringing about will be in part a function of the varieties of event-bringing about and in part a function of the varieties of sufficiency. With respect to the latter, one variety of propositional bringing about is carved out by understanding "sufficient" in the schema to express entailment (see D.1.9); another variety is based on "sufficient" expressing strict implication (see D.1.8); another variety is based on "sufficient" expressing causal sufficiency (see D.3.2); and so on. In this way, then, we may accommodate such statements as "Smith brought it about that, if Jones walked through the door, he would be drenched."³ ¹ But I shall not pursue this here.

4.6 RESOLUTION OF THE FIRST GROUP OF PROBLEMS

We may now, finally, address ourselves to the task of resolving the first group of problems, consisting of problems A1 and A2, posed in Chapter 2. We have in fact been in a position to resolve the first of these ever since the statement of A.4.1 and A.4.2. Regarding A1, why is it that Donald O'Connor acts whereas the dummy does not? The answer is, of course, that O'Connor acts by virtue of actively bringing about certain events, and that his actively bringing about certain events itself occurs by virtue of his willing certain events. Now, the dummy itself wills nothing and can will nothing. Therefore, it does not act, even though some of the events that O'Connor brings about may strongly resemble the motions of the dummy. (In fact, of course, the dummy's motions are themselves issues of actions performed by O'Connor – but that is a complication that need not be gone into here.) Problem A2 requires different treatment. O'Connor's breathing hard is a consequence – unintentional, presumably, but certainly foreseeable, and perhaps even foreseen – of his dancing. As such, it must be said, given D.4.8, to be indirectly brought about and thus, given D.4.3.c, to be the issue of an action of his. But what action? We may note that in English the verb "to breathe" has a dual function. To put it in the present vernacular, "O'Connor breathes" may, as has just been noted, be used to express an issue of some action of his; but it may also be used to express an action of his. Now, it might seem that, if "to breathe" (in one of its senses) may express an issue of an action, then the action in question ought to be expressible in terms of "to breathe" (in the other of its senses). (Compare the dual use of "to bend.") But – and here is the (slight) puzzle – this is *not* the case; for it is certainly odd, if not downright false, to say that *any* action that O'Connor performs while he dances may be properly expressed by "O'Connor breathes." The reason for this is easily discerned, however, and that is that, when "to breathe" is used in

English to express an action rather than an issue, it is used (roughly) synonymously with "to take a breath *intentionally*" and not with "to take a breath *(simpliciter)*." Now, it has been acknowledged that O'Connor does not intentionally take breaths while he is dancing – his mind is on other matters.[3][2] Nevertheless, he does take an occasional breath, and his doing so is an (unintentional) action whose issue is expressible by "O'Connor breathes" (in the non-action sense of "breathes").

Finally, there is a bonus to be derived from the foregoing discussion. Ludwig Wittgenstein is famous for having asked: "What is left over if I subtract the fact that my arm goes up from the fact that I raise my arm?"[3][3] Wittgenstein himself feared the answer forever elusive. Other philosophers have provided their own answers.[3][4] My answer may now be given fairly easily (even if a little roughly). If I subtract the fact that my arm goes up from the fact that I raise it, the remainder (in typical cases, at least) is an instance of my willing that my arm should go up together with my so willing's contributing causally to its going up. That, of course, is an answer rooted firmly in the tradition against which Wittgenstein (and others) so vehemently objected. Whether such objections are cogent is a matter that I shall take up in Chapter 10. Before that is done, the theory of action begun in this chapter requires completion, and I shall turn next to a discussion of matters pertaining to the individuation of actions and the issues internal to them.

Notes

1   On collective actions, see Gruner (1976), Londey (1978), Copp (1979).

2   The account to be given could, however, be refined. For instance, I shall not seek to distinguish between actions, acts, and activities, although there are undoubtedly important distinctions to be drawn here. *Cf.* Ware (1973), Roberts (1979).

3   Prichard (1949), p.62. This contention has been recently en-

dorsed by Davis (1979), p.41.

4   However, I should perhaps say that the reason why I think ef-
     fortful attempts are actions and effortless ones are not is that
     the former, but not the latter, *do* require that a volition be
     efficacious. For a little more on the concept of trying, see
     Chapter 9.

5   Note that clause (i) is strictly superfluous, in so far as clause
     (ii) could not be true if clause (i) were not true. Nevertheless, I
     include clause (i) for the sake of clarity. This point holds simi-
     larly for many of the definitions that follow in this and other
     chapters. It should perhaps be emphasized that, given the as-
     sumption that events are "eternal" entities, locutions of the
     (rough) form "S brings about e " should of course *not* be taken
     to imply that S brings e into *existence* (just as locutions of the
     form "e contributes causally to f" do not imply that e brings f
     into existence). What is implied is that the event in question is
     caused to *occur*.
         While I have said that I accept A.4.1, it should be acknowl-
     edged that I later talk of a type of action which I call synthetic
     and which *perhaps* is such that the truth of A.4.1 is not re-
     quired for such action. (See D.4.10.) Even so, the truth of
     something close to A.4.1 definitely would be required. See note
     22 to this chapter.

6   G.H. von Wright (1971), p.66.

7   I owe the expression to Donagan (1979), p.216.

8   *Cf.* von Wright (1981), p.10, where no commitment on this
     point is made. Also, *cf.* Chapter 1, Section 1.2 above, where it
     is said that a time may be a period or a moment. Clearly, the
     time at which [Smith's arm rises] occurs is a period, while that
     at which [Smith's arm is risen] occurs may not be.

9   G.H. von Wright reserves "cause" for issues (which he calls
     results) and "bring about" for consequences, but this seems to
     me unnecessarily at odds with common usage of these terms.

10   I say "commonly" for reasons already given in Chapter 3, Section 3.1. See the discussion of A.3.3 through A.3.6.

11   See note 2 to Chapter 5 below.

12   Davidson (1967), p.128.

13   But it should be noted that there are perhaps more phrases available in English to express events internal to actions than one might at first suspect. For instance, those intransitive verbs which, as Thomson puts it (1977, p.134), "match" transitive verbs lend themselves to the construction of such phrases. *Cf.* Hornsby (1980), Appendices A and B.

14   *Cf.* Donagan (1979), p.217. It may be thought that I am overstating my case here. After all, why not say that "a roast is being carved" expresses that event internal to the carving of a roast, *i.e.*, that [a roast is being carved] is the issue internal to [someone carves a roast]? Why it would be wrong to say this is perhaps best seen by means of an analogy. It has been said that [Smith's arm rises] is the issue internal to [Smith raises his arm]. Note that it was not said that [Smith's arm is raised] is the issue in question – and for good reason. For it seems to me that [Smith's arm is raised] is the same event as [something raises Smith's arm], and this is certainly distinct from [Smith's arm rises]. In the same way, then, "a roast is being carved" cannot properly be said to express that issue internal to the carving of a roast.

15   *E.g.*, Davidson (1971). *Cf.* also Sellars (1976), p.49.

16   *Cf.* Hornsby (1980), Chapter 1.

17   Nevertheless, the thesis is surely false on two scores. First, some actions are not bodily at all, at least in so far as their issues essentially involve nothing physical but only something mental – unless, of course, the mental may be reduced, in some sense, to the physical. I shall have nothing further to say here concerning any such "identity thesis," although I shall mention "mental" action later. Secondly, some (straightforwardly)

physical actions do not require bodily *movement*; remaining at attention is one example of such an action.

18 See Chisholm (1976), p.71 and p.206, n.21.

19 Bruce Aune (1977, p.46) in effect says that, if an ontology which admits of events and actions is accepted (something that he is inclined *not* to accept), then it really makes no great difference whether what is called by the name "action" is a volition, an issue, or the hybrid volition-*cum*-issue that I favor. In a sense he is right, in that what is philosophically important is that the conceptual distinction between these three alternatives be acknowledged. But in a sense he is not right, for, if we are engaged in an attempt not just to draw such distinctions but also to accommodate our everyday thinking about such concepts, it *is* important to try to make sure that what is called an action is that which we commonly think of as an action. And it seems plain to me that what we commonly think of as an action is a volition-*cum*-issue, and not either the volition or the issue taken separately.

20 The criticism to follow also applies to statement (5) on p.15 in Davis (1979).

21 Once again, I acknowledge that the rejection of D.4.3.a has not been conclusively argued for, just as the earlier rejection of D.4.1 was not conclusively argued for. But I do think that its rejection clearly conforms with what we commonly take action to be.

22 It will nevertheless turn out, given the analysis of the concept of action below (D.4.3.c), that the following is true: Necessarily, S acts relative to T and T' if and only if there are an event e and a time T^* earlier than or identical with T' such that (i) S wills e at T, and (ii) [S wills e] contributes causally relative to T and T^* to e.

23 The formula that follows is, of course, still imprecise in that it fails to make explicit mention of the determinate events to which the causal contribution is relative. But, as noted earlier,

I shall try to simplify the discussion by not explicitly mentioning such determinate events.

24 Notice that the relation of constitution is non-symmetric (whereas some might take the "just is" relation to be symmetric). It is important to recognize this, for all that is being contended when it is claimed that, on the occasion in question, Jones's calling Smith names constitutes his insulting Smith is that whatever contributes causally to the former contributes causally to the latter. It is clearly possible, indeed likely, that something should contribute causally to the latter and not to the former.

25 It is especially important to remember that the causal contribution at issue in this definition is implicitly relativized to determinate events; for, if it were not, then the causal chain could "go astray." For instance, S may bring about an event f directly relative to T and T^* (in Alaska, say) and f may contribute causally relative to T^* and T' to e (in Hawaii, say), and yet S will not bring about e indirectly relative to T and T'. This disparity in location is inconsistent with the requirement implicit in D.4.8 concerning determinate events.

26 Walton (1979) discusses what I have called (and what he also calls) direct and indirect action at some length. However, he does not discuss what I call synthetic action, as I am about to do.

27 Note that D.4.9 constitutes an analysis of the concept of *ordered* composition. For instance, to say that e is composed of $f1$, $f2$, ..., fn is not the same, according to D.4.9, as saying that e is composed of $f2$, $f1$, ..., fn. Although I think it is clear how one would go about the task of distilling from D.4.9 a general analysis of the part-whole relation (as it applies to events), where the order of composition is not relevant, it is also clear that the task is a technically forbidding one.

28 Note that, according to D.4.9, every event, when it occurs, is, if caused to occur, composed of itself. Hence, according to D.4.10, all such events that are direct bringings about or indirect

bringings about are also (trivially) synthetic bringings about.

29   A notable exception is Taylor (1966), Chapter 2. *Cf.* note 17 to this chapter.

30   Cf. Walton (1979) and works cited therein.

31   Cf. Walton (1979), p.204.

32   Even this is not clearly true. For while he is dancing O'Connor is at times also singing, and it is perhaps the case that while he sings he *does* on occasion take a breath intentionally.

33   Wittgenstein (1953), Section 621.

34   For what is perhaps the most recent published discussion of this issue (apart from the present discussion) — there are too many such discussions in the literature for them all to be cited here — see Hornsby (1980), p.23.

Chapter 5

THE INDIVIDUATION AND
TIMING OF ACTIONS AND ISSUES

5.1   *THE INDIVIDUATION AND TIMING OF ACTIONS*

If we assume that D.4.3.c is correct, then we may expect actions and issues to fall into three main categories: those which are direct, those which are indirect, and those which are synthetic. We may say first of all:

D.5.1: e is a direct action of S's =df. there is an event f such that e is [S brings about f directly].[1]

We may also say:

D.5.2: e is an indirect action of S's =df. there is an event f such that e is [S brings about f indirectly].

And we may say:

D.5.3: e is a synthetic action of S's =df. there is an event f such that e is [S brings about f synthetically].

We may then say:

D.5.4: e is an action of S's =df. either
    (i) e is a direct action of S's; or
    (ii) e is an indirect action of S's; or
    (iii) e is a synthetic action of S's.

An event cannot be an action on one occasion and not on another. For instance, [Smith multiplies 928 by 254] is an action of Smith's whenever it occurs; indeed, it is an action of his even if it never occurs.[2] But when exactly does an action that occurs occur? This is a tricky question, but I think that the following is accurate.

If the action is a direct action, then it occurs at least at the time at which the volition involved occurs and at the time at which the issue involved occurs. That is, if S brings about e directly relative to T and T', then [S brings about e directly] occurs at T and T'. Whether or not it occurs at any or all of the times in between T and T' (if there are any such times) is a moot point. Its resolution presumably depends on what to say concerning the times at which causal contributions occur. For instance, suppose that e contributes causally relative to T and T' to f. When does [e contributes causally to f] occur? This was a point which I intentionally neglected in Chapter 3, but it ought no longer to be neglected. Clearly, [e contributes causally to f] occurs at least at T and at T', but I find it difficult to argue either for the claim that it does, or for the claim that it does not, occur at any other times. I am inclined, in fact, to say that it occurs from T up to and including T', although I recognize this to be controversial – especially when T and T' are set far apart. The only reason that I can give for this is that I think we want to say that [e contributes causally to f] occurs (in straightforward cases) exactly once when e contributes causally relative to T and T' (and to some determinate events d and d') to f, and that, if we want to say that it occurs both at T and T', then, unless we say that it is a measure-event (which is something that seems intuitively wrong), we must say that it occurs from T up to and including T'.[3] But this is all pretty weak, and I acknowledge that the alternative positions that one might adopt on this matter could be more fully investigated. Nevertheless, I think that resolution of this matter is not something that is required in order for the present account of action to be acceptable. However, for the sake of completeness, I shall adopt the view – for the reason just given – that, when S brings about e directly relative to T and T', [S brings about e directly] occurs from T up to and including T'.

The times of indirect actions may be similarly treated. If S brings about e indirectly relative to T and T' by virtue of his bringing about f directly relative to T and T^* and of f's contributing causally relative to T^* and T' to e, then we may safely say that [S brings about e indirectly] occurs at least at T, T^*, and T', and, for the sake of completeness, I shall adopt the view that it in fact occurs from T up to and including T'. The question of the times at which indirect actions occur has recently generated considerable interest. For instance, consider the case of Smith's killing Jones relative to T and T', and suppose that he kills Jones by virtue of pulling the trigger of his gun relative to T and T^* and of that event internal to this pulling of the trigger contributing causally relative to T^* and T' to Jones's death. Now the current account of times at which indirect actions occur has it that [Smith kills Jones] occurs at least at T, T^*, and T'; whether or not it occurs at any or all of the times between T and T' other than T^* is an issue left essentially unresolved, although I have stipulated, for the sake of completeness, that it occurs at all such times. It should be acknowledged in this respect that the contention that, if S brings about e indirectly relative to T and T', then [S brings about e indirectly] occurs at each of T and...and T', perhaps becomes less plausible as the temporal lapse between T and T' increases. For instance, suppose that Smith kills Jones by virtue of his pulling the trigger of his gun relative to some closely related times on April 6 and by virtue of Jones's dying the following December 17. To say that the killing occurs at those times to which the pulling of the trigger is relative and at the time of Jones's death is clearly reasonable. To say that the killing occurs throughout the months in between sounds odd. Nevertheless, with some trepidation, I shall in this regard accept not only what it sounds reasonable to say but also what it sounds odd to say.[4]

At what times, finally, does a synthetic action occur? It is reasonable to say that it occurs at least at the times at which the volition (or volitions) involved occurs (or occur), and at the time at which the issue (or issues) involved occurs (or occur), and also, if any of the issues involved are indirect, at the times to which the causal contribution (or contributions) involved is (or are) relative. But I shall, as before, go further than this and endorse the view that it occurs from the time of the first volition up to and including the time of the last issue.

It should be noted that, according to the present account, it is possible for an action to occur at a time which is indefinitely later than the time at which the agent involved passes from this world. This may sound odd, but I do not think that it is truly objectionable. For it is *not* possible, according to the present account, for an action to occur and yet occur at *no* time at which the agent involved is alive; and this is so simply because, first, every action involves a volition and, second, a person cannot will an event and not be alive when he does so. It is, of course, possible (and this is especially obvious in the case of indirect action) that an issue should occur and yet not occur at any time at which the agent (or, indeed, agents) involved is (or are) alive, but this, I think, raises no problems.[5]

5.2   *THE INDIVIDUATION AND TIMING OF ISSUES*

The foregoing, limited account of the nature of actions is of course in keeping with the account of events in general given in Chapter 1, according to which events (indeed, states of affairs in general) are finely-grained, abstract entities (see A.1.6). (Whether this gives rise to any special problems is a matter that will be treated later when problems B1 through B5 are discussed.) Issues, too, being events, are finely-grained, abstract entities. But there is this difference (among other differences) between actions and issues, and that is that, although an event cannot be an action on one occasion and not on another, it is nevertheless the case that an event may be an issue on one occasion and not on another; for it is an issue when and only when it is actively brought about by an agent. Hence the concept of an issue must, strictly speaking, be relativized to times. That is, we should say:

D.5.5:   *e* is a direct issue of an action of *S*'s at *T'* =df. there is a time *T* such that *S* brings about *e* directly relative to *T* and *T'*.

D.5.6:   *e* is an indirect issue of an action of *S*'s at *T'* =df. there is a time *T* such that *S* brings about *e* indirectly relative to *T* and *T'*.

D.5.7:   *e* is a synthetic issue of an action of *S*'s at *T'* =df. there is a time *T* such that *S* brings about *e* synthetically relative to *T* and *T'*.

D.5.8:   *e* is an issue of an action of *S*'s at *T'* =df. either

(i) e is a direct issue of an action of S's at T'; or
(ii) e is an indirect issue of an action of S's at T'; or
(iii) e is a synthetic issue of an action of S's at T'.[6]

However, we should not let the accuracy of these definitions blind us to the occasional problems that arise in applying them, problems in fact inherited from problems which arise in the application of D.4.7, D.4.8, and D.4.10. (I shall raise here two problems concerning the application of D.5.5 – and its "parent" D.4.7 – only, although similar problems could be raised concerning the application of D.5.6 through D.5.8 and their "parents.") Consider, first, a case where Smith brings about [Smith's arm rises] directly relative to T and T'. Clearly, [Smith's arm rises] is a direct issue of an action of Smith's at T'. So too, in virtue of this, is [an arm rises]. But how long does the latter remain a direct issue of an action of Smith's? Suppose that [an arm rises] never ceases to occur after T' – not because Smith is always raising an arm, but because someone or another is. Clearly, [an arm rises] does not remain a direct issue of an action of *Smith's* for ever after T'. Does D.5.5 imply that it does? No, for we may safely say, given D.4.7, that, while Smith may bring about [an arm rises] directly relative to T and several times just after T', he does not bring it about directly relative to T and all times after T'. So this first "problem" is really not too problematic; but it is just as well to see how it should be handled. However, consider now this slightly different, and more difficult, case. Suppose that Smith brings about [Smith's arm rises] directly relative to T and $T1$ and...and relative to T and Tn in a "normal" way; then [Smith's arm rises] is a "normal" direct issue of an action of his at $T1$ and...and Tn. But suppose that a machine takes over at $Tn+1$ and that from that moment on Smith's arm rises because of the machine's intervention until it finally ceases to rise at $Tn+m$. Now, it might at first seem reasonable to say that [Smith's arm rises] ceases to be a direct issue of an action of Smith's at $Tn+1$; but it is not clear that this is really so. For is it the case that Smith ceases to bring about [Smith's arm rises] directly at $Tn+1$? Notice that it may well be that (i) he ceases to desire that his arm should rise at $Tn+1$, (ii) he ceases to intend that his arm should rise at $Tn+1$, and (iii) his arm's rising ceases to be in his control at $Tn+1$, but *none* of these has been said to be necessary for his bringing about his arm's rising directly, and I think it is clear that none of them *should* be said to be so. Notice also that it *may* be that Smith's original volition (which, for simplicity's sake, we may assume to be a volition that his arm should rise) *continues* to contribute causally to his arm's rising at $Tn+1$ onward (up until $Tn+m$); this seems indeed to be the case if the machine would not have been in a position to make Smith's arm continue to rise had Smith not obliged by raising it to the level that it had reached at Tn. If this is so, and given that [Smith's arm rises] constitutes itself, then, according to D.4.7, Smith brings about [Smith's arm rises] directly not simply relative to T and $T1$ through Tn but also relative to T and $Tn+1$ through $Tn+m$. Hence [Smith's arm rises], according to D.5.5, is a direct issue of an action of Smith's from $T1$ not just through Tn but through $Tn+m$. This may be surprising, but I think that it is correct – *if*, as I assume (and this is where D.4.7 and hence D.5.5 are on occasion difficult to apply), Smith's original volition does in fact continue to contribute causally to [Smith's arm rises] beyond Tn up until $Tn+m$.

At this point it should be acknowledged that there is a certain element of arbitrariness in the foregoing account of the individuation and timing of actions and issues. While this account is of course tailored to the ontology of events laid out in Chapter 1, it remains somewhat arbitrary since it inherits certain features of that ontology, the rationale for the adoption of which was at best loosely defended. Now, the theory of events presented in Chapter 1 has certain features which I take to be desirable (foremost among which are ontological economy – of one sort – and clarity of exposition), but there are of course rival theories which, had they been adopted, would have resulted in a quite different account in this chapter of the individuation and timing of actions and issues. Moreover, I do not think that any of the main rival theories can be conclusively defended or undermined,[7] and so I also do not think that any of the main rival accounts of the individuation and timing of actions and issues can be conclusively defended or undermined – hence the element of arbitrariness, just noted, in the account presented in this chapter.

Nevertheless, it should perhaps be stressed that, while (as pointed out at the outset of Chapter 1) it seems to me that all of the main rival theories of events – and, it may now be added, all of the main rival accounts of the individuation and timing of actions and issues – have certain counterintuitive features, the theory of events proposed in Chapter 1 – together with the account of actions and issues proposed in this chapter – has many intuitive features and few counterintuitive ones. For instance, where events and actions are taken to be coarsely-grained, concrete entities, we are forced to talk of actions "under a description," something the present account successfully and happily avoids. I say "happily," for one problem with such talk is that we cannot of course infer "(action) a has (property) F" from "a has F under (description) d," since a may have F under d but fail to have F under another description d'.[8] Hence, just what being-a-property-under-a-description amounts to is not immediately clear; moreover, whatever it is, it appears to introduce certain entities (namely, concrete events and descriptions) into one's ontology which the present account, economically, does without. (I shall have more to say shortly concerning act-descriptions when discussing problem B4.) Moreover, an account of actions as concrete entities is subject to certain further objections – many of which have been raised by Alvin Goldman.[9] For instance, if John's pulling the trigger is the same act as John's killing Smith, then surely John's pulling the trigger occurs just when John's killing Smith does. But suppose that Smith dies several months after John pulls the trigger. It seems that we must say that John killed Smith several months before Smith died – and this sounds very odd. Or again, John's pulling the trigger caused Smith to die, but it sounds very odd to say that John's killing Smith caused Smith to die. And so on and so forth. Now let me emphasize straight away that neither of these (or any such) objections seems conclusive (although I do find some of them telling); replies may be, and have been, given to them.[10] Nevertheless, an account of actions which avoids these objections – as the present account does – is, I think, in so far forth to be preferred.

But only "in so far forth"; for an account, such as the present one, which takes actions to be finely-grained, abstract entities is also *prima facie* objectionable in its own right. The most serious objection is that it appears to multiply actions unacceptably. Now, in response to this, it must be acknowledged that, on the present account, there are many more actions than would be recognized by someone who accepts an account of actions as coarsely-grained; but I deny that this proliferation of actions is unacceptable. In one sense, such proliferation renders one's ontology "bloated," but I deny that *this* sort of bloatedness is in general to be shunned.[1][1] Moreover, while I recognize that pre-analytic intuition may incline one to think otherwise, I deny that this sort of bloatedness with respect to actions in particular is to be shunned; for we may still (in one sense) *count* actions as intuition would have us do, as I argued at the end of Chapter 1.

I have also acknowledged, earlier in this chapter, that claiming that, for example, a killing lasts from the time of the original volition all the way up to the death of the victim, may itself seem objectionable, especially if the stretch of time involved is considerable. But the alternatives seem to me no more palatable, and, anyway, I have already pointed out that the theory of events given in Chapter 1 does not *commit* me to this view of the time of a killing. Now, there are undoubtedly still other objections that could be raised against the present account of the individuation and timing of actions and issues, but I shall not consider them here. For a satisfactory response to them would require consideration of the relative merits and demerits of rival accounts and, while I have touched upon these here for purposes of preliminary comparison, it should be clear that a thorough consideration of such accounts would necessitate a great deal of detailed investigation and would lead me far from my main purpose here.[1][2] For my main purpose here is to provide resolutions to problems· B1 through B5, as presented in Chapter 2, and at this point I propose simply to turn to an attempt to provide such resolutions – resolutions which, while admittedly· arbitrary to a certain degree (for the reasons just given), appear to me nevertheless reasonable and straightforward.

5.3   *RESOLUTION OF THE SECOND GROUP OF PROBLEMS*

Problem B1 has in effect already been dealt with. It was asked how many actions Jones performed, after he opened the front door, when he flipped the light-switch, thereby turning on the light, thereby illuminating the room, and thereby alerting the prowler. The answer, according to the present account, is of course that at least four actions occurred (namely, [Jones flips the light-switch], [Jones turns on the light], [Jones illuminates the room], and [Jones alerts the prowler]) and indeed many more besides (such as [Jones flips the light-switch in the hallway], *etc.*); hence, also, at least four issues occurred (namely, those internal to the actions just mentioned) and indeed many more besides.[13] There is a sense, of course, in which [Jones flips the light-switch] "just is" [Jones turns on the light], and so on, but this is not a question of these events' being identical but of their being related by the "by"-relation. This matter will be discussed further in Chapter 7.

What of problem B2? Does Jones perform an infinite number of actions when he takes one step forward by virtue of his taking half a step forward, a quarter of a step forward, and so forth? Intuitively, I think, we are inclined to say that he does not, and the present theory accords with intuition here.[14] Or more precisely, the present theory implies that, if (where e is the event internal to [Jones takes one step forward]) Jones brings about e *directly* (and let us say that he does this by virtue of his willing e and of this volition's causing e to occur), then Jones's half-step, quarter-step, and so on, are not actions of his. This is because the events internal to his half-step, his quarter-step, and so on, far from being *constituted by e*, themselves appear to *constitute e*. That is, e is *composed* of them (see D.4.9); indeed, e is a *measure-event* and they are *fractions* of it (see D.1.30 and D.1.31). Of course, if Jones brings about e *synthetically* (and *not* directly) – this would be an odd thing to do, but nevertheless this would be the case if, for instance, Jones brought about his leg's going half-way forward directly and then brought about his leg's going the rest of the way forward directly – then some of the fractions of e will indeed be issues of actions of Jones's; but *only* some, and not all.

As for problem B3 and the matter of the accumulability of actions, it begins to look as if D.4.3.b might be preferable to D.4.3.c after all. Given D.4.10, it turns out that Jones brings about the event internal to his walk synthetically and that therefore, by D.4.3.c, D.5.4, and D.5.7, his walk is an action of his and the event internal to it is, on that occasion, an issue. Now, perhaps this is not too objectionable. But is it not theoretically possible that direct actions be accumulated *ad indefinitum* so that a person's entire life (if, as is perhaps practically impossible, the person is continually active) turns out to be one big synthetic bringing about, and hence an action, of his? It seems so; and perhaps it would be better if the present theory did not have this implication. But we are caught in a dilemma here. For if we rule out one synthetic bringing about on the grounds that it is just too big to count as a single action, how are we still to rule in as actions those synthetic bringings about, such as [Jones hits a forehand], [Jones drives around the corner], and [Jones multiplies 928 by 254], which appear to have a legitimate claim on the title "action"? For my part, I can find no acceptable way to rule in the more compact synthetic bringings about and to rule out the larger synthetic bringings about as actions. My decision has been, as in the case of indirect bringings about, to bite the bullet and call *all* synthetic bringings about actions. Hence I have claimed the truth of D.4.3.c (as opposed to D.4.3.a), D.5.4, and D.5.7. The alternative (to claim that only direct and indirect actions and issues are genuine actions and issues), though simpler, seems to me even less palatable.

When it comes to problem B4 and the distinction between actions and consequences, however, the advantages of the relative simplicity of the present theory of action are clear. In one of his papers J.L.Austin says:

> [A] single term descriptive of what he [the agent] did may be made to cover either a smaller or a larger stretch of events, those excluded by the narrower description being called the "consequences" or "results" or "effects" or the like of his act.[1 5]

Since Austin wrote this, it has become somewhat of a commonplace to say that there is no hard-and-fast distinction between act and consequence, that the distinction is more linguistic than ontological. For instance, Eric D'Arcy proposes the thesis that the term which denotes the act, in the description of a given incident, may often be elided into the term which denotes the consequence of the act,[16] especially when the consequence is anticipatable.[17] Indeed, he says:

> As a rule...the line between "act" and "conse-quence" may be drawn at different points when the elements of a given episode are being ana-lyzed.[18]

Joel Feinberg calls the phenomenon that Austin points to the "accordion effect,"[19] and Donald Davidson[20] and Bruce Aune[21] speak approvingly of his discussion of this. But, clearly, if an act is an event and a consequence is another event which is an effect of that act, no amount of linguistic legerdemain will be able to accomplish the miracle of merging these two separate and distinct entities into one. In fact, both Davidson and Aune explicitly recognize this point (although Austin, D'Arcy, and Feinberg do not) by stipulating that what is stretched and squeezed when the accordion effect is operative is the *description* of the act concerned, and not the act itself. A proposed example of the accordion effect is the case of Jones's flipping of the switch, thereby turning on the light, illuminating the room, and alerting the prowler. In this example, for instance, the term "Jones flipped the switch" is presumed to "cover a smaller stretch of events" than the term "Jones alerted the prowler." Perhaps, on a Davidsonian ontology of events, according to which a single event often bears several descriptions and according to which Jones's flipping the switch and Jones's alerting the prowler are (in this case) identical, there is some reason for saying that the accordion effect is operative here. For there may be, indeed there surely is (given the distinction between direct and indirect bringing about) a legitimate sense in which "Jones alerted the prowler" "covers" the event of the prowler's becoming alarmed whereas "Jones flipped the switch" does not; and given that, on such an ontology, "Jones flipped the switch" and "Jones alerted the prowler" nevertheless describe the *same* action, perhaps there is good reason to talk about the "stretching and squeezing" of descriptions in this case. But, to repeat, there is no good reason to talk of the stretching and squeezing of actions themselves.

On the ontology of events and actions proposed in this chapter, however, talk of the accordion effect would appear unwarranted. For Jones's flipping the switch and Jones's alerting the prowler are *not* identical, on this theory, and so the fact that the description of the former fails to "cover" an event that the description of the latter "covers" is of no special importance. It seems to me a considerable advantage of the present theory that talk of the accordion effect may be dispensed with; for having to account for the description of actions, as well as the actions themselves, can only serve to complicate matters.

In the present context I am of course taking a consequence of an event *e* to be any event to which *e* contributes causally (on the occasion in question). Note that, although it is obviously true that, if *f* is a consequence of *e*, *f* may be and indeed very often is distinct from *e*, it is yet possible for an action or issue to be a consequence of an action or issue. We have already seen that all indirect issues are themselves consequences of direct issues. That an action may be a consequence of an action is made clear by the fact that, if Smith hypnotizes Jones and Jones walks around in circles as a consequence, then both [Smith hypnotizes Jones] and [Jones walks around in circles] are actions, even though the latter is a consequence of the former.[2 2] I believe in fact that, in general, an action has exactly the same consequences, on a particular occasion, as the issue internal to it, but I am not sure how this might be proven.

What of problem B4 in particular, however? When Jones kills Smith, is Smith's death a part or a consequence of what Jones does? We are now in a position to see how this question requires clarification. When Jones kills Smith, he brings about Smith's death indirectly. Smith's death, therefore, is an issue, and hence a *part*, of the action which is Jones's killing Smith and which is composed in addition of a volition of Jones's and of a direct issue of an action of Jones's, an issue which contributes causally to Smith's death. But although Smith's death is part of Jones's killing him, and although it is of course true that it is logically impossible that Jones kill Smith and Smith yet live, it is also true that Smith's death is a consequence of an action of Jones's. This is because the killing is an indirect action, and every indirect action is performed partly by means of a direct action. In the present case, Jones shoots Smith. Let us assume that his pulling of the trigger is a direct action of his. We may then say that Smith's death is a *consequence* of Jones's pulling the trigger. Speaking loosely, then, we may say that Smith's death is both a part and a consequence of "what Jones does." But this is, of course, just loose talk; the way in which to render it more precise has just been shown.

Finally, with regard to B5, it is clear that, on the present account of action, [Jones butters something], [Jones butters toast], [Jones butters toast in the bathroom], and [Jones butters toast in the bathroom with a knife] are all distinct actions of Jones's. [Jones butters toast in the bathroom with a knife at midnight] is a different matter. If we take "midnight" to designate a particular midnight (as we clearly should, given the wording of the illustration), then this state of affairs is a proposition, and hence not an event, and hence not an action. There may yet be some sense in which the manner, the place, and the time are "circumstances" of the particular occurrence of [Jones butters something] in question, but the temptation to clarify this sense is diminished in so far as, given the present finely-grained individuation of actions, not only [Jones butters something] but also [Jones butters toast], and so on, may safely be said to be actions of Jones's.

In this connection it should be mentioned that there is another sense of "circumstance" which is often invoked in action-contexts. In this sense, a circumstance is an event which occurs around about the time at which the action occurs but which is neither the action itself, nor a cause of the action, nor a consequence of the action. I shall forgo trying to render this sense of "circumstance" more precise here.

Notes

1   [S brings about f directly] is that event whose occurrence at T and T' is entailed by S 's bringing about f directly relative to T and T', for any times T and T'. This point holds analogously of [S brings about f indirectly], [S brings about f synthetically], and, indeed, of all states of affairs thus "constructed" from time-relativized concepts. Similarly, [e contributes causally to f] is that event whose occurrence at T and T' is entailed by e's contributing causally relative to T and T' to f, for any times T and T'.

2   It may be thought that the remark that an event is always or never an action is false for the following reason. Suppose that, on one occasion, John causes a mild sensation by streaking at a formal cocktail party and that, on another occasion, John causes a mild sensation by falling asleep during an important meeting. Should it not turn out, given my account of action, that [John causes a mild sensation] is a genuine action of John's on the first occasion but not an action of his on the second? I think not. The correct move here is, I believe, to note that it is the *phrase* "John causes a mild sensation" that is ambiguous; on some occasions it may properly be employed to express a genuine action and on some occasions it may properly be employed for some other purpose. It is not the *event* [John causes a mild sensation] that is an action on one occasion and not on another. The question arises, however: is [John causes a mild sensation] an action or not? I am not sure how this question ought to be answered, for an adequate answer would involve treatment of the issue of how best to express and to designate states of affairs – an extremely important issue, but one that I have for the most part studiously avoided. (For instance, it is certainly incorrect to claim that there is a one-one correspondence between well-formed assertoric English sentences and states of affairs – states of affairs which may be perspicuously designated by placing their corresponding sentences in square brackets. And it may be incorrect, too, to say that every placing of a well-formed assertoric English sentence

inside square brackets results in the designation of a state of affairs. (*Cf.* Chisholm (1981), pp.54-5.) But what restrictions should be put on this device of designation is a matter that I cannot enter into here.) Perhaps the proper answer is that there *is* no event that is adequately expressed by "John causes a mild sensation," even though the phrase "John brings about a mild sensation actively" does adequately express a particular event (an event which is of course an action).

3   On measure-events, see Chapter 1, Section 1.4.

4   Thomson (1971, 1977) also argues for the strong, at times odd-sounding thesis that I have tentatively endorsed here.

5   Cf. Walton (1979), p.182.

6   Are actions observable? Melden (1961, pp.21-2), claims that they are, but that the volitional theory of action requires that they be unobservable. Without entering into this controversy here, I suggest that this matter may be settled by distinguishing between actions and issues (the former cannot be physically observable in their entirety – unless volitions may be said to be so – while some of the latter can be physically observable in their entirety), and also between physical observability and propositional observability (on which see Chisholm (1976), p.135). *Cf.* Hornsby (1980), Chapter 3.

7   See Chapter 1, notes 2 through 5, for a listing of such theories. See also note 60 to that chapter.

8   See Chisholm (1971b), pp.187-8.

9   Goldman (1970), pp.1-10.

10   Goldman himself considers some replies (see Goldman (1970), pp.1-10). See also Aune (1977), p.12ff.; Grimm (1977); Davis (1979), Chapter 1; Anscombe (1979).

11   In Chapter 1, Section 1.1 I distinguished two sorts of bloatedness in ontologies. First an ontology may be bloated with re-

spect to the number of *entities* it posits, and, second, it may be bloated with respect to the number of *types* of entities it posits. The present ontology is bloated in the former way, but respectably lean in the latter – and it is only the latter sort of bloatedness that I think is objectionable. One reason why I regard the former sort of bloatedness unobjectionable is that it seems to me almost impossible to avoid – for, even if events are considered coarsely-grained, it is highly likely that other entities which one is forced to admit into one's ontology (including propositions, properties, and perhaps even sets and concrete individuals) will be recognized as finely-grained.

12   There are, indeed, accounts of the individuation and timing of actions and issues that I have not even touched on here, including especially the "middle ground" between particularists – such as Anscombe and Davidson – and multiplicationists – such as myself – favored by Thalberg (1971), Beardsley (1975), and others.

13   Note that some of these issues will be consequences of others. For instance, the issue internal to [Jones illuminates the room] – namely, [the room lights up] – is a consequence of the issue internal to [Jones turns on the light] – namely, [the light goes on]. It is interesting to note that Chisholm (1979, p.366) – despite his advocacy of a fine-grained approach to the individuation of events – says that just *one* action is involved in a case such as this. This characteristically surprising move is, however, based on a definition of "action," one undesirable implication of which seems to be that my action of writing this note will continue to occur indefinitely.

14   Rescher (1970) has urged that one resist advocating the "infinite divisibility" of actions; Melden (1961, p.64) agrees.

15   Austin (1956), p.40.

16   D'Arcy (1963), p.15.

17   D'Arcy (1963), p.32.

18 D'Arcy (1963), p.16.

19 Feinberg (1965), p.40.

20 Davidson (1971), p.53ff.

21 Aune (1977), p.5.

22 I assume, of course, that Smith's hypnotizing Jones does not preclude Jones's willing certain events and this willing's having certain effects.

Chapter 6

INTENTIONAL ACTION

Not all action is intentional action. Philosophers sometimes forget this; worse, they sometimes deny it. But it is clear that people sometimes act unintentionally and that the account of action in general given in Chapter 4 (especially that portion contained in D.4.7 through D.4.11 and D.4.3.c) is compatible with this fact. (See again the discussion following the presentation of D.4.7 where Smith's knocking over Brown's Ming vase was said to be an unintentional action.) But what is it, then, that distinguishes intentional from unintentional action? In order to facilitate the discussion of this question, I shall begin by concentrating solely on intentional direct action.

6.1   DEFECTIVE ANALYSES

Let us first consider a proposal which, although apparently sometimes endorsed in the literature,[1] is clearly inadequate, and that is that acting intentionally is simply doing what one intends to do. More precisely, the proposal in the present context is this:

D.6.1.a: S intentionally brings about e directly relative to T and T' =df.
      (i) S intends e at T;[2] and
      (ii) S brings about e directly relative to T and T'.

Now, although both clause (i) and clause (ii) of this definition do, I think, state necessary conditions for the truth of the definiendum, they do not state, singly or jointly, a sufficient condition for its truth. Consider this counterexample. Let e be the event internal to Smith's hitting Jones. Suppose that Smith is talking to Brown and, also, that he intends that e should occur, and suppose that, in the course of his talk with Brown, he becomes excited and starts gesticulating wildly, thereby inadvertently hitting Jones, who happens (unknown to Smith) to be standing close by. Certainly Smith does not intentionally bring about *e* directly, and yet according to D.6.1.a he does.

Before an attempt is made to improve on D.6.1.a, it should be recognized that some philosophers dispute the claim that clause (i) of the definition states a necessary condition of the truth of the definiendum. Two main reasons have been given for the claim that one may (to put it somewhat roughly) intentionally do something without intending to do it. First, some claim that intending to do something requires that one believe that one has "at least a fifty-fifty chance" that one will succeed in doing it (if one tries, perhaps), whereas one may intentionally do something even when one thinks it probable that one will fail to do it.[3] Second, some claim that, when one intends to do something, the intention precedes the doing, whereas one may act intentionally even when no thought or intention precedes one's action.[4] Now, with respect to the first claim, I accept that one may intentionally do something even when one thinks it probable that one will fail to do it. For instance, I may intentionally shoot a target even if I think it probable that I will fail (I am not an expert gunman, the target is far away, the wind is up, and so on). But since I take clause (i) of D.6.1.a to state a necessary condition of the truth of the definiendum, what I think that this point shows is that intending to do something does not require that one believe that one has "at least a fifty-fifty chance" of success.[5] With respect to the second claim, I accept that one may intentionally do something "spontaneously," that is, without one's action being preceded by a (relevant) intention. For instance, braking to avoid hitting a dog that darts out into the street may well be an intentional action of this sort. But, again, since I take clause (i) of D.6.1.a to state a necessary condition of the truth of the definiendum, what I think that this point shows is that intending to do something may accompany, and need not precede, the doing of it. This point is, I think, rendered more plausible when it is acknowledged that willing requires intending (see A.3.10) and yet also that willing is a part, and not a precursor, of action.

Now, my replies to the objections in the preceding paragraph are perhaps not terribly convincing. For the objections are of the form "*P, Q*, therefore *R*," and my replies are simply of the form "*P*, not-*R*, therefore not-*Q*." I am not sure how to defend my replies, other than to say that I take it to be very plausible to claim that doing something intentionally requires (again, to put it somewhat roughly[6]) intending to do it and that, therefore, this claim ought not to be given up except to avoid the sacrifice of an even more plausible claim. I find neither the claim that intention requires a belief that one has a "better than fifty-fifty chance" of success, nor the claim that intention must precede the (relevant) action, to be more plausible than the claim that doing something intentionally requires intending to do it.[7] Others, of course, may, and presumably do, find differently. Perhaps this impasse may be avoided through further argumentation, but I am not sure how this may be achieved. Henceforth, then, I shall simply take it as given that clause (i) of D.6.1.a does state a necessary condition of the truth of the definiendum. As noted, however, D.6.1.a requires modification. Given that clauses (i) and (ii) are not to be rejected, such modification must take the form of supplementing these clauses with further clauses which state necessary conditions of the truth of the definiendum, until a point is reached where the clauses, taken jointly, also state a sufficient condition of the truth of the definiendum. Now, several candidate conditions are to be found in the literature. Foremost among these are conditions concerning desire and knowledge. I shall consider these, briefly, in turn.

Sometimes it is claimed that doing something intentionally requires desiring or wanting to do it, and, indeed, this seems plausible when one attempts to draw a distinction between intention and (mere) foresight.[8] I think that this is claimed only because it is thought that intentionally doing something requires intending to do it, and that intending to do it requires wanting to do it. Now, I have already noted (when discussing statement 10 in Chapter 3, Section 3.2) that I think that the connection between intention and desire is tenuous at best, and so I am not of the opinion that bringing desire into the picture when discussing intentional action will be of any help, even if such introduction of desire is warranted (which I doubt).

Sometimes it is claimed that doing something intentionally requires knowing that one is doing it.[9] This is false. A counterexample to the claim has been given by Davidson:

[I]n writing heavily on this page I may be intending to produce ten legible carbon copies. I do
not know, or believe with any confidence, that I
am succeeding. But if I am producing ten legible
carbon copies, I am certainly doing it intentionally.[1][0]

The claim may be modified by talking of "non-observational"
knowledge, or by talking of knowing that one *may* be performing the
action in question, or both,[1][1] but I do not think that such
modifications, even if accurate, will be of any real help, although I
shall not seek to demonstrate the reasonability of my doubts.

Perhaps, given the treatment of action in general in Chapter 4,
the most obvious move, in an effort to improve on D.6.1.a, is to introduce the concept of volition and to attempt to forge a link between what S wills at T and what is thereby caused to happen. If
we look at D.4.7, the move that immediately suggests itself is to
stipulate that "e" and "g" designate the same event. That is:

D.6.1.b: S intentionally brings about e directly relative to
             T and T' =df. there is an event f such that:
             (i) S wills f at T in order that e may occur;
             (ii) [S wills f in order that e may occur] contrib-
             utes causally relative to T and T' to f; and
             (iii) f constitutes e at T'.[1][2]

Note that, as with D.6.1.a, the following are implications of D.6.1.b:
first, S intends e at T; second, S brings about e directly relative to T
and T'. But D.6.1.b will not do, and this has been a well-established
point ever since Chisholm came up with a couple of counterexamples concerning what he calls "inadvertent successes" and
"happy failures."[1][3] To fit the present discussion of direct action,
such counterexamples will have to be modified. But one will suffice,
and here is one. Let f be [S's hand rises] and e be the event internal to [S signals], and let everything which is said of f and e in the
definiens of D.6.1.b hold. But suppose that [S wills f in order that e
may occur] succeeds in contributing causally to f (and, by clause
(iii), to e) only due to the intervention of some event totally unfore-
seen and unexpected by S. (For instance, suppose that S's volition

is causally effective only by virtue of the fact that an event *g* occurs as causal intermediary, and that *g* occurs totally fortuitously; *g* may, for example, be [*S* throws a fit].[1] [4] In such a case, although the definiens of D.6.1.b is satisfied, its definiendum is surely not satisfied. Nevertheless, it is useful to note that *S* has acted successfully, even if not intentionally, in this case, and so we may say:

D.6.2:   *S* successfully brings about *e* directly relative to *T* and *T′* =df. there is an event *f* such that:
(i) *S* wills *f* at *T* in order that *e* may occur;
(ii) [*S* wills *f* in order that *e* may occur] contributes causally relative to *T* and *T′* to *f*; and
(iii) *f* constitutes e at *T′*.[1] [5]

What has gone wrong with D.6.1.b? Briefly, it fails to recognize the fact that, as the current vernacular has it, "causal chains" may be "wayward." It fails to recognize that, as Chisholm puts it, "an agent performs an *intentional action* provided there is something he makes happen *in the way he intended.*"[1] [6] But what is it for a causal chain not to be wayward? What sense are we to make of the notion of making something happen "in the way one intends"? Chisholm believes that what this amounts to is a requirement that the issue be not just *successfully* brought about, but that it be brought about in a manner which is "*completely* successful."[1] [7] His proposal, when fit into the present framework, amounts approximately to supplementing the definiens of D.6.1.b with a fourth clause in the following manner:

D.6.1.c: *S* intentionally brings about *e* directly relative to *T* and *T′* =df. there is an event *f* such that:
(i) *S* wills *f* at *T* in order that *e* may occur;
(ii) [*S* wills *f* in order that *e* may occur] contributes causally relative to *T* and *T′* to *f*;
(iii) *f* constitutes *e* at *T′*; and
(iv) for any event *g*, if *S* also wills *g* at *T* in order that *e* may occur, then [*S* wills *g* in order that *e* may occur] contributes causally relative to *T* and *T′* to *g*.

But D.6.1.c will not do either. Let *e* once again be the event internal to [*S* signals], and suppose that *S* wills two things at *T* in order that *e* may occur, namely, *f* ([*S*'s hand rises]) and *g* ([*S*'s hand is outstretched]). Suppose, further, that *S* wills nothing else at *T*. It may yet, of course, happen, just as in the case with D.6.1.b, that each of *e*, *f*, and *g* occurs fortuitously, and this would be sufficient to render *S*'s action unintentional, even though the definiens of D.6.1.c is satisfied.[18]

Several philosophers seem to accept Chisholm's insight that acting intentionally requires that the issue or issues of one's action be made to happen "in the way one intends" – as, indeed, I think they should – but they do not seem to have made it any clearer, although this is not for want of trying. For instance, Alvin Goldman proposes an account of intentional action in which a person is said to act intentionally only if his having an action-plan causes the issue in question "in a certain characteristic way."[19] Goldman is, of course, aware of the vagueness of this locution, but he claims that it is not incumbent upon him, *qua* philosopher, to seek to dispel it. He claims, rather, that this is a matter which properly concerns the neurophysiologist.[20] But such an abjuration of philosophical inquiry is, I believe, premature. Similarly, Gilbert Harman has suggested that a person acts intentionally only if an intention of his causes the issue in question "in a more or less explicitly specified way,"[21] and Richard Foley has proposed that a person acts intentionally only if a volition of his causes the issue in question "in the way envisaged."[22] But none of these substitute locutions is any clearer than that locution we are seeking to understand, namely, "in the way one intends."

At one point Foley suggests a reading of the locution "in the way envisaged" which results in the following definition (when modified to fit the present framework), one in which clause (ii) of the definiens of D.6.1.b is changed to accommodate lack of surprise on the part of the agent concerning the manner in which the event which he brings about comes about as a result of his volition:

D.6.1.d: *S* intentionally brings about *e* directly relative to
          T and *T'* =df. there is an event *f* such that:
          (i) *S* wills *f* at *T* in order that *e* may occur;

> (ii) [*S* wills *f* in order that *e* may occur] contrib-
> utes causally relative to *T* and *T'* to *f* in a manner
> which does not surprise *S* ; and
> (iii) *f* constitutes *e* at *T'*.[2][3]

But, while this is suggestive and, perhaps, close to being correct, it is in fact wrong to take "in the way one intends" or "in the way en- visaged" to mean the same in this context as "in a manner which does not surprise *S*." For consider this case. Smith is painfully in- ept and, not unreasonably, totally lacking in self-confidence. Whenever he manages to do something that he intends to do, he is astonished. Now, Jones is an insensitive, self-satisfied scoundrel who continually berates Smith, mocking his ineptitude. Smith finally becomes so exasperated at Jones's insulting behavior that he decides to teach him a lesson. He decides that, if Jones insults him just one more time, he will punch him in the mouth. The next day Jones again insults Smith and Smith carries out his intention. He punches Jones in the mouth; but, true to form, he is surprised that he succeeds in doing so (and, *a fortiori*, surprised concerning the manner in which the volition of his action contributed causally to its issue). According to D.6.1.d, then, Smith does not act intentionally when he punches Jones in the mouth. But the fact is, of course, that he does.[2][4]

There are still others who have tried their hand at analyzing the concept of intentional action. For instance, Judith Jarvis Thomson proposes an analysis in terms of the concept of hope.[2][5] This anal- ysis is, I believe, defective, but it is very complicated and I shall not discuss it here. I propose to turn, rather, to an analysis of my own. However, before I do so, brief acknowledgement should be made of a method of treating this issue which is different from the general method adopted by Chisholm, Goldman, Harman, Foley, and others. G.E.M. Anscombe has given a clear statement of this method. Rather than deal with the *causal* history of the action (or issue), Anscombe proposes to deal with the *reasons* for which the action is performed by the agent. (There are those, of course, who believe that such reasons just are causes of the action in question, but An- scombe is not of this opinion.) Her proposal amounts to the follow- ing:

D.6.1.e: *S* intentionally brings about *e* directly relative to
           T and *T′* =df. there is a rational explanation of
           [*S* brings about *e* directly relative to *T* and *T′*].[26]

Bruce Aune has given voice to the same intuition (although, as we
shall see, he also has sympathies with the causal approach) and at
one point makes a proposal which in outline is as follows:

D.6.1.f: *S* intentionally brings about *e* directly relative to
           T and *T′* =df. there are an intention *i* and a time
           T* such that [*S* has *i* at *T**] rationally explains [*S*
           brings about *e* directly relative to *T* and *T′*].[27]

This approach to the present problem is difficult to evaluate, for the
concept of rational explanation must first be clarified. Both Anscombe and, especially, Aune undertake such clarification, but their
treatment of this matter is incomplete in certain respects, as they
are themselves aware. Nevertheless, I suspect that this approach,
even if adequately clarified, would prove defective. First, I think
that there may well be intentional actions performed by an agent
for which the agent has no reason, and hence for which there is no
rational explanation.[28] Having a reason for acting is, I think, a
mark of *deliberate* action, and whereas all deliberate action is intentional, not all intentional action, I believe, is deliberate. (I shall return to the matter of deliberate action shortly.) Secondly, it would
seem to me possible to give a rational explanation of an unintentional action. Suppose that I want to please my host and, for this
reason, reach out for a second cup of coffee. But suppose that, in so
doing, I unintentionally knock over the coffee pot, spilling its con-
tents on to my host's lap. Does my desire to please my host rationally explain my knocking over the coffee pot? I am not sure,
although it seems plausible to me to say that it does. Perhaps either Aune or Anscombe would reply that it offers no *"complete"* rational explanation of this action. There may be something to this
reply but, without further details, it is one that I cannot adequately
evaluate. I would rather, therefore, turn back from reasons to
causes and see if we cannot, following the general method adopted
by Chisholm, Goldman, and the rest, come up with a satisfactory
account of intentional action. I think that we can.

6.2   *A PROPOSED ANALYSIS*

The most striking feature of an issue intentionally brought about, over and above its being successfully brought about, is that it *comes about* in the way that the agent intends. This, as has been said, is Chisholm's insight, and it is one with which I am in complete agreement. But what does this amount to? Foley puts the matter this way:

> We want, it seems, a criterion of doing something deliberately which does not require the agent to foresee a consequence with perfect accuracy, and yet we also want a criterion which does not allow the agent to be radically mistaken about how the state of affairs in question is caused.[29]

I think that this is both a correct and a useful way of looking at things. (Where Foley uses the term "deliberately" I would rather use the term "intentionally," but this is a minor point that I shall overlook for the moment.) Foley's proposed solution, as has already been mentioned, concerns the element of surprise, and it is one that has been found wanting. But we should nevertheless attempt to meet his requirements for a satisfactory criterion. The correct solution, I believe, is really rather straightforward. For an action to be intentional, it must come about in one of a certain limited number of ways acceptable to the agent. What this amounts to is, I think, roughly this. An event comes about as an agent intends just in case, first, he intends that it come about by way of at least one of a certain limited number of causal paths, and it does so, and, second, there is no causal path which occurs, culminating in the event in question, but which the agent believed would *not* occur. To put this more precisely we must invoke the concept of an event e's contributing causally to an event g via another event f, as analyzed in D.3.5. (On such an occasion, f may be said to be an intermediary.) We may then say:

D.6.3: e comes about at T', as a result of f occurring at T, as S intends at T'' =df.
    (i) there are events $g1,...,gn$ such that

(a) S intends at T''' that, for some time T^*, f should contribute causally relative to T and T^* to e either via $g1$ or...or via gn, and

(b) f (in fact) contributes causally relative to T and T' to e either via $g1$ or...or via gn ; and

(ii) there is no event g such that

(a) S accepts at T''' that, for any time T^*, if f contributes causally relative to T and T^* to e, then f does not contribute causally relative to T and T^* to e via g, and

(b) f (nevertheless) contributes causally relative to T and T' to e via g.

In this case $g1$ through gn are projected potential intermediaries, one at least of which turns out to be an actual intermediary. Moreover, there occurs no actual intermediary which was anticipated by S as *not* occurring. (Note that this is *not* to say that no intermediary occurs which was not anticipated by S as occurring.) The proposal embodied in D.6.3 in fact comes close to Foley's proposal concerning the lack of surprise; but it avoids the objection raised above against that proposal by stipulating in clause (ii)(a) that S's belief be a conditional one. Clause (ii) rules out what Foley calls "radical mistakes" – and thereby, I believe, rules out "causal chains" that are "wayward"; moreover, his stipulation that "perfect accuracy" not be required is also met (consult the preceding parenthetical remark), especially since in most cases the disjunction of $g1$ through gn of clause (i) will contain more than one disjunct. It seems, then, that we may truthfully assert the following:

D.6.1.g: S intentionally brings about e directly relative to T and T' =df. there is an event f such that:

(i) S wills f at T in order that e may occur;

(ii) [S wills f in order that e may occur] contributes causally relative to T and T' to f;

(iii) f constitutes e at T' ; and

(iv) e comes about at T', as a result of [S wills f in order that e may occur] occurring at T, as S intends at T.

The definiens of D.6.1.g is, of course, the same as that of D.6.1.b, except that it has clause (iv) attached. In this connection we may note the following theorem:

T.6.1:   Necessarily, if S intentionally brings about e directly relative to T and T', then S successfully brings about e directly relative to T and T'.

If D.6.1.g is accurate, as I claim, then the concepts of intentionally bringing about an event indirectly and intentionally bringing about an event synthetically are easily accounted for. We may say:

D.6.4: S intentionally brings about e indirectly relative to T and T' =df. there are an event f and a time T^* such that:
(i) S intentionally brings about f directly relative to T and T^* ; and
(ii) e comes about at T', as a result of f occurring at T^*, as S intends at T.[30]

D.6.5: S intentionally brings about e synthetically relative to T and T' =df. there are events $f1,...,fn$ and a time T''' such that:
(i) e is composed relative to T''' and T' of $f1,...,fn$;
(ii) for any event f, if f is identical with $f1$ or...or f is identical with fn, then there are times T^* and T^{**} such that
(a) T is not later than T^*, T^* is not later than T^{**}, and T^{**} is not earlier than T''' and not later than T', and
(b) either
(1) S intentionally brings about f directly relative to T^* and T^{**}, or
(2) S intentionally brings about f indirectly relative to T^* and T^{**}; and
(iii) S intends at T that, for some time T^*, e should be composed relative to T''' and T^* of $f1,...,fn$.

Though fairly formidable in appearance, these two definitions are
really just slightly modified versions of D.4.8 and D.4.10, respectively. And the modifications are as one would expect. That is, in
clause (i) of D.6.4, there is the added stipulation that the event that
is directly brought about by the agent is brought about intentionally, and in clause (ii) it is stipulated that the event that is indirectly
brought about comes about as the agent intends; and, as for D.6.5,
there is the added stipulation in clause (ii)(b) that the direct and indirect issues, of which the event that is synthetically brought about
is composed, are themselves intentionally brought about, and also a
third clause is added to the effect that the agent intends that the
event that is synthetically brought about be composed of the events
of which it is composed. It should of course be noted that it is a
theorem, first, that [S intentionally brings about e directly relative
to T and T'] implies [S brings about e directly relative to T and T'];
second, that [S intentionally brings about e indirectly relative to T
and T'] implies [S brings about e indirectly relative to T and T'];
and, third, that [S intentionally brings about e synthetically relative
to T and T'] implies [S brings about e synthetically relative to T and
T']. Given the foregoing definitions, we may say:

D.6.6: S intentionally brings about e actively relative to
            T and T' =df. either
                (i) S intentionally brings about e directly relative
            to T and T'; or
                (ii) S intentionally brings about e indirectly rela-
            tive to T and T'; or
                (iii) S intentionally brings about e synthetically
            relative to T and T'.

And we may also say:

D.6.7: S acts intentionally relative to T and T' =df.
            there is an event e such that S intentionally
            brings about e actively relative to T and T'.

We may of course also say that S acts unintentionally relative to T
and T' just in case he acts relative to T and T' but does not act intentionally relative to T and T'.

6.3   *TEST CASES*

Let us now see how this account of intentional action measures up to a few test cases. The most interesting ones appear to concern indirect action; at any rate, these have been the main focus of attention in the recent literature, and I shall here confine my attention to them. First, suppose that Jones is intent on shooting Smith. He takes aim at Smith's heart and pulls the trigger of his gun. His aim is a little off, however, and he shoots Smith straight between the eyes instead, nevertheless still managing thereby to kill him instantly. Now it turns out, according to D.6.4, that [Jones shoots Smith straight between the eyes] is *not* an intentional action of Jones's; for Jones has no intentions regarding the event internal to this action, and so clause (ii) of D.6.4 fails to be satisfied. But is this result not counterintuitive? No, I do not think that it is. For Jones certainly did *not* intentionally shoot Smith *straight between the eyes*. This of course leaves open the possibility of his intentionally pulling the trigger (probably a direct action) and of his intentionally shooting Smith (another indirect action). In such circumstances as those just sketched, I would think it almost certainly true that Jones *did* intentionally pull the trigger. Whether or not he also intentionally shot Smith will depend in part upon how detailed his picture was of how the bullet was to find its way into Smith's body. The fact that Jones did not intend that Smith should be shot straight between the eyes does not imply that, by shooting him straight between the eyes, he did not intentionally shoot him. For I think that it is true that, if Jones intended that the event internal to his shooting Smith in the heart should occur, then he also intended that that event internal to his shooting Smith should occur. And, as long as he did not accept that this latter event would *not* be brought about (if brought about at all) by virtue of the bullet's piercing Smith's brow instead of his heart, then Jones did intentionally shoot Smith, although, to repeat, he did not intentionally shoot him straight between the eyes.[31]

Or take these two cases given by Aune:

> I intend to frighten Smith and decide to do so by making a threatening gesture. My eyesight is poor, however, and I approach a rack full of

coats, taking it to be Smith. I make the
threatening gesture. Smith, at the other end of
the room, sees me making the gesture to the
coatrack and, thinking I have gone mad, becomes
frightened. It seems doubtful that I frightened
Smith intentionally: my decision to make the
threatening gesture does not cause Smith's fright
by the appropriate sequence of events. On the
other hand, suppose that I intend to kill Smith
and, as a means of killing him, decide to stab him
with an icepick. I then lunge with the icepick, but
I miss my target, striking his neck with my
clenched fist. A blood vessel breaks in Smith's
neck, and he dies. In this case it seems that I do
kill Smith intentionally, although I do not kill him
in the way that I intended to kill him: the sequence of events connecting my decision to stab
Smith with Smith's death would seem to be close
enough to the envisioned sequence to render my
killing intentional.[3][2]

Aune's conclusion is that "[t]hese contrasting cases suggest that the
notion of doing something with an intention is a little too vague to
be pinned down with any precise formula."[3][3] But this conclusion is
unwarranted, I think. Clause (ii) of D.6.3 gives us the clue as to
how to adjudicate these cases. Did I accept that Smith, if he be-
came frightened at all, would *not* become frightened in the manner
in which he actually did? If so (and perhaps this is likely) then I did
not intentionally frighten him.[3][4] Or again, did I accept that, if I
killed Smith at all, it would *not* be due to my clenched fist's striking
Smith's neck and breaking a blood vessel? If not (and perhaps this
is likely) then I *did* intentionally kill him. The problem in such cases, I submit, is not with the formula that I have proposed but with
whether or not there is sufficient information to know how to apply
it accurately.[3][5]

Finally, consider this intriguing puzzle posed by Ronald Butler.[3][6] Suppose that Brown hopes to throw a six in an ordinary
game of dice, throws the die, and succeeds in throwing a six. Suppose also that Jones puts one live cartridge into an empty six-

chambered revolver, spins the chamber, points the gun at Smith, pulls the trigger hoping to kill Smith thereby, and succeeds in killing Smith. Now, both Brown and Jones have a one-in-six chance of success, but, Butler claims, Brown does *not* throw the six intentionally whereas Jones *does* kill Smith intentionally. How is this disparity between the cases to be accounted for?

Butler's problem has given rise to considerable discussion. I do not intend to recapitulate this discussion in detail here; rather, I shall present a tentative solution to – or, rather, dissolution of – the problem. Two broad reactions to Butler's problem are possible: either one can accept that there is the disparity between the cases that Butler points to, or one can deny that there is such a disparity. Most commentators have taken the former tack,[37] but some have taken the latter.[38] Whichever tack one takes, it is important to note that the cases serve to highlight a fact already mentioned in Section 3.2 of Chapter 3 and in Section 6.1 of this chapter, namely, that intending that an event occur does not require that one believe that it will occur or even that one believe that there is "at least a fifty-fifty chance" of its occurring.[39] Certainly one may intentionally swat a fly, even when one believes it likely that one will fail, and this (as mentioned in Section 6.1) seems to imply that one may intend to swat a fly, even when one believes it likely that one will fail. But, as to Butler's problem in particular, I must say that I tend to favor the claim that there is *no* such disparity as that to which he points. Those who accept that there is such a disparity have proposed solutions to the problem that are intended to illuminate the disparity, but I think that these proposals have already been cogently and correctly criticized by others.[40] It seems to me that, in the cases as set up by Butler, neither Brown nor Jones acts intentionally because (roughly speaking[41]) neither Brown nor Jones can be correctly said to intend to perform his respective action. Why should this be so? The answer, I think, is that intending that an event occur requires that one have some conception as to what steps one may take to see to it that it does occur.[42] Put this way, the requirement is stated very roughly, but I am not sure how to make it more precise. The point, however, is that neither Brown nor Jones has any conception as to what steps he may take beyond his "initial action" (in Brown's case, the "initial action" is that of throwing the die; in Jones's case, the "initial action" is that synthetic action of spinning the chamber, pointing the gun, and pulling the trigger) in order to achieve what he hopes to achieve (in Brown's case, the hope is that a six will turn up; in Jones's case, the hope is that the bullet will enter Smith's body). Hence, neither Brown nor Jones may be said to intend to do what he hopes to do; hence neither Brown nor Jones may be said to intentionally do what he does.[43] This has nothing to do with the odds. Both Brown and Jones have a one-in-six chance of success, whereas another person, Green, may have (and correctly believe that he has) only a one-in-ten chance of successfully swatting the fly that has been bothering him all morning. But Green differs from both Brown and Jones in that he has some conception as to how to see his project through; he has swatted flies before, he knows how quickly they react, he knows how best to manipulate the fly-swatter in order to swat the fly, and so on.

Such is my brief and tentative dissolution of Butler's problem. I acknowledge that it may well appear unsatisfactory, for two reasons. First, it is stated very roughly and hence somewhat unclearly; secondly, it does not even attempt to accommodate the intuition that many apparently have, including Butler, that there really is a disparity between the cases. I do not know how to avoid the former problem; perhaps the latter can be alleviated by noting that one may be tempted to incorporate – irrelevantly – considerations pertaining to moral responsibility in the Jones case and not in the Brown case.[44] But I shall not pursue this; for there is a more important point to make, and that is that, if there *is* the disparity between the cases that Butler claims, it is apparently traceable to the fact that Brown does not intend to throw a six while Jones does intend to kill Smith. Hence (this may seem like a "cop-out" – and in a sense it is – but it is nevertheless a proper move, I think) the account of intentional action given in this chapter is adequate to the resolution of this puzzle, *however it is to be resolved*. For this account requires (again, speaking roughly) that an intentional action be intended. If Brown does not intend to throw a six, then he does not throw it intentionally. If Jones intends to kill Smith, then, given the facts of the case, he may be said to kill him intentionally. Thus the puzzle is pushed back a step from the concept of intentional action to the concept of intention. Of course, the puzzle is not made to disappear by such a relocation, and the question arises as to why Jones may be said to intend to kill Smith while Brown may not be said to intend to throw a six. As indicated, my inclination is to deny that Jones intends to kill Smith; but if this is wrong and Jones may correctly be said to intend to kill Smith, then I confess that I do not know how to answer the question. But this does not render the present account of intentional action incorrect. What it does is to render the present account of intentional action that much more obscure than it might at first appear, since it is based in part on a concept (the concept of intention) which turns out to be more obscure than it might at first appear. If this is so, this is an unfortunate fact that must be acknowledged; but it must not be given more than its due weight and be thought to vitiate the present account of intentional action.

6.4 RESOLUTION OF THE THIRD GROUP OF PROBLEMS

The concepts of intentional and unintentional actions and issues and related concepts may of course be formally analyzed in terms of D.6.7, but I shall not present explicit analyses of them here. I propose, rather, to turn now to a consideration of the third group of problems posed in Chapter 2.

Assuming the accuracy of the foregoing account of intentional action, encapsulated in D.6.7, problem C1 has in fact already been resolved. What of problem C2? This too may now be resolved. Given that, on the present theory, actions are finely-grained, the solution is fairly obvious. Since [Hamlet kills Polonius] and [Hamlet kills the man behind the arras] are distinct actions, there is no difficulty in seeing how the former may be unintentional and the latter yet intentional, even though Polonius was the man behind the arras. And it may still be maintained that only one killing occurred since, to invoke the strategy used earlier, [something is killed] occurred only once at the time and place at which Hamlet killed Polonius. Finally, with respect to problem C3, it is of course true that not all actions are intentional. Perhaps, however, few philosophers have claimed that all actions are intentional.[4 5] What many philosophers do say is that all actions are "intentional under some description."[4 6] Such a claim of course goes hand in hand with an ontology according to which events and actions are coarsely-grained.

But at least one implication of the claim may be put in terminology which is neutral with respect to ontologies, and that is that, whenever one acts, one acts intentionally (even if it is not the case that, whatever one does, one does intentionally). Is this claim true? According to the present account of intentional action, it is *not* true, although two closely related theses are. These theses may be stated precisely by means of the following theorems:

T.6.2:   Necessarily, if S acts relative to T and T', then there is an event e such that S intends e at T.

T.6.3:   Necessarily, if S acts relative to T and T', then there are an event e and a time T^* such that S successfully brings about e directly relative to T and T^*.[4][7]

Notice that the denial of the claim that, whenever one acts, one acts intentionally, is quite compatible with the (true) claim that certain actions cannot be performed unintentionally (first degree murder, for example).[4][8]

6.5   RELATED CONCEPTS

I mentioned a short while ago that I would use "intentionally" where Foley uses "deliberately." Perhaps this is just a question of usage; nevertheless, there is a concept distinct from that analyzed in D.6.7 which it would be useful to analyze, and I propose the following:

D.6.8: S acts deliberately relative to T and T' =df. there are events e and f such that:
             (i) there are times $T1$, $T2$, ..., Tn such that
                (a) Tn is just prior to T,
                (b) $T1$ is not later than $T2$, and..., and $Tn\text{-}1$ is not later than Tn, and

(c) S considers [S wills e in order that f may occur] at $T1$, and..., and at Tn ; and
(ii) S intentionally brings about f actively relative to T and T'.[49]

The consideration specified in clause (i) of this definition may be termed "deliberation." Often, of course, deliberation will involve a mulling of alternatives and the willing that contributes causally to e and f will then be a choice (see D.9.5 below). But I shall not discuss this issue. However, we may say, in connection with D.6.8:

D.6.9: S acts impetuously relative to T and T' =df.
          (i) S acts relative to T and T'; and
          (ii) S does not act deliberately relative to T and T'.

Voluntariness is also closely allied with intentional action. On one understanding of "voluntary," to act voluntarily just is to act intentionally. That is:

D.6.10: S acts voluntarily$_1$ relative to T and T' =df. S acts intentionally relative to T and T'.

But there are other ways to understand "voluntary," two of which are important here, the one being more liberal and the other being more restrictive than that sense captured in D.6.10. On the more liberal understanding, the concept of voluntary action may be analyzed as follows:

D.6.11: S acts voluntarily$_2$ relative to T and T' =df. S acts either intentionally or believingly relative to T and T'.

"S acts believingly" may be understood in this way: just as "S acts intentionally" is to be defined in terms of "S intentionally brings about e actively," so "S acts believingly" is to be defined in terms of "S believingly brings about e actively"; and just as "S intentionally brings about e actively" is to be compared and contrasted with "S acts with the intention that e occur" (see D.6.1.a and the discussion that follows it), so "S believingly brings about e actively" is to be compared and contrasted with "S acts with the belief that e will occur." Indeed, a definition of "S acts believingly" may, I think, be attained along lines exactly parallel to those along which the definition of "S acts intentionally" is attained in D.6.7. On the more restrictive understanding, the concept of voluntary action may be analyzed either as follows:

D.6.12: S acts voluntarily$_3$ relative to T and T' =df.
           (i) S acts voluntarily$_1$ relative to T and T'; and
           (ii) [S acts] is uncoerced at T,

or as follows:

D.6.13: S acts voluntarily$_4$ relative to T and T' =df.
           (i) S acts voluntarily$_2$ relative to T and T'; and
           (ii) [S acts] is uncoerced at T.

Of course, the term "uncoerced" in the last two definitions is undefined, but I shall not seek to define it here. As to the terms "involuntary" and "non-voluntary," it would perhaps be best to adopt the following conventions: an action may be said to be non-voluntary if and only if it is not voluntary; no action may be said to be involuntary, since an "involuntary action" is commonly held to be one in which no volition plays a part, and hence is not what I call an action at all. Of course, this *usage* of terms is not binding – this is the case with *all* of the terms introduced in this chapter, indeed, in this entire book – so long as the *concepts,* for the expression of which I propose the use of these terms, are clear.[50] In this connection, J.L.Austin in particular has provided a valuable service in several of his papers by discussing the usage of such terms as "intentional," "deliberate," "purposeful," "impetuous," and so on.[51] It is not my aim here to embroil myself in such discussion; nor do I make any claim that the concepts analyzed in D.6.7 through D.6.11 are those unfailingly expressed by the English terms "intentional," "deliberate," and so on.[52] Nevertheless, I do believe that these concepts, like the other concepts analyzed in this book, are of first importance to action-theory.

Notes

1   G.H. von Wright (1971), p.89; Beardsley (1980), p.72.

2   On the intention of events, see Chapter 3, Section 3.2.

3   See Audi (1973), pp.395-6, 401; Harman (1976), pp.432-4. Compare A.3.7 and note 16 to Chapter 3.

4   Wright (1974); Davis (1979), pp.59-60.

5   Nevertheless I do hold to A.3.7, and so the question arises: just how improbable can one believe one's chances of success to be before one must be said not to *intend* to do what one has in mind but only, perhaps, to *hope* that one will succeed in doing it? I am afraid that I have no ready answer to this question. It should be noted, of course, that the distinction between intention and hope has more to it than merely this aspect of probability of success (*if* this is something that distinguishes the two concepts at all – and I am inclined to think, but I am not convinced, that it does). For instance, presumably intending that something will occur requires, *ceteris paribus*, trying to insure its occurrence (I shall have more to say regarding this in Chapter 10), whereas hoping that something will occur does not require this.

6   Why roughly? Because, strictly speaking, what is willed, and hence intended, when one intentionally does something is not the action in question but its issue. For more on this point, see Chapters 9 and 10.

7   Notice that the claim that intentionally doing something requires intending to do it is compatible with the claim – which I also take to be true – that one may act intentionally without having a *reason* (or, perhaps, *purpose)* in so doing. For, to ask for someone's reason or purpose in doing something is to ask what his "end-intention" is, that is, what he intends (ultimately) to achieve by doing the thing that he is doing. And it may

be, of course, that sometimes one acts intentionally without having any such ulterior intention. Compare, for instance, (truthfully) answering the question "Why did you raise your arm?" in one instance by saying "To warn John that the train was coming" and in another instance by saying "Because" or "No reason." *Cf.* Grimm (1980), p.238; Beardsley (1980).

8   See, *e.g.*, Kenny (1966), p.645; Grimm (1980), p.243ff. and fn.10.

9   See, *e.g.*, Kenny (1966), p.645ff; Mackie (1977), p.204; Gorr and Horgan (1982). *Cf.* Grimm (1980), p.243ff.

10   Davidson (1978), p.92. Compare Davidson (1971), p.50. Further objections to the thesis under consideration may be found in Ross (1982).

11   See Davis (1979), p.69ff.

12   Davidson (1963) seems to espouse an account of intentional action somewhat akin to that expressed in D.6.1.b, except that events are, of course, regarded by Davidson as particulars and that he talks of primary reasons rather than volitions – but this account is repudiated later in Davidson (1973).

13   See Chisholm (1976), p.83, for their latest statement. See Chisholm (1964), p.617, for their earliest statement. Compare also Davidson's well-known "climber" case in Davidson (1973), p.79.

14   Of course, *why* S 's volition should cause him to throw a fit is perhaps a little obscure, but presumably such a train of events is possible.

15   For a notion akin to that of successfully bringing something about directly, see D.4.5.

16   Chisholm (1964), p.619.

17   Chisholm (1976), p.83.

18   Michael Corrado makes essentially the same point in Corrado (1979), p.15.

19   Goldman (1970), p.57.

20   Goldman (1970), p.62.

21   Harman (1976), p.445. Harman in fact also offers a complete analysis of the concept of intentional action (p.445n.); I shall not comment on this analysis, however, for it makes use of concepts which cannot be adequately discussed here.

22   Foley (1977), p.67.

23   Foley (1977), p.68. *Cf.* Wittgenstein (1953), Section 628.

24   Gorr and Horgan (1982), pp.257-8, believe that one cannot be surprised at what one does intentionally. The present case, and a case given by Ross (1982), pp.263-4, seem to me to show otherwise.

25   Thomson (1977), Chapter 9.

26   Anscombe (1969), p.9.

27   Aune (1977), p.101ff.

28   Anscombe explicitly disagrees. See Anscombe (1969), Section 20. Also, see note 7 to this chapter.

29   Foley (1977), p.68.

30   Davis (1980, pp.56-60) in effect says that the modification of clause (ii) in D.4.8 to read as clause (ii) in D.6.4 reads is not required. But we shall see that this modification is in fact required when discussing a couple of test cases below.

31   It should be noted that, even if this case were filled out so that it turned out that Jones did *not* intentionally shoot Smith (because he had a belief concerning the bullet's path into Smith's

body incompatible with the actual path of the bullet), this of course leaves open (and perhaps untouched) the question as to whether Jones is, or is to be held, *morally responsible* for shooting Smith.

32 Aune (1977), p.110, n.69.

33 Aune (1977), p.110, n.69.

34 Note that it is *not* enough to rule out my intentionally frightening Smith to point out that I did *not* accept that Smith *would* become so frightened. An "accept that not" clause, rather than a "not accept that" clause, is required in D.5.3 – as explained earlier – in order to avoid requiring "perfect accuracy" on the part of the agent.

35 Again, let me point out the fact, noted in note 31 to this chapter, that, whatever our final verdict on the question concerning intentional action, its implications concerning any final verdict on the question of moral responsibility will be indirect at best.

36 Butler (1978), pp.113-4.

37 See Ross (1978), Kraemer (1978), Davies (1981, 1982).

38 See Lowe (1978, 1980, 1982), Stiffler (1981).

39 See statement (3), assumption A.3.7, and note 16 to Chapter 3.

40 For a criticism of the solutions proposed by Ross (1978) and Kraemer (1978) see Lowe (1980). For a criticism of the solution proposed by Davies (1981) see Stiffler (1981) and Lowe (1982). Davies replies to both Stiffler and Lowe in Davies (1982).

41 See note 6 to this chapter.

42 This point was first brought to my attention by Paul Bowen. Stiffler (1981, p.217) makes the same point. The requirement captured in this point was not mentioned in Chapter 3, but it is

consistent with what was said in that chapter.

43 More precisely, while of course Brown intentionally throws the die and Jones intentionally pulls the trigger, Brown does not intentionally throw a six and Jones does not intentionally shoot Smith. "What he does" is intended to refer to the latter pair of actions and not to the former.

44 *Cf.* Butler (1978), p.113; Lowe (1978), p.118; Lowe (1980), pp.115, 118.

45 But see Meiland (1963).

46 See Davidson (1971), p.46. *Cf.* Goldman (1970), p.18; Hornsby (1980), p.36. Contrast Bach (1978), pp.362-3.

47 As will be seen in the next chapter, whenever one acts, one performs a *"basic"* action, and basic actions are always successful, even if not always intentional.

48 See Anscombe (1963).

49 See note 57 to Chapter 1 concerning the concept of one time's being just prior to another.

50 In light of the remarks made concerning "voluntary," "involuntary," and "non-voluntary," one might seek to draw a threefold distinction between intentional, unintentional, and non-intentional action, but I do not think that this distinction – however it were drawn up – would reflect current linguistic usage. For this reason I have stipulated (immediately following the presentation of D.6.7) that one acts unintentionally if and only if one acts but does not act intentionally. Contrast Gorr and Horgan (1982), where an account is given according to which some actions may be neither intentional nor unintentional. Their account seems to me mistaken. See notes 9, 10, and 24 to this chapter.

51 See Austin (1956, 1966).

52   Useful discussions of these concepts, other than Austin's, are to be found in Fitzgerald (1961, p.129ff.), Gordon (1966), and Aune (1977, p.84ff.).

Chapter 7

DOING ONE THING BY DOING ANOTHER

The "by"-relation – that relation which binds, for instance, Smith's signalling and Smith's raising his hand when Smith signals by raising his hand – is one which requires elucidation in any theory of action which presumes to be comprehensive. For it is this relation which constitutes much of the unity and coherence to be found in the complex structure of human action.

7.1 RESOLUTION OF THE FOURTH GROUP OF PROBLEMS

As far as I can tell, there are few restrictions on how the "by"-relation may relate one type of bringing about to another.[1] In Chapter 4 six types of bringing about were distinguished, and there are doubtless others that could be distinguished also. There are, therefore, many different types of exemplification of the "by"-relation – a point which appears hitherto to have been fully appreciated by few philosophers. (This suggests that no single definition or formula will capture the complexity of this relation, and this suggestion will be borne out in what follows.) In this chapter, however, I shall concern myself with just five of these different types of exemplification. These five strike me as being the most important; an account of the others could be generated from the account that I shall give of these five.

Consider problem D1 of Chapter 2. How are we to account for the fact that Jones alerted the prowler by illuminating the room, illuminated the room by turning on the light, turned on the light by flipping the switch, flipped the switch by raising his hand, but did not raise his hand by doing anything else? Questions of this sort have received a fair bit of attention by philosophers ever since Arthur Danto initiated discussion of what he has called "basic action."[2] Danto himself in effect says that, when Jones flips the switch by raising his hand, his raising his hand causes his flipping the switch.[3] But this is clearly incorrect, as many commentators on Danto's thesis have pointed out. What is true, rather, is that Jones's raising his hand causes the switch to go up – and this is an insight that must be accommodated by any adequate account of the "by"-relation.[4] Alvin Goldman, who, in his discussion of what he calls "level-generation," has given the most detailed account to date of the "by"-relation, claims that no actions related by the "by"-relation are what he calls "on the same level" as one another.[5] On inspection, it is apparent that this implies that we cannot truthfully say for example (where Smith is the mayor) that, by hitting Smith, Jones hit the mayor. But this is surely an appropriate thing to say on some (possible) occasion. Goldman also claims that actions related by the "by"-relation must occur at, or throughout, exactly the same period of time. But this too is dubious, especially given an account (such as Goldman's) where actions are considered to be finely-grained entities. For instance, if actions are to be finely individuated, it would seem (as argued in Chapter 5) that Jones's raising his hand ended before his alerting the prowler ended (given that the prowler's reaction to the room's illumination was not instantaneous). In fact, Goldman elsewhere argues for actions' being finely individuated on the basis of just such a disparity in times of occurrence, and his account of level-generation is thus at odds with this argument.[6]

I do not propose here to give a detailed account and criticism of other philosophers' accounts of the "by"-relation. Goldman's is the best-known and most detailed, but, as we have just seen, it is inaccurate.[7] There is no other account of which I am aware that matches Goldman's for detail, and yet detail as well as accuracy is required for adequacy in this case. It is reasonable to assume, therefore, that no one has yet given an adequate account of the "by"-relation, and I shall now focus my attention on the provision of such an account.

Given the apparatus already set up in Chapter 4, a resolution of problem D1 is in fact not hard to come by. If we assume, as I think we should, that [Jones raises his hand] and [Jones flips the switch] are direct actions of Jones's and that the remainder (i.e., [Jones turns on the light], [Jones illuminates the room], and [Jones alerts the prowler]) are indirect actions of Jones's, then we should note that there appear to be three main types of the "by"-relation involved here. These are, first, the type which binds a direct action to a direct action; second, the type which binds a direct action to an indirect action; and, third, the type which binds an indirect action to an indirect action. Let us call the issue internal to [Jones raises his hand] *e*, that internal to [Jones flips the switch] *f*, that internal to [Jones turns on the light] *g*, that internal to [Jones illuminates the room] *h*, and that internal to [Jones alerts the prowler] *i*.[8] Let us assume that Jones brings about each of *e* and *f* relative to *T* and *T'*. Now, I think that it is correct to assume that *e* constitutes *f* at *T'*, but not *vice versa*, and that it is in virtue of this fact that we say that Jones brings about *f* by bringing about *e*, but not *vice versa*. (What event is there that contributes causally to *f* but not to *e*? One such event is [someone installs the switch].) Generalizing on this, I believe that we may say:

D.7.1:   *S* brings about *f* directly relative to *T* and *T'* by bringing about *e* directly relative to *T* and *T'* =df.
          (i) *S* brings about *e* directly relative to *T* and *T'*;
          (ii) *S* brings about *f* directly relative to *T* and *T'*; and
          (iii) *e* constitutes *f* at *T'*.[9]

The type of "by"-relation that obtains between Jones's bringing about *f* and his bringing about *g*, however, is not that type analyzed in D.7.1. For it is hardly likely that it is the case – indeed, for the sake of argument, let us assume that it is not the case – that *g* also occurs at *T'*; hence *f* does not constitute *g* at *T'*, and so D.7.1 is inapplicable. We should note, however, that *g* is brought about indirectly by Jones; that this is so in virtue of the fact that he brings about *f* directly; and that it seems that we are prepared to say that he brings about *g* by bringing about *f* simply because it is in virtue of his bringing about *f* that he brings about *g*. Generalizing on this, I believe that we may say:

D.7.2:   *S* brings about *f* indirectly relative to *T* and *T'* by bringing about *e* directly relative to *T* and *T**
          =df.

(i) S brings about e directly relative to T and T^*; and

(ii) e contributes causally relative to T^* and T' to f.

(Compare D.4.8.)

Once again, however, the type of "by"-relation that obtains between Jones's bringing about g and his bringing about h is neither that type analyzed in D.7.1 nor that type analyzed in D.7.2. For it is hardly likely that it is the case – indeed, for the sake of argument, let us assume that it is not the case – that g and h occur at the same time; moreover, both g and h are brought about indirectly. But D.7.2 may nevertheless guide us here. For it appears that g contributes causally to h, and that it is in virtue of this fact that a "by"-relation obtains between Jones's bringing about g and his bringing about h. (The same, indeed, may be said of Jones's bringing about h and his bringing about i.) It would seem, then, that all that need be done to accommodate the present case is to change the "directly" of clause (i) of D.7.2 to "indirectly." But, while this modification to D.7.2 would in fact suffice for the present case, it would not suffice to accommodate other cases of bringing about one event indirectly by bringing about another event indirectly. Consider, for instance, Brown's doing what he ought not to do (call this Brown's bringing about k) by breaking his promise (call this Brown's bringing about j).[10] Let us assume that Brown brings about both j and k indirectly. It seems that, far from j's contributing causally to k, j *constitutes* k, and that this is the basis of this particular exemplification of the "by"-relation. Hence, where the "by"-relation binds two indirect actions, it seems that a disjunctive analysis is required, namely:

D.7.3: S brings about f indirectly relative to T and T' by bringing about e indirectly relative to T and T^* = df.

(i) S brings about e indirectly relative to T and T^*; and

(ii) either

(a) e contributes causally relative to T^* and T' to f, or

(b) (1) T^* is identical with T', and
(2) e constitutes f at T^*.[1][1]

We should note that it is not only the case in our example that Jones brings about i by bringing about h, that he brings about h by bringing about g, and so on, but it is also the case that he brings about i by bringing about *each* of e, f, g, and h, that he brings about h by bringing about *each* of e, f, and g, and so on. D.7.1 through D.7.3 yield this result, although I shall not attempt to establish this in detail here.

But what of e in our example? How is it that Jones brings this about directly but not by bringing about some other event directly? That is just the way it is. (As we shall shortly see, e may be said on this occasion to be a basic issue of Jones's.) There is no real mystery about this; it just happens that Jones raises his hand but not by doing anything else. It is not *necessarily* this way; it just *is* this way. Note, of course, that Jones does not raise his hand by willing e.[1][2] Given D.4.7, it is easily seen why this is so (although I again do not presume that it is *necessarily* so): [Jones wills e] is not an action, direct or otherwise, of Jones's.

Let us now turn to a consideration of problem D2. This is a little more difficult to handle. The case to be considered is that of Jones's raising his hand in order that his neurons may fire; he succeeds in his endeavor, and it therefore seems legitimate to say that he causes his neurons to fire by raising his hand. The oddness of this case consists in the fact that it is reasonable to assume both that [Jones's hand rises] is a *direct* issue of an action of Jones's and that [Jones's neurons fire] contributes causally to *and precedes* [Jones's hand rises]. Given these assumptions, it turns out that [Jones's neurons fire] is not an issue of a direct action, or of an indirect action, or of a synthetic action, and hence, according to D.5.7, not an issue of any action at all of Jones's. In order to deal with this problem we should note, first, that Jones does indeed bring about [Jones's neurons fire] (call this event f) *unrestrictedly* relative to some times T and T' (see D.4.2), and, second, that, although he would appear to bring about e unrestrictedly on every occasion on which he raises his arm, the distinguishing factor in this case is that on this occasion he *intentionally* brings about f unrestrictedly, where:

D.7.4:   *S* intentionally brings about *f* unrestrictedly
           relative to *T* and *T'* =df. there is an event *e* such
           that:
           (i) *S* wills *e* at *T* ; and
           (ii) *f* comes about at *T'*, as a result of [*S* wills *e*]
           occurring at *T*, as *S* intends at *T*.

(D.7.4 is just like D.4.2, except that it is stipulated in clause (ii) –
as we would expect – that the event that is brought about comes
about as the agent intends.) Now the type of "by"-relation at issue
in the present example seems to be that captured in the following
definition:

D.7.5.a: *S* brings about *f* unrestrictedly relative to *T* and
           T' by bringing about *e* directly relative to *T* and
           T* =df. there are events *g* and *h* such that:
           (i) *S* wills *g* at *T* in order that *h* may occur;
           (ii) [*S* wills *g* in order that *h* may occur] contrib-
           utes causally relative to *T* and *T** to *g* via *f* at *T'*;
           and
           (iii) *g* constitutes *e* at *T**.[1][3]

(This definition "combines" D.4.2 and D.4.7 in the manner that is to
be expected, given the present case of neuron-firing.) At this point
we may take either of two paths. Either we may say that an event,
such as *f*, that has been unrestrictedly but intentionally brought
about and which contributes causally to an event which is directly
brought about, is itself a genuine issue – but this is clumsy and
would, in any case, necessitate extensive revisions to D.4.3.c, D.5.4,
and D.5.7. Or we may say (and this is what I prefer to say) that
an event, such as *f*, that has been unrestrictedly but intentionally
brought about by means of directly bringing about some other event
is an *intentional side-effect* of the direct action in question. If we
take this latter path, as I propose, then we may say:

D.7.6:   *f* is a side-effect of [*S* brings about *e* directly rela-
           tive to *T* and *T**] =df. there is a time *T'* such
           that *S* brings about *f* unrestrictedly relative to *T*
           and *T'* by bringing about *e* directly relative to *T*
           and *T**.

An intentional side-effect will then be one that has been intentionally brought about unrestrictedly but will not necessarily be the issue of any action.[14] Hence my proposed resolution of problem D2 is that the type of "by"-relation at issue is that analyzed in D.7.5.a, and that [Jones causes his neurons to fire] is *not* an action of Jones's although [Jones's neurons fire] is indeed an intentional side-effect of a direct action of Jones's.

It should be noted that D.7.5.a and D.7.6, while perhaps adequate for a resolution of problem D2, will *not* suffice for a resolution of a closely related sort of problem. Suppose, for example, that Jones is an accomplished pianist who plays a certain phrase of music composed of the notes C, D, and E. It is certainly legitimate to say that he plays the phrase by playing each of C, D, and E; but, according to the account of the individuation of actions given in Chapter 5, if his playing the phrase is a direct action of his (a distinct possibility for an accomplished pianist), then his playing C, his playing D, and his playing E are not actions of his at all (just as half-steps, quarter-steps, *etc.*, are not actions if the whole step is a direct action). Still, Jones may be properly said to play each of C, D, and E intentionally when he plays the phrase composed of them, and this fact serves to show how close this case is to that given in D2. The difference between the cases consists in the fact that, in D2, [Jones's neurons fire] *causes* [Jones's hand rises], whereas in the present case the events internal to [Jones plays C], [Jones plays D], and [Jones plays E] each *constitute* (at different times) the event internal to [Jones plays the phrase]. This fact indicates that D.7.5.a requires only moderate modification in its second clause in order for both D2 and the present case to be accommodated:

D.7.5.b.: S brings about f unrestrictedly relative to T and T' by bringing about e directly relative to T and T^* =df. there are events g and h such that:

(i) S wills g at T in order that h may occur;

(ii) either

(a) [S wills g in order that h may occur] contributes causally relative to T and T^* to g via f at T', or

(b) (1) T^* is identical with T',

(2) [*S* wills *g* in order that *h* may occur]
contributes causally relative to *T* and *T** to both *f*
and *g*, and
(3) *f* constitutes *e* at *T**; and
(iii) *g* constitutes *e* at *T**.[15]

D.7.6 may be allowed to remain as before, and the diagnosis of the
present case may now be seen to be essentially similar to that given
for problem D2. That is, we may say that the type of "by"-relation
at issue in both cases is that analyzed in D.7.5.b, and that neither
[Jones causes his neurons to fire] nor [Jones plays *C*] is an action of
Jones's, although the events internal to both events are indeed intentional side-effects of direct actions of Jones's.

We may now turn our attention to problem D3. How are we to
account for the fact that Jones drives around the corner by first
signalling, then braking, then changing gear, then turning the
steering-wheel, and then accelerating out of the corner? The answer is, I think, easily given. The obvious point to make here is
that [Jones drives around the corner] is a synthetic action composed
of the direct actions (if they are direct) of his signalling, braking,
and so on; and it seems to be simply in virtue of this fact that he
performs the synthetic action by performing the direct actions.
Hence I propose:

D.7.7: *S* brings about *f* synthetically relative to *T* and *T'*
by bringing about *e* directly relative to *T** and
T** =df.

(i) *S* brings about *f* synthetically relative to *T*
and *T'*;
(ii) *S* brings about *e* directly relative to *T** and
T**; and
(iii) there are events *g1*,...,*gn* and a time *T'''* such
that
(a) *f* is composed relative to *T'''* and *T'* of
g1,...,*gn*,
(b) *e* is identical with *g1* or...or with *gn*, and
(c) *T* is not later than *T**, *T** is not later than
T**, and *T*** is not earlier than *T'''* and not later
than *T'*.

Other types of the "by"-relation could be accounted for here – perhaps the most important of those that remain unaccounted for are those of a person's bringing about an event f synthetically by bringing about an event e indirectly and of a person's bringing about an event f synthetically by bringing about an event e synthetically – but the foregoing should suffice as an indication of how these other types of the "by"-relation might be accounted for. It might be thought that, despite the detail of the foregoing account, the account is nevertheless inadequate in that it does not distinguish the four types of level-generation which Goldman calls causal, conventional, simple, and augmentation generation. But while it is true that a distinction along the lines that Goldman has given has not been drawn up, I believe that the present account may nevertheless accommodate the same data as Goldman attempts to accommodate in his account. For instance, the case of Jones alerting the prowler by illuminating the room, *etc.*, is a case of several different exemplifications of what Goldman calls causal generation. I think that D.7.1 through D.7.3 adequately account for this case. But I believe that these definitions (along with the other definitions in this chapter) also adequately account for the other types of generation that Goldman distinguishes. For example, the case of Brown doing what he ought not to do by breaking his promise is a case of what Goldman calls conventional generation, and it is handled by D.7.3. However, I shall forgo any attempt to give a precise account of the four-fold distinction of which Goldman gives an informal, though most insightful, sketch – for I do not know how to provide such an account.[1][6]

7.2   *BASIC ACTION*

I shall now turn to a brief discussion of what has come to be called basic action. The term "basic action" was first introduced by Danto and has been the subject of much discussion since that time.[1][7] Exactly what Danto himself meant by this term is not clear, however. It seems in fact that he used it to express a variety of concepts, one of which is the concept of an action which is performed, but not by performing some other action. Two points should be noted here. The first is that it is certainly true that the term "basic action" can be and has been used by Danto and others to express concepts other than that just mentioned. What these concepts are, whether the term "basic action" is usefully employed in the expression of these concepts, and what the correct analyses of these concepts are, are all matters that I shall not pursue here.[18] The second point is that Danto's analysis of the concept just mentioned, based as it is on his mis-analysis of the "by"-relation, is defective, and that this concept is still in need of an accurate, detailed analysis.

The concept, whose analysis it is that I am presently concerned with, is, then, that which is captured roughly by the words "an action which is performed, but not by performing some other action." Slight complications arise when an attempt is made to render this concept of basic action more precise, however, due to the fact, amply demonstrated above, that several types of bringing about an event may be distinguished. But, if we restrict our attention to those types of bringing about an event which are genuine instances of acting, then our task is considerably simplified. For, given D.4.3.c, only the direct, indirect, or synthetic bringing about of an event constitutes genuine action. Now, we already know (see D.4.8 and D.7.2) that, whenever one brings about an event f indirectly, one does so by bringing about an event e directly; and so we also know (see D.7.7) that, whenever one brings about an event f synthetically, one does so by bringing about an event e directly. It has also been said[19] that it seems impossible that one should bring about an event f directly by bringing about an event e indirectly (where f is not itself brought about indirectly) and also impossible that one should bring about an event f directly by bringing about an event e synthetically (where e is not itself brought about directly). Hence, when it comes to the treatment of basic action, we may confine our attention exclusively to direct action, and in light of this I propose the following:

D.7.8: S brings about e basically relative to T and T'
           =df.
           (i) S brings about e directly relative to T and T';
           and

(ii) there is no event *f* distinct from *e* such that *S* brings about *e* directly relative to *T* and *T'* by bringing about *f* directly relative to *T* and *T'*.

Note two theorems that follow from this definition and the account of action given in what precedes them. These are, first, that whenever there is action there is basic action, and, second, that whenever there is basic action there is successful action. Or more precisely:

T.7.1: Necessarily, if *S* brings about *e* actively relative to *T* and *T'*, then there are an event *f* and a time *T** such that *S* brings about *f* basically relative to *T* and *T**.

T.7.2: Necessarily, if *S* brings about *e* basically relative to *T* and *T'*, then *S* successfully brings about *e* directly relative to *T* and *T'*.[20]

I shall forgo a formal proof of these theorems. Note also that the concepts of a basic action and a basic issue may be analyzed in terms of D.7.8. It should be recognized, of course, that an action may be basic on one occasion and not on another; hence, the concept of a basic action, as well as that of a basic issue, must be relativized to times.[21] We may say:

D.7.9: *e* is a basic action of *S* 's relative to *T* and *T'* =df. there is an event *f* such that:
(i) *e* is [*S* brings about *f* directly]; and
(ii) *S* brings about *f* basically relative to *T* and *T'*.

D.7.10: *e* is a basic issue of an action of *S* 's at *T'* =df. there is a time *T* such that *S* brings about *e* basically relative to *T* and *T'*.

And, finally, we may of course say that a non-basic action or issue is simply one that, on the occasion in question, is not basic.

Notes

1   I think it is impossible for a person to bring about an event f
     directly by bringing about an event e indirectly (where f is not
     itself brought about indirectly), and also impossible for a person
     to bring about an event f directly by bringing about an event e
     synthetically (where e is not itself brought about directly), but
     many different possible exemplifications of the "by"-relation
     remain.

2   Danto (1963, 1965).

3   Danto (1963), pp.435-6.

4   See, among others, Stoutland (1968), p.469; Goldman (1970),
     p.24; Davidson (1971), p.20; Chisholm (1976), p.72; Hornsby
     (1980), pp.67-8.

5   Goldman (1970), pp.43, 45.

6   Goldman (1970), p.2ff.; see Lombard (1974).

7   There are other problems with Goldman's account not yet
     mentioned. For instance, it relies on statements couched in the
     form of subjunctive conditionals, and this is always risky, since
     the truth-conditions of such statements are notoriously contro-
     versial. There is an unsolved problem concerning causal over-
     determination, acknowledged by Goldman himself (1970,
     pp.13-14). And the requirement (Goldman (1970), pp.43 and
     45) that the occurrence of act A not entail that the level-gener-
     ated act A' occur is too strong, for reasons given by Castañeda
     (1979, p.249).

8   I think there are phrases available to express e, g, and h in
     English, but not to express f and i. I believe that "Jones's hand
     rises" expresses e, that "the light goes on" expresses g, and
     that "the room lights up" expresses h.

9 Note that, given T.4.1, the type of "by"-relation analyzed in D.7.1 is reflexive. This may strike some as inappropriate. It should be noted, however, that given the possibility that an event may occur more than once at a time, this relation is definitely neither asymmetrical nor irreflexive – suitable cases to demonstrate this are easily concocted. It may nevertheless be thought that the relation should be said to be nonreflexive rather than reflexive. I have some sympathy with this view, but it seems to me to be no serious matter to stipulate that the relation is reflexive. Nothing adverse follows, I believe, and such stipulation considerably simplifies matters. On matters pertinent to D.7.1, see Hornsby (1980), Chapter 5.

10 I borrow this case from Goldman (1970), p.25.

11 It might seem that the sort of disjunction introduced in D.7.3 ought to feature also in D.7.2. But while I accept that causal contribution may obtain between simultaneous events (see Chapter 3, Section 3.1), I can in fact think of no case where S brings about f indirectly relative to T and T' by bringing about e directly relative to T and T^* and where T^* is identical with T'. But such identity of times is required for constitution (see D.4.6), and so I have not complicated D.7.2 in the manner just mentioned.

12 Melden correctly emphasizes this point (1961, pp.40 and 65).

13 This definition relies implicitly on the following schematic definition: e contributes causally relative to T and T^* to g via f at T' =df. (exactly as in the definiendum of D.3.5, except "there are a time T' and" becomes "there is").

14 The terminology of D.7.6 should not be misconstrued. While e *is* an effect (or consequence) of a volition of S's, it is not necessarily an effect of S's bringing about f. Despite this, "side-effect" seems to me the most appropriate, readily available common term.

15 It is possible that still different cases of bringing about an event f unrestrictedly by bringing about an event directly can be con-

cocted which would require an addition of yet another disjunct to clause (ii) of D.7.5.b, but I shall not pursue this matter further here.

16   Part of such an account would presumably have to concern itself with distinguishing *modes* of constitution. For instance, Brown does what he ought not to do (call the issue of this f) *by* breaking his promise (call the issue of this e) because – on my account – whatever contributes causally to e also contributes causally to f. And this holds, likewise, of Brown's outjumping George (call the issue of this h) and his jumping six feet three inches (call the issue of this g). (See Goldman (1970), p.27.) But the former is a case of what Goldman calls conventional generation, while the latter is a case of what he calls simple generation. The distinction between these types of generation would, I think, have to be found in a distinction between the *way* in which whatever contributes causally to e also contributes causally to f and the *way* in which whatever contributes causally to g also contributes causally to h. In the former case, presumably, there are conventions which dictate the constitution in question, while in the latter there are not. But this is all very murky, and I do not know how to clear it up.

It should also be noted that in this section I have been explicitly concerned with what I have called the "by"-relation. I have not been *explicitly* concerned with what may be called the "in"-relation, a relation exemplified when S, *in* bringing about e, also brings about f. I am not at all sure that the two relations are in fact distinct, although I do acknowledge that sometimes it seems more natural to *say* "in" rather than "by," or *vice versa*. But such naturalness is not always a good guide; indeed, what some find natural in this regard, others may not (*cf.* Castañeda (1979, pp.247-8)). At any rate, two points should be made here: (i) if the "by"- and "in"-relations are distinct, then it is only the former for which I have tried to give an account here; (ii) even if these relations are distinct, it may well be that an account of the "in"-relation can be given by appealing to the concepts of constitution, causal contribution, and composition – the same concepts to which I have appealed in drawing up the foregoing account of the "by"-relation.

17 Danto (1963, 1965).

18 See Hornsby (1980), Chapters 5 and 6 for a variety of uses of the term "basic action." See Baier (1971), for a criticism of philosophers' uses of this term.

19 See note 1 to this chapter.

20 See T.6.3 and note 47 to Chapter 6.

21 Danto makes essentially the same point when he says: "I think there is nothing that is always and in each of its instances an unmistakably basic action" (1965, p.46). He goes on to distinguish those people who are "positively abnormal" *(i.e.,* those who have a greater "repertoire" of basic actions than the "normal" person) from those who are "negatively abnormal" *(i.e.,* those who have a smaller "repertoire" than the "normal" person). Some of Danto's points are penetrating, some erroneous (such as the claim that every "normal" person has the same "repertoire" of basic actions (1965, p.51)), but I shall not discuss them in detail here.

Chapter 8
OMISSIONS

Philosophers often talk of acts of omission, but such talk is immediately puzzling; for omissions (of all sorts) appear to be paradigms of not-doing rather than doing, even though no omission is *merely* a not-doing. But, as I shall seek to show, although talk of acts of omission is frequently misleading, it is not altogether inappropriate and is not to be eschewed, as some would argue.[1]

8.1   *INTRODUCTION*

My purpose in this chapter is to provide an analysis of two concepts which I shall express (roughly) by means of the phrases "omit (to bring about)" and "intentionally omit (to bring about)."[2] These two concepts are germane to action-theory, even though relatively little attention has been paid to their analysis. Interest in providing an adequate account of omissions has recently risen, however, due to a rise in interest in such ethical and legal matters as killing *versus* letting die, Good Samaritanism, and so on – matters whose resolution is taken to be dependent upon a proper account of omissions.

The term "omit" (and its cognates), like the term "action" (and its cognates), is ambiguous. But in the case of "omit" the ambiguity appears systematic (and this facilitates the present enterprise). That is, first, all senses of "omit" (and its cognates) appear to presuppose a distinction between omitting to bring about something and simply not bringing it about, and, second, there appears to be a broad sense of "omit" upon which more restrictive senses are based. In this chapter I shall focus much of my attention on this broad sense of "omit"; it is the concept expressed by *this* sense of "omit" which will be the subject of analysis. How to analyze concepts expressed by more restrictive uses of "omit" will also be indicated. In addition, I shall treat the term "intentionally omit" in similar fashion; that is, I shall seek to provide an analysis of its broadest sense and also indicate how more restrictive senses may be analyzed.

Some philosophers have seized upon the distinction just mentioned between omitting to bring about something and simply not bringing it about and pronounced omissions to be "negative actions," a sort of hybrid of doing and not-doing. For instance, in a recent article on Good Samaritanism John Kleinig claims that omissions can be said to be things that are done and calls them "active non-doings."[3] Also, Danto distinguishes between not doing *a* and doing not-*a* and calls the latter "forbearing."[4] But talk of negative actions or active non-doings is certainly odd. It is not at all clear, either, what it *means* to prefix "not" to a singular term "*a*," since negation is traditionally applied to propositions.[5] Such talk could in fact be accommodated by the account of action presented in the preceding chapters in either of two ways. One could broaden the account of active bringing about (D.4.11) by talking of the bringing about of the negations of events (see D.1.7 and D.1.25). This would require admission of the concept of causal* contribution into the analysis of the concept of bringing about. (See D.3.1 and the discussion of "negative events" in Chapter 3.) Or one could talk about bringing about propositions (see the last paragraph of Chapter 4, Section 4.5), which would *a fortiori* accommodate talk of the bringing about of the negations of propositions, since such negations are themselves propositions.[6] But whichever tack one takes, the question arises: do all omissions involve such negative action or active non-doing? I think that it will be seen that this is not the case – at least with respect to that sense of "omit" with which I am dealing here and which I take to be involved in much of the discussion of ethical and legal matters of the sort mentioned earlier. Nevertheless, I shall try to make sense of the locution "act of omission."

The elusiveness of the concept of omission has apparently prompted certain prominent action-theorists to ignore the concept altogether.[7] Nevertheless, there have been several attempts in the literature to provide adequate analyses of the concepts of omission and intentional omission. I shall discuss some of these later, once my own proposed analyses have been provided. My immediate concern is with providing my own analyses. Now, it might seem that a natural way to proceed at this point would be to attempt first to analyze the (basic) concept of omission in general and then to analyze the (basic) concept of intentional omission in particular.[8]

But the ambiguity of "omit" previously noted renders this task extremely difficult, in that it proves not at all easy to make sure, in the absence of an account of intentional omission, that one has accounted for the broadest of those senses of "omit" consonant with the distinction required between omission and mere not-doing. It is easier, I think, to tackle the analyses in reverse order, and so my strategy will be this. I shall consider what seems to be a relatively clear-cut case of a situation in which it is quite proper to ascribe an intentional omission to an agent, and then I shall seek to discern its fundamental features. On the basis of this I shall propose an analysis of the concept of intentional omission in question, and then, on *this* basis, I shall propose an analysis of that concept of omission with which I am in general concerned here.

8.2   *INTENTIONAL OMISSION*

This is the relatively clear-cut case. Last week Smith was sitting in a rocking-chair on his porch and a car-accident occurred in the street right outside his house. He witnessed the accident and debated whether or not to go to the aid of the victims. Not wanting to disturb himself, and oblivious of his moral obligations, he decided to remain where he was, knowing full well that he could go to the victims' aid but that, in remaining seated, he would not, indeed could not, go to their aid. The upshot was that Smith callously continued to rock in his chair and the victims went unaided.

I think that it is clear that Smith intentionally omitted to go to the victims' aid. The case, so described, surely warrants this claim. But what aspects of the case are *necessary* for Smith's intentional omission? This is a tricky question and, while I readily acknowledge that some of the claims that follow are not conclusively argued, I suggest that they are all true.

First, Smith did not go to the aid of the victims. This is obviously a necessary condition of his intentionally omitting to go to their aid. Second, he debated going to their aid. Such debate is, I submit, not necessary for the intentional omission to act, although *some* measure of awareness or consideration of what one intentionally omits to do or bring about surely is. That is, had Smith not debated whether or not to go to the victims' aid but merely considered or been aware of his not going, we would not, I think, be required to retract our ascription of an intentional omission to him – so long, of course, as certain other conditions also obtained. Third, Smith debated remaining where he was. Again, such debate is, I believe, dispensable, although *some* measure of awareness of what one intentionally does is required. Fourth, Smith could have gone to the victims' aid. This is, I think, indispensable, although someone might object to this as follows. Suppose that, unbeknownst to him, Smith had been secured to his rocking-chair in such a fashion that, had he decided to go to the victims' aid, he would have found himself unable to do so. Would it not then still be appropriate to say that he intentionally omitted to go to their aid? I think not. It would be better to say that he omitted to *try* to go to their aid but that, because he in fact could not go to their aid, he did not actually omit to *go* to their aid. Fifth, Smith knew that he could go to the victims' aid. I suggest that such *knowledge* is *not* necessary for one's intentionally omitting to do something, but that some measure of *belief* (and hence, given the fourth point, *true* belief) *is* necessary.[9] Sixth, Smith knew that he could not both remain where he was and go to the victims' aid. Again, such knowledge of alternatives is, I think, not required, although Smith's truly believing that there were such alternatives is required. Seventh, Smith did not want to go to the victims' aid. Such lack of desire is *not* required. Suppose that Smith's daughter had been kidnapped and that he felt that he must stay near the telephone next to his rocking-chair. He might very much have wanted to go to the victims' aid but, desiring even more to hear from the kidnappers, he intentionally omitted to go to their aid. Eighth, Smith intended not to go to the victims' aid. This is surely indispensable. Notice that Smith apparently also omitted to go to get a drink of water. Perhaps he had considered doing this as a third alternative. But if, when remaining seated, it was not his intention not to go and get a drink of water, he cannot be said to have intentionally omitted doing so then. Ninth, Smith intentionally remained where he was. This is *not* required, although something of its kind is. Suppose that, instead of remaining seated, Smith intentionally went to get that drink of water; then he would still have intentionally omitted to go to the victims' aid. So Smith's remaining seated is not required; still, *some* intentional action on his part is.[10] Tenth, Smith is to be blamed for not going to the victims' aid. This is not required for the intentional omission to act. Many intentional omissions, such as Smith's, are morally reprehensible. But many are not. Suppose, once again, that Smith's daughter had been kidnapped and also that he had noticed that many other, apparently unhindered persons had witnessed the accident. It might well be that, in this case, Smith's not going to the victims' aid is not reprehensible; yet he would still, I think, be properly said to have intentionally omitted to go to their aid.

The forgoing ruminations could doubtless be refined. Nevertheless, on their strength, I shall now propose an analysis of the relevant concept of intentional omission. For no necessary condition of the intentional omission to act has gone unmentioned, I believe, unless it be one (such as the condition that the agent exist) which is implied by one already mentioned. The analysis is basically this: in the broadest sense of "intentionally omit," intentionally omitting to do something is intentionally not doing something that one can do.[1][1] But this requires unpacking. I shall confine myself here to an account of intentionally omitting to bring about an event *e active-ly* (see D.4.11). What it is to intentionally omit to bring about an event *e* directly, indirectly, or synthetically is something that can easily be accounted for along the same lines (given D.4.7, D.4.8, and D.4.10), but I shall forgo providing such an account. In what follows, the sort of "can" at issue is that which may be characterized roughly by the statement that a person can perform an action if and only if he has the ability and opportunity to perform it.[1][2] (This sense of "can" will be discussed in detail in Chapters 11 and 12, and a tentative libertarian analysis of it will be provided in D.11.14.) The analysis, in greater detail, is this:

D.8.1:   *S* intentionally omits at *T* to bring about *e* active-ly relative to *T* and *T'* =df. there are an event *f* and a time *T** such that:
          (i) *S* can at *T* bring about *e* actively relative to *T* and *T'*;
          (ii) *S* can at *T* bring about *f* actively relative to *T* and *T**;
          (iii) *S* cannot at *T* both bring about *e* actively relative to *T* and *T'* and bring about *f* actively relative to *T* and *T**;

(iv) *S* considers at *T* each of the propositions contained in (i) - (iii);

(v) *S* accepts at *T* each of the propositions contained in (i) - (iii);

(vi) *S* intends at *T* [*S* does not bring about *e* actively relative to *T* and *T'*]; and

(vii) *S* intentionally brings about *f* actively relative to *T* and *T**.

(Notice that, apart from the mention of "can," none of the clauses in this definition contains a concept that has not yet been formally introduced.) According to D.8.1, then, and dispensing with mention of times, the important features of the Smith case are that Smith could have gone to the aid of the victims and also remained where he was, but he could not have done both; that he considered this; that he accepted it; that he intended not to go to the victims' aid; and that he intentionally remained seated where he was. Note, of course, that clauses (iii) and (vii) of D.8.1 jointly imply that *S* does not bring about *e* actively relative to *T* and *T'*. I shall refrain from explicitly stating further implications of this definition.

8.3   OMISSION IN GENERAL

The next task is to provide an analysis of the relevant concept of omission in general. This task is now facilitated by taking note of two important points. First, it is necessarily the case that, if (in the basic sense) *S* intentionally omits to bring about *e*, then (in the basic sense) *S* omits to bring about *e* ; second, it is not necessarily the case that, if (in the basic sense) *S* omits to bring about *e*, then (in the basic sense) *S* intentionally omits to bring about *e*. So our task is essentially one of whittling away at clauses (i) through (vii) of D.8.1.

One apparent instance of unintentional omission has already been cited. When Smith intentionally omitted to go to the aid of the victims of the car-accident, he also omitted, but unintentionally, to go to get a drink of water. The reason why this omission was said to be unintentional was that Smith did not intend not to go and get a drink of water. So clause (vi) of D.8.1 may now be dropped. Similarly, clause (vii) may also be dropped. Suppose that Smith had not intentionally done anything; suppose that he had been so nervous that he reached no decision as to what to do. Then, not only did he not intentionally do anything other than go to the victims' aid, but it seems that he did nothing at all. Still, he omitted to go to the victims' aid; he omitted to go to get a drink of water; and so on. What of clause (v)? Need it be the case that Smith believed that he could go to the victims' aid? No; perhaps his indecision was a function not so much of his nervousness but of a complete lack of confidence in his capabilitites. In addition, it is clear that omitting to bring about an event does not require considering whether or not one can bring it about. Cases of negligence are strong testimony to this fact. Hence clause (iv) may also be dropped. In fact, it seems to me that Smith can truthfully be said to have omitted to go to the victims' aid just so long as he *could* have gone but did not. Indeed, it is this simple fact concerning "can" that in general seems to separate omissions, in the broadest sense of "omit," from mere not-doings. (It *need* not even be the case, though perhaps it usually is the case, that there be some alternative event f that the agent can or does bring about. This point was just made concerning indecision as to what to do.) That is, as an analysis of the relevant concept of omission in general, I propose the following:

D.8.2: S omits at T to bring about e actively relative to T and T' =df.
           (i) S can at T bring about e actively relative to T and T'; and
           (ii) S does not bring about e actively relative to T and T'.

No doubt most omissions are not as "bare" as D.8.2 indicates they can be. Most cases of omission, for instance, may well involve bringing about some other event f; but all that D.8.2 says is that there is a sense (and, I would add, an important and common sense) of "omit" according to which omitting to bring about e does not *require* bringing about some other event f. Nevertheless, it may strike some that D.8.2 allows omissions to be too "bare," that it stretches the term "omit" beyond even its broadest sense and thereby admits too many not-doings into the class of omissions.

Some, for instance, may prefer to stipulate that a not-doing, to be an omission, must in some way be "untoward," that it must "stand out" in some way. But, although I have some sympathy with this, there are two problems with making such a stipulation. The first problem is that it would seem to be too strong; for instance, as argued earlier, although Smith's not going to the victims' aid was in fact morally reprehensible, the case could have been altered so that his inaction would have been seen still to be a case of intentional omission even though not morally reprehensible. The second problem is that it seems extremely difficult to make precise the requirement that the inaction be untoward. Perhaps the requirement can be understood in terms of some long disjunction such as "S's not bringing about e relative to T and T' is either morally reprehensible, or contravenes some law, or is not to be expected, or would not be expected of S if he were normal, or...(and so on)," but I for one certainly do not know how this disjunction is to be spelled out in detail. Indeed, I am not at all sure that it is required anyway. May we not simply say that some omissions are untoward and some not, and that it is only the former which are wont to engage our attention? This seems very reasonable to me. Notice that untoward omissions are of course still omissions on this account, while no toward not-doings would be omissions on the stricter account. Moreover, while there seems to be a sense of "omit" according to which an omission fails to satisfy the stricter account, there seems to be no recognized sense of "omit" according to which an omission fails to satisfy D.8.2.

Even this last statement may appear too strong, however. For it seems to be true not only that Smith omitted to *go* to the aid of the victims, but also that he omitted actually to *aid* them. But aiding them is *not* something that he could have done relative to T and T' (where these are the times relative to his omission to *go* to aid them) since going to their aid would have taken some time, and aiding them would have been possible for Smith only *after* he had *gone to* their aid; and so it seems that, according to clause (i) of D.8.2, he did not omit to aid them, when in fact he did.

But clause (i) of D.8.2 does *not* have this implication. Granted, it implies that Smith did not *at T* actually omit to aid the victims relative to T and T', but it leaves open the question whether he omitted actually to aid them altogether. This is where the double time-index comes in handy. In general, there are many actions that one can at T perform relative to some other (later) times T^* and T^{**}. The point is that Smith could *at* T have *gone* to the victims' aid relative to T and some time T' and, all things being equal, this would have enabled him actually to aid them relative to some *later* times T^* and T^{**}. So Smith could *at* T actually have aided the victims relative to T^* and T^{**}; and it is, I believe, because this is true that he may also be said to have omitted actually to aid the victims. That is to say, Smith omitted *at* T to aid the victims relative to T^* and T^{**}; this is *not* to say either that Smith omitted at T to aid the victims relative to T and some time T' or that he omitted at T^* to aid the victims relative to T^* and T^{**}. And so, generalizing on D.8.2, we may, I think, say the following:

D.8.3: S omits at T to bring about e actively relative to T' and T^* = df.
           (i) S can at T bring about e actively relative to T' and T^*; and
           (ii) S does not bring about e actively relative to T' and T^*.

Note that D.8.3 allows us to say (as, it seems, we would want to) that, for example, although I am not presently sunbathing in the Bahamas, neither am I presently omitting to sunbathe in the Bahamas – *if* what is meant by this is that I am not *now* omitting to sunbathe in the Bahamas *now*. Assuming that I can now go to (that is, start on my way to) the Bahamas and that, if I were to do so, I would soon be able to sunbathe there, D.8.3 *does* commit us to saying both that I am *now* omitting to *go* to the Bahamas *now* and that I am *now* omitting to sunbathe in the Bahamas *later* – but both of these seem acceptable to me.

D.8.2, then, is a "special case" of D.8.3. This suggests that D.8.1 is a "special case" also. That is, it suggests that we can properly say of someone S that he intentionally omits at T to bring about e relative to T' and T^*. In order that cases where T is distinct from T' may be accommodated, a comprehensive and fairly complex formula is called for. The following is, I think, what is needed:

D.8.4:   *S* intentionally omits at *T* to bring about *e* actively relative to *T'* and *T** =df. there are events *f1,...,fn*, times *T"1,...,T"n*, and times *T**1,...,T**n* such that:

(i) *S* can at *T* bring about *e* actively relative to *T'* and *T**;

(ii) *S* can at *T* bring about *f1* actively relative to *T"1* and *T**1*, and..., and *S* can at *T* bring about *fn* actively relative to *T"n* and *T**n* ;

(iii) *S* cannot at *T* both bring about *e* actively relative to *T'* and *T**, and bring about *f1* actively relative to *T"1* and *T**1*, and..., and bring about *fn* actively relative to *T"n* and *T**n* ;

(iv) *S* considers at *T* each of the propositions contained in (i) - (iii);

(v) *S* accepts at *T* each of the propositions contained in (i) - (iii);

(vi) *S* intends at *T* [*S* does not bring about *e* actively relative to *T'* and *T**]; and

(vii) *S* intentionally brings about *f1* actively relative to *T"1* and *T**1*, and..., and *S* intentionally brings about *fn* actively relative to *T"n* and *T**n.*

This definition allows us, then, to say not only that Smith intentionally omitted to go to the victims' aid but also that he intentionally omitted to aid them.

There is an asymmetry between D.8.3 and D.8.4 that should be explicitly noted here, and that is that, according to them, omitting to do something does not, in general, require doing something whereas intentionally omitting to do something does require this. Such asymmetry is perhaps *prima facie* undesirable, from a theoretical standpoint. There are two ways in which one might try to get rid of it. One way is to stipulate that omitting to do something does, in general, require doing something. But I have already argued that this is false. The other way is to stipulate that intentionally omitting to do something does not require doing something. Actually, I am not absolutely convinced that this contention is false; it is just that I can think of no way to accommodate it in an adequate analysis of the concept of intentional omission. For just as it is false to say that one acts intentionally just in case one does something that one intends to do (see the discussion of D.6.1.a in Chapter 6), so too it is false to say that one intentionally omits to do something just in case one omits to do something that one intends to omit to do. (One counterexample against this suggestion is as follows. Smith intends to insult Jones by omitting to greet him upon meeting him. With this intention in mind, but unaware that Jones is the person who has just greeted him, Smith ignores Jones's greeting and walks on. In such a case, while the omission to greet may be intentional, the omission to greet *Jones* is not.) Clearly, just as some "strong" connection must be forged between the agent's intention and what he does in order for his action to be intentional, so too some "strong" connection must be forged between the agent's intention and what he omits to do in order for his omission to be intentional. I can think of no way to do this adequately except as I have done in D.8.4. This fact tends to confirm the claim that the essential elements of the car-accident case were correctly distilled in the last section.

8.4   *EVALUATION OF THE PRESENT APPROACH TO OMISSIONS*

Let us take stock of where we now stand. D.8.3 and D.8.4 are intended to provide precise analyses of two concepts which are properly expressible in terms of "omit" and "intentionally omit," respectively, and which are supposed to be broad enough to serve as the basis for analyses of narrower but related concepts. It seems that they are well suited to this task. For instance, there is an important concept, which some choose to express simply in terms of "omit," whose analysis would require appending the following clause to the definiens of D.8.3: S is legally obligated at T to bring about e actively relative to T' and T^*. This same clause can be appended to the definiens of D.8.4 to provide the analysis of an important concept which some choose to express simply in terms of "intentionally omit." The pattern should be clear: the analysis of "concepts of omission" more restrictive than those analyzed in D.8.3 and D.8.4 may be achieved by tacking on extra clauses to the definiens of each.

Some objections to the present approach to omissions have already been addressed in this chapter. Others will be discussed shortly. At this point, however, it would be helpful, as a means of allowing for an indirect appraisal of the present approach, to consider certain noteworthy analyses of the concepts of omission and intentional omission to be found in the available literature. Eric D'Arcy, for instance, contends that a person omits to perform an action if and only if he is in some way expected to perform it and yet does not perform it.[13] In light of D.8.3, this appears both too weak and too strong. It is too weak in that it allows for the possibility of omitting to do something that one cannot do, and, as I have urged, this seems incorrect. It is too strong – at least, too strong for the broadest sense of "omit" – in that it requires that the agent be subject to certain expectations. Consider the case of Jones, who is in the habit of running a mile on all and only weekday mornings and who does not run a mile on the third Sunday in April. He is not in any way expected to run that day (he is under no obligation to do so; anyone who knows him well would not expect him to do so; and so on); nevertheless, it seems correct (though possibly pedantic) to say that he omits to run on that day. On the other hand, Michael Gorr has recently offered an analysis of a concept expressed in terms of "omit" which is very close to D.8.3 and runs as follows: S omits to perform a at T if and only if (i) it is not the case that S performs a at T, and (ii) S had the ability and the opportunity to perform a at T.[14] My only real criticism of this analysis concerns, first, the substitution of "had the ability and opportunity to" for "could" (for the two are only *roughly* synonymous[15]), and, second, the absence of mention of times relative to S's ability and opportunity to perform a at T. The double time-index provided in D.8.3 and D.8.4 is, I have urged, necessary for a precise account of omissions. For instance, it seems odd to say "S omits to perform a at T," even if clauses (i) and (ii) of Gorr's criterion are satisfied, when it is also true that S is dead at T. On the other hand, S's being dead at T is clearly compatible with his omitting at some earlier time T' (when he was alive) to perform a at T.

Myles Brand claims that a person refrains from performing an action a if and only if he does not perform a but performs some other action b in order that he may thereby prevent himself from performing a.[16] There are problems with this. First, Brand offers his criterion as a criterion of the broadest type of not-doing which is not merely a not-doing. As such, it is considerably stronger than D.8.3 and, in fact, much too strong. For it makes all such not-doing intentional, while it is surely possible for there to be unintentional omissions. (Standard cases of negligence, as mentioned earlier, involve unintentional omissions.) Of course, "refrain" has connotations of intentionality, and so it might be better to compare Brand's criterion with D.8.4. But, once again, the criterion seems inadequate. As Douglas Walton has pointed out, if Smith gives his wife the keys to the liquor cabinet and unsuccessfully attempts to break it open two weeks later to get a glass of sherry, he can hardly be said to have refrained from drinking the glass of sherry.[17] But D.8.4 is adequate to ruling out this case, in so far as it appears to fail to satisfy clause (vii) of that criterion.

Other accounts of refraining have appeared recently (and I take refraining from doing something to be very similar to, if not the same as, intentionally omitting to do that thing). For instance, O.H.Green says that a person refrains from performing an action a if and only if he can perform a and is aware of this, but does not perform a and is aware of this.[18] But, if by "refrain" is meant what is meant by "intentionally omit," this is surely too weak. The person concerned might simply be suffering from indecision such that, although he is aware that he can perform a and yet is not performing it, this is not due to any intentional omission on his part but merely to vacillation. So, too, Gorr says that a person intentionally omits to perform an action if and only if he omits to perform it and is aware of this.[19] But this account is too weak, just as Green's is. Too weak, also, is the following account of deliberate omission provided by Chisholm: S deliberately omits to perform a if and only if S considers performing a and yet does not perform it.[20] For, even if we grant that S can perform a, his not performing it might simply be due to vacillation on his part, in which case it would hardly be appropriate to say that he deliberately omits to perform it. As a final example, Elazar Weinryb offers an analysis of the concept of refraining according to which the agent need not be able to perform the action in question but only *believe* that he can.[21] As argued above, however, it seems that it would have been incorrect to say, for instance, that Smith refrained from going to the victims' aid if he had unwittingly been secured to his chair. In addition, Weinryb makes no mention of intentionally performing an alternative action (or actions), but only (to put it a little roughly) of intending not to perform the omitted action and believing that one can perform it, while not performing it. But it was noted in the last section that some stronger connection than this must be forged between what one intends to omit to do and what one omits to do in order for one's omission to be intentional.

Still more accounts of omission and intentional omission are to be found in the literature,[22] but none appears to escape the sorts of criticism just drawn up, criticisms to which D.8.3 and D.8.4 seem to me not to be subject. This is not, of course, to deny that D.8.3 and D.8.4 are immune to criticism, and two objections seem to me particularly to deserve discussion here. First, it might be objected that it is in fact possible to do something while omitting to do it and that, since D.8.3 and D.8.4 both rule this out, they are defective. To support this objection the following case might be given.[23] Brown is a professional assassin. He is also cautious. He always has a back-up plan in order to make doubly sure that his intended victim will die. On a certain day Brown's intended victim is Jones. As part of his back-up plan, Brown places a bomb in Jones's car, and then waits in the shadows, gun in hand, for Jones to appear. Jones appears; Brown raises his gun, but then lowers it, curious whether or not the new type of plastic explosive that he affixed to Jones's car is efficacious. He discovers that it is. Now, Brown has killed Jones (the car blew up), but it seems that he has also omitted to kill Jones (he lowered his gun, but had he shot at Jones he would have killed him). Does this show the foregoing analysis to be defective? The answer is that it does not, for two reasons. First, there is the question of time. Even if S omits at T to bring about e relative to T' and T^*, this is compatible with his bringing about e relative to some *other* times. Secondly, there is the question of exactly what action is involved. Suppose that, in order for the explosive device to work, Brown had to push a button, and that his killing Jones thereby occurred relative to exactly the same times (T' and T^*, say) as those to which his killing Jones *would* have occurred had he shot Jones. It of course follows that, despite his lowering his gun, there is no time T such that Brown omitted at T to *kill* Jones relative to T' and T^*. Still, this is perfectly compatible with his omitting at some time T to *shoot* Jones relative to T' and some time T'''; moreover, it seems perfectly correct to say also that there is a time T such that Brown omits at T to *kill Jones* relative to T' and T^* *by shooting him* relative to T and T'''.[24] Hence, it seems to me, the present account has no counterintuitive features in this respect.

Another objection might be that D.8.3 and D.8.4 are not much help in determining why omissions are often thought to have such great moral and legal significance. But this seems to me an inappropriate objection for three main reasons. First, there is *some* help to be found in clause (i) of D.8.3 and clause (i) of D.8.4: the agent *can do otherwise*, and this is often an indication that moral or legal responsibility is properly ascribable to the agent. I say "indication" only, since being able to do otherwise is clearly not sufficient for being morally or legally responsible for what one does in fact do; indeed, as Harry Frankfurt persuasively argues, it may not even be necessary.[25] Of course, if Frankfurt is right, the question arises as to whether one may be morally or legally responsible for a not-doing which is not an omission. I suspect that one may; but this is an issue that cannot be done justice here.

Secondly, and more importantly, it is wrong to demand of an analysis that it be of significant help in resolving problems in areas where it is thought that the concept analyzed is applicable. Although one might *hope* for more, all that one should *demand* of an analysis is that it be accurate. I believe that D.8.3 and D.8.4 satisfy this condition. By way of comparison, I should point out that no even close-to-adequate analyses of the concept of action and related concepts of which I am aware (including those proposed in earlier chapters) are of much help – just by themselves – in affording comprehension of how it is that one might be morally or legally responsible for one's actions and their consequences. In this connection, it is also worth noting that some philosophers[26] have claimed that one's moral responsibility for the harm that one omits to prevent must be accounted for (if at all) in a fashion radically different from that in which one's moral responsibility for the harm that one causes is to be accounted for, and they base this claim on the contention that omissions cannot have consequences. But while it may be true that omissions cannot have *causal* consequences (and even this is far from clear), it is surely false to say that they cannot have consequences of *any* sort; moreover, it is not at all clear that the consequences that omissions may have are not of that sort which is pertinent to the ascription of moral responsibility (and, perhaps, of which *causal* consequences are also instances).[27]

Lastly, it should be noted that the hope that some philosophers have vested in an analysis of the concept of omission in terms of its providing the means for resolving such matters as killing *versus* letting die, Good Samaritanism, and so forth, has been based on the contention that letting something happen is obviously identical with, or to be especially closely allied with, omitting to prevent its happening. But let us examine this contention for a moment, for matters are not nearly so simple as it seems to imply. Before we seek to understand what it is to omit to prevent something's happening, we need to understand what it is to prevent something's happening. Roughly, preventing an event *e*'s happening is doing something that renders it impossible for *e* to occur. More precisely:

D.8.5:   *S* prevents# *e* relative to *T* and *T'* =df. there are
         an event *f* and a time *T** such that:
           (i) *S* brings about *f* actively relative to *T* and *T**;
           (ii) it is not possible# that *e* occur at *T'* and *f* occur at *T**; and
           (iii) it is possible# that *e* occur at *T'*.

The symbol "#" is intended as a variable that may be instantiated in the following sort of way. Suppose that *S* kills *S**; then *S* prevents [*S** lives], for (to suppress mention of times for the moment) it is not possible for both [*S* kills *S**] and [*S** lives] to occur. What *sort* of possibility is at issue here? Logical (or metaphysical), I think.[28] Hence we may say that *S* logically (or metaphysically) prevents [*S** lives]. Now compare the case where *S* locks the liquor cabinet and throws away the key, thereby preventing himself from drinking a glass of sherry. We may say that this is a case of prevention due to the impossibility that both [*S* locks the liquor cabinet] and [*S* drinks a glass of sherry] occur. What *sort* of possibility is at issue here? Causal, I think.[29] Perhaps yet other sorts of possibility may be invoked here, and thus yet other sorts of prevention also. But I shall not pursue this. On the basis of D.8.5, "letting happen" – "the omission to prevent" – may be defined thus:

D.8.6:   *S* lets# at *T e* happen at *T'* =df. there are an
         event *f* and times *T''* and *T** such that:

(i) *S* omits at *T* to bring about *f* actively relative to *T'''* and *T**;
(ii) it is not possible# that *e* occur at *T'* and *f* occur at *T**; and
(iii) *e* occurs at *T'*.

(The variable "#" functions as before.) On the basis of D.8.5 and D.8.6 it seems reasonable also to say:

D.8.7:   *S* intentionally prevents# *e* relative to *T* and *T'*
           =df. there are an event *f* and a time *T** such that:
           (i) *S* intentionally brings about *f* actively relative to *T* and *T**;
           (ii) it is not possible# that *e* occur at *T'* and *f* occur at *T**;
           (iii) it is possible# that *e* occur at *T'*;
           (iv) *S* considers at *T* each of the propositions contained in (ii) and (iii);
           (v) *S* accepts at *T* each of the propositions contained in (ii) and (iii); and
           (vi) *S* intends at *T* that *e* not occur at *T'*.

We may also say:

D.8.8:   *S* intentionally lets# at *T e* happen at *T'* =df. there are an event *f* and times *T'''* and *T** such that:
           (i) *S* intentionally omits at *T* to bring about *f* actively relative to *T'''* and *T**;
           (ii) it is not possible# that *e* occur at *T'* and *f* occur at *T**;
           (iii) it is possible# that *e* occur at *T'*;
           (iv) *S* considers at *T* each of the propositions contained in (ii) and (iii);
           (v) *S* accepts at *T* each of the propositions contained in (ii) and (iii);
           (vi) *S* intends at *T* that *e* occur at *T'*; and
           (vii) *e* occurs at *T'*.

With respect to both definitions, compare D.8.4.[30]

But, even if all of this is accurate, does it help us resolve such matters as killing *versus* letting die, Good Samaritanism, and so on? If it does, I cannot see that it helps very much. For instance, on the issue of killing *versus* letting die, compare the following two cases involving what have come to be called active and passive euthanasia. In the first case, doctor A, for purposes of euthanasia, injects his patient with a lethal solution; doctor B witnesses this; also, doctor B could administer an antidote within ten seconds of the injection and save the patient, but does not; and so the patient dies. In the second case, doctor C, for purposes of euthanasia, pulls the plug on his patient's respirator; doctor D witnesses this; also, doctor D could replace the plug within ten seconds of its being pulled and save the patient, but does not; and so the patient dies. It seems clear from the description of these two cases that what doctor A does is very similar in relevant respects to what doctor C does, while what doctor B does (or does not do) is very similar in relevant respects to what doctor D does (or does not do). Do D.8.5 through D.8.8 help us here? Well, according to D.8.8, doctors B and D intentionally let their respective patients die. This seems right. But note that, given that doctors A and C could have refrained from doing what they did, *they too* intentionally let their patients die. Perhaps, when the issue of "killing *versus* letting die" is raised, the distinction that is supposed by many to be at issue is really that of killing *versus* "*mere*" letting die, where "merely" letting someone die is "merely" letting his death occur, which in turn may be understood in terms of the following definition:

D.8.9: S merely lets# at T e happen at T' = df.
     (i) S lets# at T e happen at T'; and
     (ii) there is no time T^* such that S brings about e actively relative to T^* and T'.

Does *this* help? Not really. For notice that, while, given D.8.9, it *is* true that doctor A does not *merely* let his patient die, *nor* does doctor C, although both doctors B and D do. Yet pulling the plug is a commonly cited example of what has come to be called passive euthanasia, and the distinction between passive and active euthanasia is supposed to consist in, or partly in, the distinction between killing and letting die. But, given the foregoing definitions, this common diagnosis of pulling the plug cannot be correct. Either pulling the plug is not a case of passive euthanasia, or passive euthanasia is not to be distinguished from active euthanasia solely on the basis either of the distinction between killing and letting die or of the distinction between killing and merely letting die. In my opinion, it is the latter that is correct. That is, it *does* seem to me that there is a distinction, and possibly a morally relevant distinction, between what doctor *A* does and what doctor *C* does. For while both doctors bring about their respective patient's death, it seems to me perhaps correct to say that only doctor *A* *kills* his patient. (While all killing involves the active bringing about of a death, the converse does not hold.) For the death of doctor *C*'s patient seems to be brought about not only by what doctor *C* does but *also* by "natural causes" – whatever they may be exactly; and this seems not to be the case with doctor *A*'s patient. The upshot of this brief discussion is that the sort of distinction that underlies the distinction between active and passive euthanasia seems *not* to be that of killing *versus* letting die or that of killing *versus* mere letting die, but rather that of killing *versus* either mere letting die or actively bringing about a death in such a manner that one does not kill. Perhaps this distinction is morally relevant; perhaps not. The point is controversial.³ ¹ Be that as it may, it is not surprising that the foregoing discussion is not too helpful in deciding this issue, although it is perhaps helpful in a "negative" way, in that it helps clarify what distinctions are *not* involved. This seems to me to be true also of the moral issues involved in such matters as Good Samaritanism, the Doctrine of Double Effect, and so on. Perhaps the foregoing analysis could be used to help clarify just what distinctions are at issue in these matters, but, as to the question of how best to decide whether there is any *moral relevance* to these distinctions, I doubt whether the analysis will be of much help.

8.5   *RESOLUTION OF THE FIFTH GROUP OF PROBLEMS*

Problems E1 and E2 of Chapter 2 are resolved by D.8.3 and D.8.4, respectively – if these definitions are accurate. Problem E3 still requires resolution, however. That is, the question still remains: what are acts of omission? If D.8.3 is correct, it is possible for someone to omit to do something and yet not act. In such a case, it is clear that there is an omission but no act or action. Hence, it is quite misleading to talk of omissions in general as "negative actions" or "active non-doings" which are "committed." On the other hand, it is true that omissions are in fact often accompanied by actions – it is perhaps the case that they in fact are *always* so accompanied, although I doubt this – and it is true that we often accept that a person omitted to do something *by* doing, or *because* he did, or *in virtue of* doing, something else.[3][2] In such cases as this, we may, I think, legitimately talk of acts of omission. But, if we do, are we thereby forced to admit that some omissions, at least, are actions or that some omissions are "committed"? Of course not. If a coarsely-grained ontology of events had been adopted in this work, then perhaps there would have been reason at this stage to have accepted the possibility that one and the same event be an action "under one description" and an omission "under another description." But working, as we are, with a finely-grained ontology of events and states of affairs, such an identification of omissions and acts or actions is ruled out, even in those cases where we omit to do something by doing something else. Rather, omissions may be seen to be complex states of affairs consisting (roughly) of a person's being able (in the sense of "can" specified earlier) to do something and his not doing it. Intentional omissions may be seen to be even more complex, that is, to be states of affairs consisting (roughly) of a person's being able to do each of at least two incompatible things, his considering this, his accepting it, his intending not to do one of them, and his intentionally doing the other or others. But even on such an ontology as this, we may – as indicated at the outset of this chapter – still legitimately speak of acts of omission. For intentional omissions will still be seen as necessarily having actions as a part, and many unintentional omissions are clearly intimately connected – by the "by"-relation and other relations – to actions, and so in both cases it appears appropriate to speak – carefully – of the actions in question as "acts of omission."

Notes

1   *E.g.*, Thomson (1977), p.212ff.

2   Some may find the phrase-form "*S* (intentionally) omits to bring about *e* " awkward, despite its being grammatically proper. If they wish, they may substitute "*S* (intentionally) omits bringing about *e* " for it.

3   Kleinig (1976), p.393.

4   Danto (1966, p.51; 1973, Chapter 6).

5   See Brand (1971), p.46.

6   *Cf.* Walton (1980), p.321.

7   *E.g.*, Goldman (1970).

8   Note that the term "basic," as used in this sentence, is *not* being used in a the same manner as that in which it was used in the last section of the last chapter.

9   The reason that I take knowledge of what one can do not to be necessary for intentional omission is simply that it seems to me that, if the case under discussion were complicated so that it was apparent that Smith was *not justified* in believing that he could go to the victims' aid but (correctly) believed this nevertheless, we would not be required to retract the ascription of an intentional omission to him. If this is correct, and if – as I assume – justified belief is necessary for knowledge, then knowledge of what one can do or bring about is not necessary for intentional omission.

10 I assume here that Smith's remaining seated is an action of his, even though it may involve no change. This is, of course, in keeping with the account of action given in earlier chapters.

11 There is a danger that the Smith case has features which appear to warrant this analysis while other cases of intentional omission lack these features. This is a danger which the reader can dispel by concocting cases of his or her own. When this is done, it will, I think, be found that the proposed analysis of the concept of intentional omission is confirmed rather than disconfirmed. This matter will be mentioned again at the end of the next section.

12 This is of course a popular characterization of the concept. (See Nowell-Smith (1960).) Note that the characterization is not only rough but in some respects inaccurate. (See Lehrer (1976), p.242.)

13 D'Arcy (1963), p.41.

14 Gorr (1979), p.97. G.H. von Wright (1963, p.45) provides an analysis of the concept of forbearing which is superficially also quite similar to D.8.3. The discussion and use of that concept that follow, however, differ markedly in certain respects from the remarks that I make concerning omissions.

15 See note 12 to this chapter.

16 Brand (1971), p.49.

17 Walton (1980), p.322.

18 Green (1979), p.107.

19 Gorr (1979), p.97.

20 Chisholm (1976), p.73.

21 Weinryb (1980), pp.7-8.

22   Robert Moore (1979) offers an analysis of the concept of refraining which both resembles and differs from D.8.4 in ways too complex and numerous to be discussed here.

23   This case is liberally adapted from Chisholm (1976), pp.83-4.

24   I have not formally introduced the "by"-relation into my discussion of omissions; nor shall I seek to do so. Still, it seems clear that it *could* be so introduced – and introduced, presumably, along the lines of the discussion furnished in Chapter 7.

25   Frankfurt (1969).

26   *E.g*, Weinryb (1980), p.10.

27   This issue is also discussed in Gorr (1979), pp.100-2; Mack (1980), pp.230-259; Husak (1980), 318-326.

28   See Chapter 1, Section 1.2.

29   See D.3.3.

30   Compare also Brand (1971), p.52 and Walton (1980), p.322, both of whom restrict "letting happen" to *causal intentional* letting happen.

31   For some fine discussions on this topic, see Steinbock (1980).

32   See note 24 to this chapter.

Chapter 9

WILLING, DECIDING, CHOOSING, AND TRYING

The account of action presented in the preceding pages may be used to clarify the relations and distinctions between the concepts of willing, deciding, choosing, and trying. In this chapter I shall briefly attempt the beginnings, but only the beginnings, of such clarification.

9.1   *DECIDING*

In Chapter 3, Section 3.3 it was mentioned that there are two main categories of decision-making, the practical and the theoretical. We should now note that there are, moreover, two distinct ways to make a practical decision that a state of affairs should occur. One way is simply to form an intention that the state of affairs should occur; the other is to will the state of affairs. As an illustration, consider the case where, at one point in the afternoon, Smith decides to watch television later that night and, when night comes, he turns on the television. It seems correct to say that Smith has made at least two decisions in this case. The first is the one he makes in the afternoon; the second immediately precedes the television's going on – indeed, it is a or the cause of the television's going on. Despite their close relation, these two decisions are of distinct types. The first, I shall say, is a $decision_1$, and the second a $decision_2$. Neither type of decision is reducible to the other.

A $decision_1$ is the formation of an intention. Such a decision may or may not come about as a result of deliberation. Smith's decision to watch television later that night may be impetuous, or it may be based on the facts that a good program will be on, that he has no other commitments, and so on. Whether impetuous or deliberate, however, the decision itself to watch television later that night seems to consist in nothing more than his beginning to intend to watch television later that night. I therefore propose the following:

D.9.1: S decides$_1$ e at T = df.
  (i) S intends e at T ; and
  (ii) there is a time T' such that
   (a) T' is just prior to T, and
   (b) S does not intend e at T'.[1]

Two points are noteworthy concerning D.9.1. First, it may seem to some that a third clause should be added to this definition, to wit, "(iii) S considers e at T." But I am not persuaded that all decision$_1$-making is or must be "conscious" (although I am sure that most of it is), and so I have not supplied such a clause. Secondly, whereas, when I make a decision$_1$ that an event e should occur, there is no necessity that I intend that e should occur as a result of my decision, this is not so when I make a decision$_2$. For decisions$_2$ just are volitions. Or more precisely:

D.9.2: S decides$_2$ e at T = df. there is an event f such that S wills f at T in order that e may occur.

Hence A.3.10 and A.3.12 apply to decisions$_2$, even though they do not apply to decisions$_1$.

Decisions$_1$ and decisions$_2$ alike may or may not be the outcome of deliberation.[2] We may say (where 1 is less than or equal to i and i is less than or equal to n):

D.9.3: S deliberately decides$_1$ e at T = df. there are times $T1$, $T2$, ..., Tn such that:
  (i) Tn is just prior to T ;
  (ii) $T1$ is not later than $T2$ and...and Tn-1 is not later than Tn ;
  (iii) for any time Ti, either S considers [S decides$_1$ e] at Ti or S considers [S does not decide$_1$ e] at Ti ;
  (iv) there is a time Ti such that S considers [S decides$_1$ e] at Ti ; and
  (v) S decides$_1$ e at T.

(Compare D.6.8.) An analogous analysis of the concept of deliberate decision$_2$-making (where "decides$_2$" replaces "decides$_1$" in D.9.3) may be given.

Despite the fact that a sharp distinction must be drawn between the concept of a $decision_1$ and that of a $decision_2$, it is nevertheless often the case that when a $decision_2$ occurs a $decision_1$ occurs also. Given A.3.9 and A.3.11, it follows, from S's willing e at T in order that f may occur, that S intends both e and f at T. Now, it may be that S did not intend either of these just prior to T. If this is so, then S's $deciding_2$ both e and f is accompanied by his $deciding_1$ them. But what if S has $decided_1$ some time prior to T that both e and f should occur and his intention has not lapsed in the interim? In such a case, although it is true that he $decides_2$ both e and f at T, he does not $decide_1$ them. Nevertheless, there is, I think, something that he does $decide_1$ should occur, and that is that, for some time T', [S wills e in order that f may occur] should contribute causally relative to T and T' to f. (Compare A.3.10 and A.3.12.) The example of Smith's turning on the television is a case in point. Let us say that in this case it is at T that Smith $decides_2$ the event (call it e) internal to his turning on the television; he does not at the same time $decide_1$ e, for he already $decided_1$ it earlier in the afternoon (and his intention has not lapsed in the interim). However, when he $decides_2$ e he *does* $decide_1$ that, for some time T', [Smith $decides_2$ e] should contribute causally relative to T and T' to e. Nevertheless, I do *not* think that we can correctly assume the truth of the following: necessarily, if S $decides_2$ e at T, then there is an event f such that S $decides_1$ f at T. The following case renders this assumption dubious. Suppose that in the afternoon Smith $decides_1$ to watch television later that night, but suppose that he has two particular times T and T' in mind and that he $decides_1$ in the afternoon that a $decision_2$ of his, that the event (call it e) internal to his turning on the television should occur, should contribute causally relative to T and T' to e. In this case it is not true that Smith $decides_1$ at T that his $decision_2$ that e should occur should contribute causally relative to T and T' to e. Nor is there any other plausible candidate for a $decision_1$ by Smith at T. In such a case, then, it seems that the agent $decides_2$ an event e and yet does not also $decide_1$ an event f.

9.2 *CHOOSING*

The concept of a choice may be analyzed in terms of the concepts of a decision and an alternative. The latter concept involves the concept of "can" already used in D.8.1 through D.8.4 and tentatively analyzed in D.11.14 below. We may say that one event is an alternative to another for an agent just in case he can bring about each but not both. That is:

D.9.4: e is an alternative to f for S at T =df. there are times T', T^*, T'', and T^{**} such that:

    (i) S can at T bring about e actively relative to T' and T^*;

    (ii) S can at T bring about f actively relative to T'' and T^{**}; and

    (iii) S cannot at T both bring about e actively relative to T' and T^* and bring about f actively relative to T'' and T^{**}.

(Compare clauses (i) - (iii) of D.8.4.) It might be thought that the definiens of D.9.4 should include a belief-condition of some sort. This is not so. A distinction must be made between the concept of a genuine alternative and that of an apparent alternative, and it is the former that I have tried to capture by means of D.9.4. Nevertheless, a belief-condition should be included in the analysis of the concept of choosing, and I shall include such a condition. Note that there are two main types of choice, just as there are two main types of (practical) decision. We may say, roughly, that a choice is a deliberate decision between two apparent alternatives. Or more precisely (where 1 is less than or equal to i and i is less than or equal to n):

D.9.5: S chooses$_1$ e at T =df. there are an event f and times $T1$, $T2$, ..., Tn such that:

    (i) Tn is just prior to T ;

    (ii) $T1$ is not later than $T2$, and..., and $Tn-1$ is not later than Tn ;

    (iii) S accepts [e is an alternative to f for S at T] at $T1$, and..., and at Tn ;

(iv) for any time Ti, either S considers [S decides$_1$ e and does not decide$_1$ f] at Ti or S considers [S decides$_1$ f and does not decide$_1$ e] at Ti ;
(v) there is a time Ti such that S considers [S decides$_1$ e] at Ti ;
(vi) there is a time Ti such that S considers [S decides$_1$ f] at Ti ; and
(vii) S decides$_1$ e at T.

An analogous analysis of the concept of choosing$_2$ (where "decides$_2$" replaces "decides$_1$" in D.9.5) may be given. Note that the following is a theorem:

T.9.1:   Necessarily, if S chooses$_1$ e at T, then S deliberately decides$_1$ e at T.

An analogous theorem for choices$_2$ and decisions$_2$ may of course also be given. It may seem that T.9.1 and its analogue ought not to hold, that is, that it is possible for some choices (whether choices$_1$ or choices$_2$) to be impetuous. While I agree that some choices may indeed be capricious or whimsical, it seems to me impossible that they should be impetuous (or, at least, impetuous in the sense that I use the term "impetuous" here, *i.e.*, not deliberate). If there has been no consideration or deliberation at all on the part of the agent as to what he takes to be alternative events, then the agent cannot choose between them.

9.3   TRYING

I shall turn now to a discussion of the concept of trying. This concept was discussed briefly when D.4.1 was under consideration. At that point I made the following claims: whenever one wills something, one makes an attempt; some attempts are actions, while others are not; and some attempts involve effort, while others do not. I shall now elaborate these theses, although I must stress at the outset that this elaboration is both tentative and slight.

It might seem at first that all attempts involve some degree of effort, but I think that this thesis has recently been fairly conclusively refuted by a number of philosophers. For instance, Brian O'Shaughnessy argues that, if a person S raises his arm intentionally, then he tries to do so, although O'Shaughnessy acknowledges that we do not often *speak* of S's trying to do this in the absence of his failing to do it.[3] His argument is essentially based on the claim that, had S attempted to raise his arm but failed, we would not hesitate to ascribe such an attempt to him, and such ascription would not be predicated on S's having made an effort ("tried *hard*") to raise his arm. Indeed, and this is the crucial point, what S "does" when he attempts to raise his arm but fails may be no different from what he "does" when he attempts to raise his arm and succeeds – with respect to that component of raising his arm which is his attempting to do so. It is perhaps odd to say that S tried to raise his arm when he succeeded in doing so, and far less odd to say that he tried to do this when he failed. But the oddness of ascribing attempts to persons in the case of successful actions should not be allowed to obscure the strict correctness of such ascription. The fact is that we commonly use the "language of attempts" only when there is *doubt* (in *our* minds) as to whether the action will be, is being, or has been successfully carried out.[4] If we see that it has already been successfully carried out, then there is no such doubt at all, and if it is a common action easily performed (such as raising one's arm), then there is very little such doubt. In either case, we tend not to ascribe an attempt to the agent; but, given that such ascription is strictly a function of a spectator's doubt *(our* doubt) as to the outcome of the attempt, and not at all a function of what the agent "does" (or, better perhaps, what happens to the agent, or goes on in his mind), we must acknowledge the correctness, while appreciating the oddness, of such ascription.

O'Shaughnessy's argument for the contention that, whenever one acts intentionally, one tries to do so, has been echoed in other philosophers' writings.[5] I accept his argument and thus his contention. More precisely, it seems to me that the following is correct:

D.9.6: S makes an attempt at T that e occur =df. there
           is an event f such that S wills f at T in order that
           e may occur.

(Compare D.9.2. The reason for the awkward locution "makes an attempt that" will become apparent shortly.) That is, making an attempt, or trying, in the broad sense of these terms (a sense which does not require that any effort take place), just is, it seems to me, willing or deciding$_2$. Hence, I agree with O'Shaughnessy *et al.* that, whenever one acts intentionally, one makes an attempt. Indeed, given D.9.6 and the account of action in preceding chapters, it is apparent that it is a theorem of the present treatment of attempts that, whenever one acts (whether intentionally, successfully, or neither), one makes an attempt. But it is not a theorem that, whatever one does, one attempts to do; nor is it a theorem that, whenever one makes an attempt, one acts.[6]

But to claim that, whenever one acts, one makes an attempt, is not to claim that, whenever one acts, one makes an effort, although it must be acknowledged that use of the word "attempt" is sometimes restricted to, and is in any case often applied to, cases of making an effort. While what it is to make an effort is something which is very familiar to most of us, *exactly* what it is (how best to describe the matter phenomenologically and how best to analyze the concept of making an effort, if it is amenable to analysis) is something for which I do not know how to provide an account.[7] Nevertheless, it certainly seems true that, whenever one makes an effort, one makes an attempt (in the broad sense analyzed in D.9.6). Indeed, it seems to me that, whenever one makes an effort, one acts, for the volition involved must, I think, be efficacious if an effort is to have taken place.[8] For instance, I take it that part of what happens when one effortfully tries to lift a heavy object is that one wills that a certain event occur and that this event *does* occur as a result. (The event in question might be the tensing of certain muscles.) Hence all efforts, it seems, constitute at least partially successful actions (but perhaps only partially: one might succeed in tensing one's muscles but fail to lift the object). On the present account, then, a totally paralyzed person cannot make a physical effort, although he may make an attempt to move some part of his body.[9]

9.4   *RESOLUTION OF THE SIXTH GROUP OF PROBLEMS*

Deciding, choosing, and trying may, then, all be closely allied, in some respects, with willing. But a problem arises as to how best to describe the objects of these mental attitudes. The problem is, in essence, that, given the foregoing characterizations of the concepts of willing, deciding, choosing, and trying (and, indeed, of intending – in Chapter 3), it would seem commonly to be the case that actions are *not* the objects of these attitudes, and yet it also seems to be the case that, commonly, the English language implicitly classifies the objects of these attitudes as actions. What I have in mind here is the fact that phrases such as "intend to do," "will to do," "decide to do," "choose to do," and "try to do" are commonly and naturally uttered – and they appear to imply that the objects of the attitudes in question are actions; yet in this and earlier chapters I have employed, for the most part, not phrases such as those just mentioned, but rather phrases (or phrase-forms) such as "intends that *e* should occur," "wills that *e* should occur," and so on. While there is some tension between my treatment of these matters and common English, this tension is in fact not as great as it might at first appear; still, the issue demands discussion.

Strictly speaking, I have said,[10] intention, volition, decision, choice, and trying are propositional attitudes. But I have also said that there is a convenient way of abbreviating talk of these attitudes so that, on the surface, it appears that events are the objects of these attitudes. But even when such abbreviation is employed, there is no guarantee that the events in question be actions. Indeed, in the case of volition (and, hence, in the case of deciding$_2$, choosing$_2$, and making an attempt), it will hardly ever, if ever, be the case that the events in question are actions. Briefly put, the reason for this (which should be fairly clear by now) is that a volition, if effective, is (on the current account) a *component* or *part* of, rather than a cause of, an action, and it is thus that the agent intends it. Now, how far common English usage accords with my technical usage of the concept of volition is moot. The term "will" (used to express the concept of volition) is not all that common in English anyway; and, when it is used, it is not clear how often it is used in a phrase such as "will to do." For instance, "he wills to move the card" is perhaps not as natural as "he wills the card to move."[11] Be that as it may, my aim here is not to accommodate common English. If it is at variance with my present treatment of the concepts in question, that is an unfortunate fact that must be duly recorded; but I do not deem this fact, if it is a fact, as sufficient reason to alter the present treatment.[12] Still, it should be noted that one *clear* case where common English is at variance with the present treatment is that of trying. "He intends/wills/decides/chooses that the card should move" is passable English and is what I should choose to say when trying to express matters more accurately than "he intends/wills/decides/chooses to move the card" allows. But "he makes an attempt that the card should move" (see D.9.6) is execrable English; still, I shall stick with it, for at least it does not suggest that his moving the card (rather than the card's moving) is the object of the attempt in question, and this certainly cannot be said of the far more natural phrase "he tries to move the card."

Now, it should not be inferred from the preceding paragraph that actions (or, strictly speaking, propositions involving actions) are hardly ever, if ever, the objects of intention, $decision_1$, or $choice_1$. For these are in a different boat from that occupied by volition (and, hence, $decision_2$, $choice_2$, and making an attempt). For instance, when Smith $chooses_1$ in the afternoon to turn on the television in the evening, it is clear that [Smith turns on the television] is the object of his $choice_1$ (and hence of a $decision_1$, and hence of an intention, also).[13] However, come evening, when Smith turns on the television, the television goes on as a result of a $choice_2$ (and hence of a $decision_2$, and hence of a volition, and hence of an attempt) of his. If his action is intentional, then his $choice_2$ is that the television should go on (and the television's going on is something that he intends); it is *not* that he should turn on the television.

I shall conclude this chapter by noting explicitly some prominent implication-relations and non-implication-relations between the concepts that have been discussed. The following are theorems:

T.9.2:   Necessarily, if S $chooses_1$ e at T, then S $decides_1$ e at T.

T.9.3:   Necessarily, if S decides$_1$ e at T, then S intends e
           at T.

T.9.4:   Necessarily, if S chooses$_2$ e at T, then S decides$_2$
           e at T.

T.9.5:   Necessarily, S decides$_2$ e at T if and only if there
           is an event f such that S wills f at T in order that
           e may occur.

T.9.6:   Necessarily, S decides$_2$ e at T if and only if S
           makes an attempt at T that e occur.

Recall, too, the following:

A.3.9:   Necessarily, if S wills p at T, then S intends p at
           T.

T.3.2:   Necessarily, S wills e at T if and only if S wills e
           at T in order that e may occur.

A.3.11:   Necessarily, if S wills e at T in order that f may
           occur, then S intends f at T.

Note, finally, that the contrapositives of T.9.2, T.9.3, T.9.4, A.3.9,
and A.3.11 are *not* theorems; indeed, they are all false. Noting
these theorems and non-theorems constitutes a resolution of
problem F1 of Chapter 2. As for problem F2, the distinction between what was called a "short-range" decision (or choice) and what
was called a "long-range" decision (or choice) is the same as that
between a decision$_2$ (or choice$_2$) and a decision$_1$ (or choice$_1$). With
the resolution of these final two problems we may now turn from an
exposition of the proposed theory of action to a brief consideration of
certain fundamental objections to it, some of which have been

forcefully voiced in the past against accounts of action which share some basic features with the present account.

Notes

1 Two points should be noted concerning this definition. First, in it "*e*" is restricted to ranging over events. Strictly speaking, deciding is a *propositional* attitude – like intending and willing – but it is convenient here to employ the sort of abbreviation that was employed when discussing intending and willing (in Chapter 3, Sections 3.2 and 3.3) and to talk of *events* as the objects of decisions$_1$ and decisions$_2$. Second, clause (ii)(a) of D.9.1 relies on the notion of one time's being just prior to another, concerning which see note 57 to Chapter 1.

2 The word "outcome" is loaded. Giving an account of it here would require giving an account of practical reasoning. But this is a complex topic and I shall not try to deal with it here. In this connection, however, see Binkley (1965), Sellars (1966), and also Aune (1977, Chapter 4 – where other relevant writings are listed).

3 O'Shaughnessy (1973), p.365ff.

4 I am so using "doubt" here that, if we know that the action will not be, is not being, or has not been successfully carried out, then, *a fortiori*, we doubt whether it will be, is being, or has been successfully carried out.

5 *E.g.*, McCann (1975); Hornsby (1980), Chapter 3; Corrado (1983), p.197.

6 O'Shaughnessy (1973, p.371) and McCann (1975, pp.436-7) both ally trying with willing. Hornsby (1980, Chapter 4) divorces the two.

7   Corrado (1983) provides an interesting discussion concerning how one *decides* or *tells* that an attempt has been made – and he is (mostly) concerned with attempts which involve effort.

8   A more cautious, and perhaps more plausible thesis, is that, whenever one makes an effort, one brings about some event *unrestrictedly* (see D.4.2). But I am prepared in fact to accept the stronger thesis that, whenever one makes an effort, one brings about some event *actively*.

9   *Cf.* McCann (1975, pp.428-9) who claims that total paralysis is consistent with making an attempt, and Taylor (1966, pp.76-84) who claims that total paralysis is inconsistent with making an effort. McCann, perhaps correctly, takes Taylor to task for his remarks, but once effortless attempts are distinguished from effortful ones, as in the present chapter, both McCann's and Taylor's theses may be accommodated.

10   In this chapter and in Chapter 3, Sections 3.2 and 3.3.

11   *Cf.* Hornsby (1980), p.54.

12   Of course, it might well be claimed that I ought to pay more attention to English usage than I do, especially where there is a clear conflict between it and the present treatment – as is the case with the concept of trying, a matter noted immediately below. I disagree; but I shall not enter into this debate.

13   Again, strictly speaking, the object of Smith's choice$_1$ is of course the *proposition* [there are times T and T' such that [Smith turns on the television] occurs relative to T and T'] (where T through T' is understood to be a stretch of time contained in the forthcoming evening). See again Chapter 3, Sections 3.2 and 3.3.

Chapter 10

OBJECTIONS

The point made at the outset of Chapter 4 bears repeating. In this book I have not attempted to account for every legitimate use of the term "action" and its cognates; nor have I attempted to legislate as to their use. The point also holds of such terms as "intention," "omission," "decision," and so on. What I have sought to do is to isolate and to analyze some particularly important concepts and to show how they may be co-ordinated so that an acceptable theory of human action results – a theory, moreover, which may serve as a basis for the resolution of problems in other areas of philosophy (but a theory which ought not to be *expected* to point the way to the resolution of any particular problem). However, in order to bolster the claim that the theory is acceptable, some important objections to it must be dealt with. Certain objections to the theory of action furnished in the foregoing chapters have already been addressed. But there are three broad categories of objections which raise such fundamental questions that they deserve special consideration, and it is to these questions that I shall now turn.

10.1   *INTENTION*

The first category of objections concerns the concept of intention and the use to which I have put this concept. Judith Jarvis Thomson says:

> My suspicion is that those who think intentionality is the mark of action would do best to give up the idea of defining either "act" or "agent."[1]

This suspicion is one to which I have paid no heed. But have I perhaps not been too hasty? Annette Baier, for instance, claims that the proper objects of intention are actions, and this claim has been echoed by others.[2] It is a claim which seems to have a certain plausibility, for is it not the case that whenever I intend something, I intend to do something, and is it perhaps not more accurate to say that the doing rather than the something is the object of my intention?

This issue is, of course, one which has in effect been dealt with in the last chapter. But it is worthwhile pointing out the highlights of my response once again. First of all, I take the objects of intention, strictly speaking, to be propositions, and not events (and, thus, not actions). Of course, the spirit of the present objection can be preserved so as to accommodate this, and the objection would then run thus. There seems to be an objectionable conceptual circularity inherent in the proposed theory of action, in that this theory seeks to analyze the concept of action (and related concepts) in terms of the concept of intention, while the objects of intention are of necessity propositions involving actions. My response to this is simply the following. The phrase "of necessity" renders the objection unsound, for while propositions involving actions *may* be the objects of intention, there is no *necessity* that this be so. While "Jones intends to go to lunch" (equivalently, but more awkwardly, "Jones intends that he should go to lunch") is a clear case of a sentence in which a proposition involving an action features as the object of someone's intention, there are just as clear cases of sentences in which a proposition involving no action or actions features as the object of someone's intention. Witness "Smith intends that Jones should be happy," "I intend that Smith's car should be waiting in front of the bank at 3 p.m. sharp," and so on.

An objection concerning conceptual circularity may be drawn up in another way, however. It might be argued that, while it is admittedly possible that some object of intention be a proposition involving no action (that is, a proposition of which no constitutent is an action[3]), still all intention is a *disposition to act*, and hence the concept of intention cannot legitimately feature in an analysis of the concept of action (and related concepts). But, while I accept that it is quite possibly true to say (given an appropriate understanding of the term "disposition") that intending that an event *e* occur is or implies a disposition to act so as to ensure that *e* occurs, I nevertheless reject the charge of conceptual circularity. For I believe that it is also true that the phrase "disposition to act" (or some equivalent phrase) need not be understood in order for the term "intend" to be understood. Moreover, having offered no analysis of the concept of intention, I have of course not offered any such analysis in which the phrase "disposition to act" (or some equivalent phrase) occurs.

10.2   *VOLITION*

The second category of objections concerns the cogency of the concept of volition. In the past it has been both vigorously asserted and vigorously denied that the concept of volition is incoherent. Perhaps Gilbert Ryle is the first in recent times to have mounted a sustained attack against the concept of volition. In particular, Ryle makes the following points.[4] First, he says, the concept of volition is a philosopher's artifice that serves no useful purpose; secondly, there are no predicates by which volitions may be described other than indirectly by means of a description of the events willed; thirdly, the existence of volitions is not asserted on empirical grounds ("ordinary men," he says, are never aware of their own volitions, and no one can witness the volitions of others); fourthly, a theory of volitions requires a transaction between mind and body where there can be none; and finally, there is a danger of infinite regress if volitions are themselves regarded as the issues of actions, such that they themselves must be willed.

Richard Taylor has taken up Ryle's banner and proposed the same and related arguments. He says:

> Surely when I say I can move my finger, and know that what I am saying is true, I am not expressing the idea of a causal connection between the behavior of my finger and some such internal hocus-pocus as this [*i.e.*, a motion-of-this-finger volition], the occurrence of which I can seriously doubt. Besides, even if this picture were not quite fantastic from the standpoint of ordinary experience, we can wonder whether I *can* bring about such an internal mental cause... If I *can*, then to what further internal events are *these* causally

related? And if I *cannot,* how can we still say
that I can move my finger after all?[5]

Taylor states that the theory of volitions is not based on any empirical evidence and claims that the theory is the "offspring of the
marriage" between the metaphysical presupposition that every
event must be caused by some other event and the "bewitchment of
grammar" which is responsible for the move from "voluntary" to
"volition."[6] (He does not mean to imply by this, however, that actions or issues are uncaused, but only that volitions do not feature
in their causal ancestry.) Taylor also claims that volitions are referred to always in terms of their alleged effects and never in terms
of themselves and, further, that it is impossible to refer to them
otherwise.[7] He argues that, since in any true causal relationship, if
one knows what the relata are, one can always describe the relata
independently of each other, volitions are purely fictional.[8] He says
that it is "absurd" to suppose that every voluntary motion is and
must be caused by anything like a volition.[9] (In this connection, by
"anything like" Taylor means to include decisions, choices, desires,
tryings, intentions, and so on.[10]) Moreover, Taylor claims that, in
order for a volition to be *my* volition, *I* must cause it; and hence, if *I*
can cause a volition, why not cut volitions entirely out of the picture
and say simply that *I* cause my actions?[11]

Several philosophers have been persuaded by arguments such as
those proposed by Ryle and Taylor. For instance, H.L.A.Hart opposes the volitional theory.[12] D'Arcy is content to say[13] simply
that the volitional theory has been successfully undermined by the
arguments of Ryle, Hart, Wittgenstein,[14] and Anscombe.[15] Arthur Danto has denounced the concept of volition.[16] And there are
many others who have done likewise. In particular, A.1.Melden
has inveighed against the concept of volition. Like Ryle, he asks: if
I perform an act by performing a volition, by what means do I perform the act of volition? By another act of volition? If so, an
infinite regress of willing quickly ensues. If not, there is no need for
the concept of volition in the first place.[17] Melden also relies particularly heavily on the argument that, if a volition (or, indeed, any
mental event, such as a motive, a desire, a choice, a decision) is to
be the cause of an action, then it must be describable independently
of its alleged effect, but that this cannot be accomplished.[18] He
says:

This then is the logical incoherence involved in the doctrine of acts of volition. Acts of volition are alleged to be direct causes of certain bodily phenomena...just as the latter are causes of the raising of one's arm... But no account of the alleged volitions is intelligible that does not involve a reference to the relevant bodily phenomena. And no interior cause, mental or physiological, can have this logical feature of volition. Let the interior event which we call "the act of volition" be mental or physical (which it is will make no difference at all), it must be logically distinct from the alleged effect: this surely is one lesson we can derive from a reading of Hume's discussion of causation. Yet nothing can be an act of volition that is not logically connected with that which is willed; the act of willing is intelligible only as the act of willing whatever it is that is willed. In short, there could not be such an interior event like an act of volition since...nothing of that sort could have the required logical consequences.[19]

Melden also argues that if (to paraphrase) my moving my finger leftward is distinct from my moving my finger rightward, then each of the volitions which allegedly cause these movements must be distinct, and this in turn implies, first, that it must be possible to offer a set of characterizations for each of these acts of volition and, secondly, that I have learnt that each volition corresponds to its appropriate effect.[20] However, neither of these, he claims, is the case.

Those who reject the theory of volitions naturally do not reject the applicability of the concepts of decision and choice; but they do of course deny that a decision or choice may be a volition, and hence D.9.2 and other such definitions in Chapter 9 are unacceptable to them. Perhaps J.L.Evans was the first seriously to attempt to accommodate Ryle's criticisms of the theory of volitions in a theory of choice.[21] According to Evans, there is a radical distinction to be made between the concepts of decision and choice; for, whereas deciding constitutes a *preparation* for action, choosing, on Evans's account, *is* acting (in the "standard" sense of "choosing"). That is, all choosing is acting, although not, of course, *vice versa* ; in particular, choosing is "doing this-rather-than-that" or "taking this-rather-than-that." Evans's theory is based mainly on the claim that the proposition expressed by the sentence "I chose to do *A* but did not do it" is self-contradictory, whereas the proposition expressed by "I decided to do *A* but did not do it" is not. P.H.Nowell-Smith proposes a theory similar to Evans's theory, where choosing is regarded as an act of selecting. He says:

> Choosing is not *just* doing, nor is it something other than doing and causally connected to it, it is doing-this-rather-than-that.[2 2]

Taylor has adopted a similar theory of choice and has constructed a parallel theory of trying.[2 3] According to him, both choosing and trying constitute types of acting. Desires, motives, and so on may also, presumably, be accounted for without recourse to a theory of volitions. And so it is that the anti-volitionists claim that perfectly satisfactory theories of readily acknowledged mental phenomena such as choice, desire, and so on may be constructed without having to invoke the repugnant notion of volition.

There is, then, a considerable philosophical tradition in opposition to the theory of volitions. Nevertheless, I believe that it is ill-founded. It will not have escaped the reader's attention that much of the so-called argument against the theory of volitions is nothing more than an intriguing exercise in philosophical rhetoric. What genuine arguments there are embedded in all of this may, I think, be fairly easily dealt with. In what follows I shall make no attempt to answer the anti-volitionists point for point but shall settle simply for addressing myself to their more important criticisms.

I think that it is a measure of the weakness of the anti-volitionists' position that their alternative accounts of deciding, choosing, and so on are so obviously wanting. To consider their preferred account of choosing: surely it is plainly false that a chosen act is identical with the choosing of the act. May not a person, whose arm is paralyzed and who is ignorant of this fact, choose nevertheless that his arm should rise? (I am here talking of that type of choice that in Chapter 9 was called choice$_2$.) Surely he may, and yet just as surely his arm will not rise (at least, if it does rise, its rising will not be of his choosing).

Moreover, it is surely not the case, as Evans claims, or at least not obviously the case, that the proposition expressed by the sentence "I chose to do *A* but did not do it" is self-contradictory. W.D.Glasgow points out that the seeming oddness of such a sentence is due to the fact that "chose," when so used, normally performs an "umbrella" function and is used to mean the same as "chose and did."[24] It is obviously inconsistent for a person to say "I chose and did *A* but did not do it."[25] But, when "chose" does not perform an "umbrella" function, there is nothing inconsistent in saying "I chose to do *A* but did not do it." After all, a person may choose to take a vacation and never live to see his choice fulfilled. In fact, when the distinction between the concepts of choice$_1$ and choice$_2$ is made explicit, it is clear that the anti-volitionist theory of choice favored by Evans, Nowell-Smith, and Taylor is, ironically, in general unable to account for those *non*-volitional choices that I have called choices$_1$.[26]

Similarly troubling points concerning anti-volitionist theories of deciding, trying, and so on may be raised, I believe. But the most telling point of all is that there is no need even to entertain such alternative theories, for the anti-volitionists' criticisms of the theory of volitions are unsound. I shall consider in turn their three most important criticisms, namely: that based, first, on the claim that the theory of volitions has no empirical basis; secondly, that based on the claim that the theory requires an infinite (and presumably vicious) regress of willing; and finally, that based on the claim that a volition and its effect must admit of logically independent descriptions.

In order to evaluate the first criticism we must ask what sort of things volitions or willings are. Two of the staunchest advocates in recent years of the theory of volitions are Wilfrid Sellars and Bruce Aune, and according to them volitions are thoughts. Sellars sometimes says that volitions are thoughts of the form "I shall now bring about *X* (or avert *Z*) by *Y*-ing" or of the form "I shall now do *A* in order to bring about (or avert) *B*."[27] Sometimes he says that they are thoughts of the form "I shall do *A* here and now."[28] Aune regards volitions to be thoughts of the form "I will do *A* here and now."[29] By stipulating that volitions are thoughts of this type of form, both philosophers apparently regard volitions to be a species of "occurrent" intention. Now, I think that talk of the "form" of thoughts is unclear and that the distinction between "occurrent" and "dispositional" intentions is also unclear. Still, there is some degree of concurrence between Sellars's and Aune's accounts and mine. It will be recalled that I have assumed that willing an event *e* implies intending it (see A.3.9), and that I have some inclination to accept that willing an event *e* implies considering it (see statement (14) of Chapter 3). Clearly, it is possible, and perhaps also necessary, for volitions to be conscious and, when they are, I see no reason to disagree with the claim made by Sellars and Aune that willing an event is having a thought which is a species of occurrent intention. The question that must now be treated is: what empirical evidence do we have that volitions occur?

Presumably, if there is any empirical evidence of volitions themselves, it will be more easy to come by in the case of conscious rather than unconscious volitions, and I shall here confine my discussion to the question of the existence of any empirical evidence of conscious volitions. Although we obviously do not have empirical evidence of all our thoughts, it is clear that we do have such evidence of some of them, if introspection (whatever that is, exactly) may be said to yield empirical evidence. I believe that introspection reveals the existence of conscious volitions. This is of necessity a personal matter, but I see absolutely no reason to bow to the assertions, so forcefully voiced by such anti-volitionists as Ryle and Taylor, to the effect that no one ever has any experience of volitions. For instance, if I attend introspectively to an occurrence of my raising my arm, it seems to me simply to be true that I am fully aware of a practical decision on my part to the effect that my arm should go up, a decision which immediately precedes my arm's going up. But perhaps the objection is, not that there is no evidence of such decisions occurring, but that there is no evidence of such decisions having the causal efficacy attributed to them by the sort of theory of action that I have espoused. But this, too, is surely false. Whatever evidence there is in general for causal contribution in cases of what Hume called "constant conjunction" – and surely it is most implausible to deny that such conjunction gives good evidence for causal contribution – is present in the constant conjunction of volitions and issues. Finally, it is appropriate to point out that the presence or absence of empirical evidence for volitions is not strictly necessary for the acceptability of a volitional account of action such as that proposed in this chapter. Simply put, theories do not have to be empirically founded to be acceptable – if they did, the acceptability of the theory of events proposed in Chapter 1 would be seriously questionable – and the anti-volitionists' insistence that the theory of volitions be empirically founded seems to me to be an outmoded legacy of logical positivism. Of course, empirical evidence of volitions cannot hurt the volitionists' attempt to render their position acceptable; but, as I have said, I believe that such evidence is forthcoming anyhow.

With regard to the second point concerning an infinite regress of willing, the proper answer to this criticism is easily given. Even though volitions are often called "acts of will," they are not in general (if ever) either actions or the issues of actions.[30] This being so, there is absolutely no ground for assuming that an infinite regress of willing arises on the theory of volitions.[31] It may seem to the reader that, in admitting that volitions are not in general (if ever) actions or the issues of actions, the volitionist is unable to provide a satisfactory theory of *free* human action. This is not so; indeed, the questions of free action and of volitions' causal relation to action seem to me entirely separate, as I shall seek to show in Chapters 11 and 12.

Finally, what of the claim that volitions and their causes ought to be independently describable? Again, this claim is entirely unwarranted. Note, first, that the anti-volitionists' point has absolutely no bearing on the analysis of the concept of action proposed in Chapter 4 where action is *unsuccessful* (for, in the case of unsuccessful action, the description of the effect of the volition, *i.e.*, of the issue of the action, will be quite independent of the description of the volition), and that, if it has any bearing at all, it has this only with respect to successful action. But this is certainly an odd situation, sufficient to give the objector pause. Moreover, Sellars argues that the logical relation between a volition and its effect, if there is one, is not that of entailment or implication but of "aboutness"; he says that, if the present objection of the anti-volitionists were sound, an analogous argument could be made to the effect that a red book could not be the cause of the perceptual belief that one is confronted with a red book.[32] This is, I think, a telling point. But perhaps it is Bruce Goldberg who, when commenting on Melden's argument as it pertains to the concept of desire in particular, has best brought out the fallacy inherent in the present criticism. Goldberg says (and his point has equal force when "volition" is substituted for "desire"):

> Melden's strongest case *seems* to be where the description of the desire includes a description of the event which it is alleged causally to explain... The general principle here seems to be that if a description of *A* involves a description of *B*, then *A* cannot be the cause of *B*. This is supposed to follow, I take it, from the incompatibility between (1) *A* does not entail *B*, and (2) a description of *B* is contained in the description of *A*. But there is no such incompatibility.[33]

Certainly, according to Hume's model of causation, to which Melden makes appeal, if *e* entails (or, simply, strictly implies) *f* then *e* is not the cause of *f*.[34] But since, as Goldberg correctly points out, *e*'s not entailing (or not implying) *f* is compatible with a description of *f* being contained in a description of *e*, there is nothing (or at least nothing that the anti-volitionists have presented) to prevent *e*'s contributing causally to *f* when a description of *f* (perhaps the only available adequate description of *f*) is contained in a description of *e* (perhaps the only available adequate description of *e*).

But perhaps the anti-volitionists' point, though this is not clear, is that a description of the "relevant bodily phenomena" *must* be contained in any adequate description of the volitions which are their alleged causes, and that it is *this* position which is incoherent. Yet this version of the argument is as poor as that just considered. First of all, it is not at all obvious that it is true that a description of a volition *must*, to be adequate, contain a description of its object. And even if this is the case, still I cannot see that there is any incompatibility between the proposition that *e* does not entail (or imply) *f* and the proposition that it is necessary that a description of *f* be contained in the description of *e*; and yet this version of the anti-volitionists' argument requires such incompatibility.

Of course, even if the foregoing responses to the main criticisms of those who oppose the concept of volition are successful, no evidence has been adduced in this chapter which can afford a conclusive demonstration that what I claim on behalf of that concept, that is, concerning the existence and nature of volitions, is true. Indeed, I know of no way to supply such demonstration; but, if there is any strength to be found in numbers (there is certainly comfort), it should be noted that the theory of volitions seems once again to be gaining support amongst philosophers. Both Sellars and Aune, as mentioned, believe that volitions occur, and they also believe that these volitions cause actions.[35] Goldman, too, has propounded a theory of action where actions are events that are always brought about by wants and normally brought about by a combination of wants and beliefs.[36] He has called this a volitional theory of action,[37] although he recognizes that volitions, though commonly regarded as a species of desire, are also commonly regarded as a species of intention.[38] Goldman's view concerning the causal connection between wants, beliefs, and actions is echoed in the writings of Kurt Baier,[39] Donald Davidson,[40] and others. And Lawrence Davis identifies actions and volitions.[41] There has, then, been considerable philosophical opinion expressed in favor of the concept of volition, and its applicability in an account of action, as well as in opposition to it, although it has been my responsibility here to pay greater attention to that which has been expressed in opposition to it.

10.3   *ANALYZING THE CONCEPT OF ACTION*

The third and final category of objections to be considered here concerns the very propriety of the attempt to analyze the concept of action. It might be said that on the present theory there is nothing really distinctive about actions that marks them off from all other events, that is, that the present account fails to highlight the peculiar nature of actions which does in fact serve to separate them from all other events.[42] For instance, Taylor and Chisholm, especially, insist that action consists (at least partly) in an event's being caused in a *special* way *by an agent,* and that no other phenomenon can boast of this.[43] In this connection, Taylor says:

> [W]hen I think and act – as distinguished from
> merely having thoughts occur to me, or having
> motions occur in my body, as in the case of my
> heartbeats or the growth and shedding of my hair
> – I seem to be *making something happen*, initiat-
> ing something, or bringing it about. I do not in
> this case just passively *undergo* changes, whether
> of body or of thought, but seem actively to *pro-
> duce* those very changes in myself and, conse-
> quently, in my environment.[4 4]

It is Taylor's contention that there is an "absolute distinction" between the concept of acting and the concept of being acted upon, and
that the concept of acting cannot be analyzed in terms of the concepts sufficient for the description of inanimate behavior or, indeed,
in terms of *any* simpler concepts.[4 5] His claim is that, in order to
give an account of action, one must invoke the concept of an active
agent and that this renders worthless the notion of action consisting
in the causal efficacy of certain mental phenomena.[4 6] He says:

> There is...an inherent implausibility in the sug-
> gestion that, whenever I can truly say that I am
> doing something, this ought to be understood to
> mean that something not identical with myself is
> the cause of whatever is being done.[4 7]

And he urges: if a volition were to cause my hand to move, but I did
not move it, my hand's moving would *not* be (or be part of) an act of
mine.[4 8] To illustrate this fact, Taylor considers the following four
sentence-schemata:

> (1) *e* occurs.
> (2) Something makes *e* occur.
> (3) *A* does *e*.
> (4) Something makes *A* do *e*.[4 9]

(Possible substitution-instances of (1) - (4) are:

> (1a) My finger moves.
> (2a) Something makes my finger move.

(3a) I move my finger.
(4a) Something makes me move my finger.)[50]

Now Taylor claims that the only entailment-relations that hold between (1) - (4) are these: (4) entails (3), (3) entails (2), and (2) entails (1). In particular, (2) does not entail (3), as the volitionists would have it.

Taylor's reasoning, however, is not persuasive. I would readily grant that, in the case of *free* action, an agent seems "actively to produce" the issues in question, but this is very different from saying that he does so in all cases of action. Suppose that determinism is true.[51] On such a supposition it would seem that any *special* type of causation that might be effected by agents would be wholly superfluous and hence it would seem that there is no reason to believe that such causation ever takes place. Yet even under such conditions, that is, even if determinism is true, there still occur such things as actions.[52] Although Taylor explicitly and repeatedly states that his theory of action is independent of the truth or falsity of determinism,[53] it seems nevertheless to be the case that his theory of action is based on an intuitive model of free (that is, undetermined) action. Taylor is of course right to point out that the only entailment-relations (or, perhaps better, implication-relations) that hold between (1) and (4) are those that he cites; but he is wrong to attribute to the volitionists the view that (2) entails (or implies) (3). The volitionists would rather say that (2b) (or something like it) entails (or implies) (3), where (2b) is as follows:

(2b) *A*'s willing that *e* should occur makes *e* occur.

There seems to be no way, simply by looking at the form of the sentence-schemata (2b) and (3) (which is the method Taylor seems to rely on), to decide whether or not (2b) entails (or implies) (3).

There may well be, I believe, a proper role for the concept of a special type of agent-causation to play in a theory of action (that is, a type of agent-causation which is *not* reducible to event-causation in the fashion indicated at the end of Section 3.1 of Chapter 3). But, *contra* the contentions of Taylor and Chisholm, this role is not that of providing an opportunity for an account of the concept of action in general, but rather that of providing an opportunity for an account of the concept of *free* action. Indeed, it is tempting to think that Taylor and Chisholm, by considering agent-causation (of the special sort) to be necessary for *all* action, free and unfree, have misapplied the insight which led them to embrace the concept of agent-causation in the first place. For instance, it seems clear that Chisholm first latched on to the concept of a special type of agent-causation when seeking a solution to the well-known problem that the ascription of moral responsibility to persons for (certain of) their actions appears to be inconsistent both with the supposition that determinism is true and with the supposition that indeterminism is true (and yet either determinism or its contradictory, indeterminism, must be true).[54] Chisholm's solution, very roughly, is that a person may be morally responsible for his actions because *he* contributes causally to them. When first presenting this solution, Chisholm likened the agent to a "prime mover unmoved"[55] and characterized agent-causation thus:

> In doing what we do, we cause certain events to
> happen, and nothing – or no one – causes us to
> cause those events to happen.[56]

Chisholm would no longer accept this as completely accurate, however. In *Person and Object* he does *not* say that "nothing or no one" causes a person to contribute causally to certain events; rather, he says that the person himself contributes causally to his own causal contributions. This is required, according to Chisholm, because the problem of the ascription of moral responsibility being consistent with the truth of indeterminism would arise once again if there were no cause at all (*i.e.*, neither an event-cause nor an agent-cause) of a person's contributing causally to an event. Hence, a necessary condition of a person's being morally responsible for an event is that he contribute causally both to it and to his causal contributions.

It is not clear whether or not, when he first introduced the concept of agent-causal contribution, Chisholm thought that an agent's contributing causally to an event was not only necessary but also sufficient for his being morally responsible for it. If he did, then he would have had the sort of criterion that he was looking for, a criterion by which one might distinguish those events for which one is morally responsible from those for which one is not. Be that as it may, by the time he wrote *Person and Object* Chisholm certainly did *not* believe that an agent's contributing causally to an event is sufficient for his being morally responsible for it. For there he contends that, *whenever* one acts, one contributes causally to an event; and yet (reasonably enough) he does not accept that, whenever one acts, one incurs moral responsibility for an event. Indeed, in *Person and Object* he implicitly accepts the view that an agent *S* is morally responsible for an event *e* only if *e* is within *S*'s power, and that *e* is within *S*'s power only if there is an event *f* which *S* is free to undertake. Moreover, he says that it is not the case that everything that one undertakes is such that one is free to undertake it.[57] But, this being the case, there has clearly been a shift in emphasis over the years in Chisholm's use of the concept of agent-causal contribution. Originally invoked to handle the thorny problem of how it can be that one sometimes is and sometimes is not morally responsible for one's actions (and other events), the concept of agent-causal contribution comes to be used by Chisholm in *Person and Object* to characterize *all* action, whether or not moral responsibility is incurred as a result of performing an action. The shift is perhaps understandable, but it results in a loss of explanatory power. As originally conceived, the concept of agent-causation (of a special sort) seemed to be useful as a tool for solving the problem just mentioned concerning the ascription of moral responsibility. But when applied to *all* action, including that for which the agent is *not* morally responsible, the concept seems no longer to be useful in this respect. Nor does it seem useful in any other respect. In particular, if agent-causation (of a special sort) and agent-causation alone is regarded as *both* a necessary *and* a sufficient condition for *all* action (and this is how both Taylor and Chisholm *seem* to regard it), and if the concept of such causation is regarded as unanalyzable (as Taylor regards it, and apparently Chisholm also[58]), then the concept of action is effectively cut off from analysis. Hence, invocation of the concept of agent-causation in this manner serves to render human action far more mysterious than I have taken it to be in this work. Taylor, clearly, is prepared to accept this consequence, and perhaps Chisholm is also; but I am not. More to the point, I have sought to show in this section that there is no *necessity* that this consequence be accepted *a priori*; in particular, there is no necessity that the concept of action be allied with some concept of a special sort of agent-causation, and there is no necessity that the concept of action be regarded as immune to analysis.

The concept of a special sort of agent-causation will be discussed further in the next two chapters, where its role in providing a coherent account of *free* action (and, thereby, an account of the ascribability of moral responsibility to persons for certain states of affairs) will be considered in greater detail. But at this point my exposition and defense of the present theory of action is completed. It is clear that the theory could be filled out in various ways. For instance, closer attention could be paid to the concepts of a part, a purpose, a means, an end, a reason, deliberation, and so on, some of which have received only cursory discussion in the preceding chapters, and some of which have not been discussed at all. Nevertheless, I believe that the truly key concepts have been adequately discussed, and the project that I wish now to undertake is that of giving a tentative, but fairly detailed, account of *free* human action. The remaining two chapters will be concerned with the completion of this project.

Notes

1   Thomson (1977), pp.44-5.

2   Baier (1970), pp.648, 649, 652; Baier (1977), p.398. See also Audi (1973).

3   I shall not attempt to furnish an account of the sense of "involves" (as used *here*, and its use here is not to be confused with its use in D.1.4) or "constituent." I assume that these terms are fairly readily, even if roughly, understood.

4   Ryle (1949), p.62ff.

5   Taylor (1966), pp.49-50.

6   Taylor (1966), pp.65-7.

7   Taylor (1966), p.68.

8   Taylor (1966), pp.68-9.

9   Taylor (1966), p.71.

10   Taylor (1966), pp.72-4, 78.

11   Taylor (1966), pp.116-7.

12   Hart (1968). Hart has in mind in particular the theory of volition propounded by John Austin, in which volition is taken to be a form of desire.

13   D'Arcy (1963), p.99.

14   Wittgenstein (1953), Section 611ff.

15   Anscombe (1969), Section 7ff.

16   Danto (1963, 1965).

17   Melden (1961), p.45.

18   Melden (1961), pp.46, 77, 78, 80, 113, 114, 116-7, 202-3.

19   Melden (1961), p.53.

20   Melden (1961), pp.48-50.

21   Evans (1955).

22   Nowell-Smith (1958), p.68.

23   Taylor (1966), pp.76, 77, 79-84.

24   Glasgow (1957).

25   The "umbrella" function of "chose" is more often in evidence when "chose" is followed by a noun, in which case it means the

same as "chose and took," as in "He chose tea rather than coffee."

26   Nichols (1973, p.51) raises a similar point.

27   Sellars (1966a), p.109.

28   Sellars (1976), p.47.

29   Aune (1977), p.63ff.

30   There is no necessity that a person not will to will, but the only occasions for this that I can think of (at least, for a rational person) are either when the resolution of some overly long deliberation is required or when an attempt is made to gather introspective evidence of volitions.

31   Both Sellars (1966b, pp.156-7; 1969, p.243) and Goldman (1976, pp.68-9) have stressed this point.

32   Sellars (1969), pp.243-5.

33   Goldberg (1965), p.72.

34   On the distinction between entailment and strict implication, see D.1.8 and D.1.9. Notice that, on the present finely-grained ontology of events, Hume's thesis must be modified to be acceptable. See A.3.6.

35   Sellars (1966b, pp.144, 150, 159; 1976, p.49); Aune (1977, p.44). In fact, Aune concedes this point only on the assumption that there are such things as actions, an assumption which he is reluctant to make. Nevertheless, he would be prepared to accept an analogous relation between willing and acting even in a theory of agency according to which there are no such things as actions. (Note: I would rather say "issues" than "actions" in this context.)

36   Goldman (1970), pp.67, 72-6.

37 Goldman (1976), p.67.

38 Goldman (1976), p.68; see also Grice (1971), p.277. My disagreement with Goldman's characterization of the concept of volition is encapsulated in my denial that an analogue of statement (10) of Chapter 3, where "wills" replaces "intends," is true and my assertion that A.3.9 is true.

39 Baier (1965), p.193.

40 Davidson (1963), pp.4, 5, 12.

41 Davis (1979), Chapter 1.

42 This sort of objection is raised by Taylor (1966) (see the notes that follow for detailed references), by Frankfurt (1978), p.157ff., and, perhaps most recently, by Brand (1979).

43 Taylor (1966), pp.111-2; Chisholm (1976), Chapter 2.

44 Taylor (1966), p.13.

45 Taylor (1966), pp.60-1.

46 Taylor (1966), pp.74, 109, 111.

47 Taylor (1966), pp.110-1.

48 Taylor (1966), p.113.

49 Taylor (1966), pp.123, 165.

50 Of course, (1a) through (4a) do not exactly match the form of (1) through (4), but the principle of substitution being implicitly applied should be obvious enough.

51 By "determinism" I mean, roughly, the doctrine that there is a sufficient causal condition of every event. See D.3.2.

52 Unger's argument (1977) to the contrary notwithstanding. See

note 7 to Chapter 11.

53   Taylor (1966), pp.113-5, 128-9, 263.

54   Chisholm poses the problem, sans solution, in Chisholm (1958).
     See Section 11.1 of Chapter 11 below.

55   Chisholm (1966), p.20.

56   Chisholm (1966), p.23.

57   Chisholm (1976), Chapter 2, Section 3.

58   I say "apparently," for although Chisholm *does* present (1976,
     p.70) a definition of "*S* (an agent) contributes causally at *t* to
     p " (indeed, this definition is explicitly presented in order to
     "bridge the gap" between agent- and event-causation), he *also*
     implies (1964; 1966; 1970b; 1971a; 1976, p.66) that compre-
     hension of the concept of undertaking, which he invokes unan-
     alyzed, requires comprehension of the concept of agent-causa-
     tion – and yet the concept of undertaking features in the
     definiens of the definition just mentioned.

PART III
FREE HUMAN ACTION

Chapter 11

A LIBERTARIAN ACCOUNT OF FREEDOM OF ACTION

11.1 *BACKGROUND TO THE ACCOUNT*

Just as not all action is intentional action, so not all action is free action. But, as in the case of intentional action, philosophers sometimes forget this fact; some even deny it. The sort of freedom of action with which I wish to concern myself here is that which is, in my opinion and the opinion of many others, necessary for a person's being morally responsible for some state of affairs. The sort of account of freedom of action that I wish *tentatively* to propose is one which implies the falsity of the second premise in the following familiar argument:

> (1) If determinism is true, then no one ever acts freely.
> (2) If indeterminism is true, then no one ever acts freely.
> (3) Either determinism is true or indeterminism is true.
> (4) If a person is morally responsible for some state of affairs, then he is acting or has acted freely.
> Therefore
> (5) No one is ever morally responsible for any state of affairs.

But all of this requires careful introduction.

It has often been assumed, by philosophers of quite disparate persuasions, that each of the first two of the following three propositions implies its successor:

(6)   *S* (a person) is morally responsible for *a* (an action).

(7)   *S* does (or did) *a* freely.

(8)   *S* can do (or could have done) other than *a.*

But there are major problems with this assumption, even when we overlook the manifestly rough presentation of these propositions.[1] There are two such problems that I wish to point to in particular. The first concerns the fact that it is fairly apparent that (6) does *not* imply (7). This fact has been widely recognized. If Smith freely takes a drug, which he knows from experience will induce in him an irresistible desire to commit violence, and then, as a result, commits violence, it seems correct to say that he is morally responsible for committing violence (and for the damage that results therefrom), even though his doing so was something he could not resist. But, if this case undermines the contention that (6) implies (7) – and I presume that it does – it does *not* undermine, indeed it seems to confirm, the contention that (6) implies the following proposition:

(7')   Either *S* does (or did) *a* freely, or there is an ac-
              tion *b* such that *S* did *b* freely and *a* is (or was) a
              consequence of *b*.

Hence, freedom of action still seems to be a necessary condition of moral responsibility. So that the "chain of implication" from "morally responsible" through "free" to "can do otherwise" may be preserved on this modification of (7) to (7'), (8) may be correspondingly modified as follows:

(8')   Either *S* can do (or could have done) other than *a,*
              or there is an action *b* such that *S* could have
              done other than *b* and *a* is (or was) a consequence
              of *b*.

But at this point the second major problem arises, and that is that it is arguable that the chain of implication breaks down even when the propositions which feature in it are modified as above. This claim (or something very close to it) is presented by Harry Frankfurt in a paper that has excited a good deal of comment.[2] Actually, the claim to which Frankfurt explicitly addresses himself is the following:

(9)   A person is morally responsible for what he has
done only if he could have done otherwise.

But, if Frankfurt is right (and I shall not attempt here to determine
whether or not he is right[3]), the question that arises is: given that
(6) does not imply (8'), *which* of the following claims is false: (6)
implies (7'), or (7') implies (8')? It seems to me arguable that, if
Frankfurt is right at all, it is only the *latter* of these claims that is
false.[4] If this is so – and I shall henceforth assume that it is – then
the force of the dilemma that was presented in the opening paragraph of this chapter is not at all diminished, Frankfurt notwithstanding. That is, premise (4) may still be seen to be true and still
be seen to constitute (along with the surely undeniable premise (3))
the common ground in the debate between compatibilists and incompatibilists.

But perhaps I am proceeding too quickly. What, after all, are
"compatibilists" and "incompatibilists," and what is the debate between them? A compatibilist is one who rejects premise (1); more
precisely, he is one who believes the truth of determinism to be
compatible with the (metaphysical) *possibility* that some person act
freely; an incompatibilist is one who denies this compatibility (and
hence accepts premise (1)). In order to render this debate compre-
hensible, I must say what I mean here by "determinism." But this
is a straightforward matter. I mean by "determinism" the proposition that every event is caused by an event or, more precisely, the
proposition that, for any event e and any time T, if e occurs at T,
then there are an event f and a time T' such that f contributes causally relative to T' and T to e.[5] (It is important to note that, given
A.3.2, it follows from this definition of "determinism" that, if determinism is true, there is a *sufficient causal condition* of every event
that occurs.) By "indeterminism" I mean the contradictory of determinism. Now, traditionally (though by no means necessarily),
compatibilists have been determinists, and the position that they
advocate has come to be known as "soft determinism." Incompatibilists have not been so united. Some have been and are determinists (and the position that they advocate has come to be known as
"hard determinism"[6]); others have been and are indeterminists.
The former (given their acceptance of premise (4)) are committed to
the truth of (5); the latter are not so committed. Indeed, traditionally (though again not necessarily), indeterminists have been

advocates both of incompatibilism and of the falsity of premise (2), and it is their advocacy of the latter which, in their eyes, "salvages" moral responsibility.[7] Such incompatibilists have come to be called "libertarians." In recent years, the compatibilist-incompatibilist debate has in fact been, for the most part, a soft determinist-libertarian debate; both parties to the debate are committed to the falsity of (5), that is, they are committed to showing how it is that some people may be, indeed are, morally responsible for some states of affairs.

Usually, compatibilists – adhering, often tacitly, to the claim that (7') implies (8') – have attempted to argue for the truth of their position by providing a definition of the phrase "he could have done otherwise" according to which the truth of determinism does not rule out the possibility that a person can do otherwise than he does. The vast majority of such attempts have been based on a "conditional" analysis of "can," an analysis which conforms roughly to the pattern: S can do a if and only if he would do a if he chose. This is a tradition which stems from Hobbes (if not before) and continues to the present day.[8] Any such attempt with which I am familiar seems to me to fall victim to an argument of the sort presented by both Chisholm and Keith Lehrer.[9] But I shall not seek to demonstrate this here; for my purpose is not to refute compatibilism. Indeed, even if one admits that the "conditional" analysis of "can" is defective, this does not of course require one to admit that compatibilism is false. In fact, Lehrer himself attempts to defend compatibilism by providing an alternative analysis of "can" in terms of possible worlds.[10] In my opinion, the analysis that Lehrer provides, even if correct, lends no clear support to compatibilism. I have argued this elsewhere, however, and so, once again, I shall not pursue the issue here.[11] For it is of course still true that, even if Lehrer's analysis fails to lend support to compatibilism, compatibilism may yet be true. Nevertheless, the following points should be noted. The only truly sustained efforts to support compatibilism to date seem to have been those provided in the tradition of Hobbes on the one hand and that provided by Lehrer on the other. If both are defective, then compatibilism remains essentially unsupported. Moreover, both appear to be premised on the claim that (7') implies (8'); if this claim is false, the efforts seem irrelevant to the issue at hand. Now, none of this shows compatibilism to be false; indeed, I know of no way to show this. But I am inclined to think that it is false, and so what I want to do here is to construct in some detail an incompatibilist account of free human action, an account that is based on the theory of action provided in the foregoing chapters. I shall call this account not just incompatibilist but libertarian. Strictly speaking, this is somewhat inaccurate. What I am primarily interested in giving is an account of freedom of action which implies the falsity of premise (2) of the argument presented at the outset of this chapter. Now, a determinist can consistently reject (2); but it is clearly the libertarian whose position is *founded* on the falsity of (2). Even though the account that follows does not go beyond a rejection of (2) to the claim that determinism is indeed false, the underlying purpose of its presentation is that of seeing how much can be done to "clear the way" for libertarianism, and it is as a reminder of this purpose that I call the account a libertarian one. Finally, let me stress here that what follows is a *tentative* proposal. Just why it is tentative will become clear in the next chapter, where objections to the account will be entertained.

11.2   *THE ACCOUNT*

The libertarian account of freedom of action that is to be given in this section is not only tentatively proposed; it is also severely restricted. The nature of this restriction can best be brought out by means of a familiar example. Suppose that Smith walks into a bank, goes up to Jones (a teller), points a gun at Jones, and orders him to hand over all the money in the till. Suppose that Jones does so. Is Jones morally responsible for handing over the money? This question is, on investigation, a tricky one. But I think that the proper answer, after such investigation (and I shall not undertake such investigation here), is the same as that to which we are initially inclined, and that is that Jones is *not* morally responsible for handing over the money to Smith. (At least, this is so in the absence of any further information.) *Why* is Jones not morally responsible for handing over the money? Because he acted under extreme duress; he was strongly coerced to act as he did; he did not act freely; he had no choice in the matter; he could not have done otherwise.

Rough as it is, this analysis of the case seems to me essentially correct. But note that, while it seems correct to say that, in a sense, Jones did not act freely (he had no choice in the matter, he could not have done otherwise), it *also* seems correct to say that, in a sense, he *did* act freely (he *did* have a choice in the matter — not a pleasant one, admittedly — and he *could* have refused to hand over the money). I propose that we distinguish two senses of "freedom" (and of "choice," and of "can") here and that we say that, in the *broad* sense, Jones did *not* act freely (he had *no* choice, he could *not* have done otherwise), while, in the *strict* sense, he *did* act freely (he *did* have a choice, he *could* have done otherwise). Given this rough distinction, it is apparent that the example shows that premise (4) may be understood so that "freely" is taken in the broad sense. But I think that premise (4) also holds true where "freely" is understood in the strict sense; and it is in *this* sense that I propose to take it here. That is, I shall seek here to provide a libertarian account of *strict* freedom only; how to supplement this so that an account of broad freedom emerges is a matter that I shall leave entirely to one side. The reasons for this restriction are basically three in number. First, it seems to me that libertarians have traditionally been primarily concerned with giving an account of strict freedom of action,[1][2] and it is at this basic level of freedom that they have injected the element of indeterminism; secondly, I think it correct to seek the element of indeterminism at this level; thirdly, I do not really know how to supplement an account of strict freedom so that an account of broad freedom may emerge.[1][3]

In their accounts of freedom of action, libertarians appeal almost without fail to a concept which has traditionally been called the concept of agent-causation. There is good reason for appealing to this concept. As will be seen, it is the linchpin of the libertarian account. But the name "agent-causation" is unfortunate, since it conjures up the notion of (event-)causal contribution; yet the concepts of agent-causation and (event-)causal contribution have little in common, and any attempt to compare them is liable to mislead. For this reason, I prefer to talk of *"agent-effectuation"* rather than agent-causation.[1][4] Nevertheless, it should be acknowledged that the concepts of causal contribution and agent-effectuation (or, as I shall henceforth call it, effectuation) have a common origin; hence the tendency to confuse them.

We may, I think, trace the origin of the concept of effectuation at least as far back as to the writings of Aristotle. Aristotle of course distinguishes various kinds of cause.[15] But of particular note is his discussion of the concept of an efficient cause.[16] He seems to say that an efficient cause is always a substance; what it causes may be the generation of another substance or a change in another substance.[17] There is at least *prima facie* evidence, then, that Aristotle regards efficient causation to be a relation that holds between substances on the one hand and events on the other (though just how events fit into his ontology is unclear). Prior to this century, the most forceful advocate of the concept of effectuation in modern times is Thomas Reid. Action, he says, is the exertion of "active power," and whatever exerts such power is the cause of the changes that such exertion brings about.[18] The means of such exertion, according to Reid, is the agent's will.[19] A person is free in so far as he, and not some other agent, is the cause of the "determination" of his will.[20] Indeed, Reid does not explicitly discuss the possibility that causation be a relation that binds an *event* to an event.[21] Immanuel Kant does explicitly discuss this possibility, however, but also seeks to distinguish between agent-causation and event-causation.[22] According to him, a rational agent may himself be the cause of effects that take place in the phenomenal world.[23] In this century, C.A. Campbell stands out as a strong supporter of the concept of effectuation. He insists that, for an agent to act freely, he must be the sole cause of his act.[24] According to Campbell, free action is, in some sense, a matter of "self-determination."[25] Richard Taylor, with the sort of argument concerning moral responsibility given at the outset of this chapter explicitly in mind, is just as insistent that the concept of effectuation be accorded its proper place in the philosophy of action.[26] But Taylor, as we saw in the last chapter, regards *all* action, and not just free action, as essentially involving this concept. Finally, as we also saw in the last chapter, Chisholm's theory of action is also dependent on this concept.[27] The fact that some prominent philosophers have espoused the concept of effectuation should not of course be taken to provide conclusive evidence that this concept is applicable to the situations to which they take it to be applicable. Indeed, it is not at all clear that it is exactly the same concept that is invoked by each of these philosophers. Nevertheless, it is from such philosophers' writings that the concept of effectuation to which I shall appeal is drawn, and the use to which I shall put this concept is strongly influenced by these writings.

Rather than talk of (agent-)effectuation *simpliciter*, I think that it will be useful to distinguish two types of effectuation, to wit, direct and indirect effectuation. The unanalyzed concept will be that of direct effectuation, and the primitive locution that I shall adopt is: "*S* directly effectuates *e*." A partial characterization of the concept of direct effectuation is contained in the following assumptions:

A.11.1:   Necessarily, if *S* directly effectuates *e* at *T*, then
          (i) *S* is a person and *S* exists at *T*, and
          (ii) *e* is an event and *e* occurs at *T*.[28]

A.11.2:   Necessarily, if *S* directly effectuates *e* at *T*, then there is no event *f* which strictly implies *e* and which is such that, for some time *T'* not later than *T*, there is a sufficient causal condition relative to *T'* and *T* of *f*.

A.11.3:   Necessarily, if *S* directly effectuates *e* at *T*, then *S* directly effectuates [*S* directly effectuates *e*] at *T*.[29]

A.11.4:   Necessarily, if *S* directly effectuates *e* at *T* and there is no event *f* such that *e* strictly implies [*S* directly effectuates *f*], then there is an event *f* such that *e* strictly implies [*S* decides *f*].[30]

And we may say:

D.11.1:   *S* indirectly effectuates *e* relative to *T* and *T'* =df. there is an event *f* such that:
          (i) *S* directly effectuates *f* at *T* ; and
          (ii) *f* contributes causally relative to *T* and *T'* to *e*.[31]

This calls for some comment. A.11.1 is, I think, self-explanatory. A.11.2 and A.11.3, combined, are intended to constitute the essential weaponry needed in the libertarian's attack on premise (2). Roughly put, A.11.2 ensures that whatever is agent-caused is not event-caused; this expresses the indeterministic underpinnings of libertarianism. A.11.3 ensures that every agent-causing is itself agent-caused; this constitutes the libertarian attempt to rebut the objection that, if an event occurs un-(event-)caused, it occurs "out of the blue" and cannot be in any person's "control" (in the sense of "control" supposed to be essential to freedom of action). Of course, the libertarian is aware of this sort of objection; hence his invocation of the concept of direct effectuation to begin with. That is, the libertarian seeks to counter the objection that any event that occurs un-(event-)caused lies beyond anyone's control by pointing to direct effectuation as the source of a person's control over an un-(event-)caused event. But, in doing this, he is tacitly conceding that an event which is neither (event-)caused nor directly effectuated *does* lie beyond anyone's control, and so, unless he assumed A.11.3, he would be open to the objection that direct effectuations are *themselves* beyond the agent's control, and, if this were so, then any reason to assume that what is directly effectuated is under the agent's control would appear undermined.[3][2] A.11.4 allows us to say, roughly, that, whenever an agent directly effectuates an event which is not itself a direct effectuation, then that event is a decision by the agent. (It should be recalled — see T.9.5 — that every volition is a decision.) Finally, D.11.1 is of use to one who attempts to give an account of moral responsibility based in part on the notion that an agent is morally responsible not only for some of his free actions but also for some of the consequences of those actions.

Armed with A.11.1 through A.11.4, we may proceed to give a libertarian analysis of what it is to act freely. Such analysis must be undertaken piecemeal. First, we need the concept of an agent's being free to will something. Roughly, we may say that an agent is free to will an event just in case there is no sufficient causal condition either of his doing so or of his not doing so. More precisely:

D.11.2: S is free at T to will e at T' in order that f may occur =df. for any time T^* not later than T:

(i) there is no sufficient causal condition relative
to T^* and T' of [S wills e in order that f may oc-
cur]; and
(ii) there is no event g such that
(a) it is physically necessary that, if g occurs
at T', then S does not will e at T' in order that f
may occur, and
(b) there is a sufficient causal condition relative to T^* and T' of g.

Clause (ii) would be simpler if it read "there is no sufficient causal
condition relative to T^* and T' of [S does not will e in order that f
may occur]," but [S does not will e in order that f may occur] is not
an event, and so this reading would be inadequate. Why have such
a clause at all? If such a clause were not included, then it might be
physically impossible, given the conditions that obtain at T, for [S
wills e in order that f may occur] to occur at T', and this certainly
seems inconsistent, from an incompatibilist point of view, with S's
being free at T to will e at T' in order that f may occur.[33] We may
also say that a person freely wills an event when he directly effectuates his volition. That is:

D.11.3: S freely wills e at T in order that f may occur
            =df. S directly effectuates [S wills e in order that
            f may occur] at T.

This is an important definition; for, to put it roughly, it is whether
or not an action is freely willed that determines whether or not it is
freely performed. (Note that, given A.11.1 through A.11.3, [S
freely wills e at T in order that f may occur] implies both [S wills e
at T] and [S is free at T to will e at T in order that f may occur].)
Definitions analogous to D.11.2 and D.11.3 may be drawn up for
the purpose of defining the phrases "S is free at T to decide e at T,"
"S freely decides e at T," "S is free at T to choose e at T," "S freely
chooses e at T," and so on. (Consult D.9.1 through D.9.5.) But I
shall forego giving these definitions here.

    Given that, on the sort of libertarian account that I am con-
structing here, freedom of volition determines whether or not one
acts freely, the analysis of what it is to act freely is fairly easily

given. We may say, on the basis of the definitions provided in Chapter 4, the following:

D.11.4: S freely$_1$ brings about e directly relative to T and T' =df. there are events f and g such that:
(i) S freely wills f at T in order that g may occur:
(ii) [S wills f in order that g may occur] contributes causally relative to T and T' to f; and
(iii) f constitutes e at T'.

Note that the only feature that distinguishes the definiens of D.11.4 from that of D.4.7 (where "S brings about e directly relative to T and T'''" is defined) is the addition of "freely" to clause (i) in the former. This is, however, an important feature. (The reason for talking of "freedom$_1$" rather than just "freedom" will become clear shortly.) An analysis of the concept of freely$_1$ bringing about an event indirectly can be given along the same lines as D.4.8, with D.11.4 incorporated, and the result is the following:

D.11.5: S freely$_1$ brings about e indirectly relative to T and T' =df. there are an event f and a time T^* such that:
(i) S freely$_1$ brings about f directly relative to T and T^*; and
(ii) f contributes causally relative to T^* and T' to e.

Note that the only distinguishing feature is the addition of "freely$_1$" to clause (i). Finally, an analysis of the concept of freely$_1$ bringing about an event synthetically can be given along the lines of D.4.10, with D.11.4 and D.11.5 incorporated, and the result is the following (presented schematically):

D.11.6: S freely$_1$ brings about e synthetically relative to T and T' =df. there are events $f1,...,fn$ and a time T''' such that:
(i) (as in clause (i) of D.4.10); and
(ii) (preamble as in clause (ii) of D.4.10)

        (a) (as in subclause (a) of clause (ii) of
D.4.10), and
        (b) either
            (1) S freely$_1$ brings about f directly rela-
tive to T^* and T^{**}, or
            (2) S freely$_1$ brings about f indirectly rela-
tive to T^* and T^{**}.

Once again, the only distinguishing feature is the addition of
"freely$_1$" to subclause (b) of clause (ii). And then we may of course
say:

D.11.7: S freely$_1$ brings about e actively relative to T and
          T' =df. either
          (i) S freely$_1$ brings about e directly relative to T
          and T'; or
          (ii) S freely$_1$ brings about e indirectly relative to
          T and T'; or
          (iii) S freely$_1$ brings about e synthetically relative
          to T and T'.

And, finally, we may say:

D.11.8: S freely$_1$ acts relative to T and T' =df. there is
          an event e such that S freely$_1$ brings about e ac-
          tively relative to T and T'.

    The foregoing account is, I hope, clear enough. One limitation
(that it is restricted to an account of *strict* freedom) has already
been noted. Another limitation should now be noted. The account
says nothing of the concept of "can." We cannot tell whether the
account sanctions the inference – as it surely ought – from "S freely
brings about e" to "S can bring about e." Indeed, the account
seems *not* to sanction the inference from "S can bring about e" to
"S can do otherwise," an inference which, if Frankfurt is wrong, it
apparently ought to sanction. I shall now endeavor to get rid of this
second limitation.
    Compatibilists, we have seen, have often tendered this definition
of "can": S can do a if and only if he would do a if he chose. Some-

times one finds "wanted," "tried," or some such verb, in place of "chose"; but the weight of tradition is in favor of "chose." Given the account of human action in earlier chapters, it is obvious that this definition of "can" requires revision before it can be considered even initially plausible. First, it is questionable whether the concept of choice is in fact best suited for the role which it plays in the definition. The closely related concept of willing would appear more appropriate here.[34] For the concept of choice (see D.9.5) involves the concept of an alternative, whereas the concept of willing does not; and the concept of an alternative seems more pertinent (if pertinent at all) to the matter of what one is *free* to do rather than to the matter of what one *can* do. Secondly, the fact that the definition requires that what would actually occur, if the choice were made, be identical with the object of choice (the event is designated by "a" in both cases) suggests that, even if otherwise adequate, it would be unable to account for those actions which one can perform but which, were one to perform them, would be instances of unsuccessful action (see D.6.2). Thirdly, the definition glosses over the distinction between direct, indirect, and synthetic action (see D.4.7, D.4.8, and D.4.10); one would suspect that this distinction would play a role in constructing an adequate account of the concept of "can," just as it did in constructing an adequate account of the concept of action in general. Finally, there is no mention of times in the definition, and this is a grave omission. In fact, three distinct designations of times should be made, namely, that of the time at which the "can" in question is operative and those to which the bringing about in question is relative.[35] For instance, there are presumably many things that I can now do, some of which I can now do now and some of which I can now do later. An adequate account of "can" must be able to deal with all such cases.

Given these considerations, it would appear that the phrase that is in need of definition in this context is not "S can do a" but rather "S can at T bring about e actively relative to T' and T^*." But it is plausible to assume that, in order to arrive at a definition of this phrase, one must first arrive at definitions of each of "S can at T bring about e directly relative to T' and T^*," "S can at T bring about e indirectly relative to T' and T^*," and "S can at T bring about e synthetically relative to T' and T^*." Moreover, it appears that, in order to arrive at a definition of the phrase "S can at T bring about e directly relative to T' and T^*" one must first arrive at a definition of the phrase "*S* can immediately at *T* bring about *e* directly relative to *T* and *T'*." The distinction between these last two phrases (highlighted by the presence of "immediately" in the second and its absence from the first) concerns the times to which the bringing about of *e* is said to be relative. In the second, one of these times (that designated by "*T* ") is stipulated as being the same as that at which the "can" is operative; in the first, no such stipulation is made. This distinction between the phrases reflects the fact that "cans" may operate on actions not in the immediate future as well as on actions in the immediate future. For instance, I can now stop writing now; but I can also now start writing tomorrow. In fact, some of the "cans" that now apply to me have no definite limit in the future. Suppose that someone discovers the secret of immortality, harnesses it in a pill, and that I take this pill twenty years from now; if this is possible, it may (for all I know) be true that I can *now* read a book not just in 1983 but in 8983. An adequate account of "can" must accommodate this possibility. Or let us take a more mundane example. I can immediately stop writing. However, I cannot immediately drink from a glass of water, for I am sitting at my desk in my study and the nearest glass is in the kitchen; but I can now drink from a glass of water in a very short while, for the kitchen is just a few yards away. I need not do anything first in order to stop writing; that is (partly) why I can immediately stop writing. I must do something first if I am to drink from a glass of water; I must stop writing, get up out of my chair, walk a few yards, open the door, go into the kitchen, and so on. In a case such as that of my drinking from a glass of water, I can now perform this action by virtue of the fact that I can immediately perform some other action (that of ceasing to write) and, if I were to perform this action, I would then be in such a position that I could *immediately* perform another action, and then another, and then another, and so on until I could *immediately* drink from a glass of water.

Given the foregoing, it is apparent that one's first attempt at defining "can" ought to be by way of defining the phrase "*S* can immediately at *T* bring about *e* directly relative to *T* and *T'*." Now, a definition of this phrase may be drawn up in traditional compatibilist spirit as follows:

D.11.9.a: *S* can immediately at *T* bring about *e* directly relative to *T* and *T'* =df. there are events *f* and *g*
such that, if *S* were to will *f* at *T* in order that *g*
might occur, then
(i) [*S* wills *f* in order that *g* may occur] would
contribute causally relative to *T* and *T'* to *f*, and
(ii) *f* would constitute *e* at *T'*.

(Compare D.4.7.) But I have already noted that such a definition
seems to me defective, given the sort of argument presented by
Chisholm and Lehrer.[3][6] Moreover, the definition is of course *com-
patibilistic* and thus inconsistent with my current libertarian enterprise. However, it seems to me that both problems may be circum-
vented by amending the definition so that it explicitly incorporates
the notion of freedom of volition. What results is the following
slightly, but importantly, amended version of D.11.9.a:

D.11.9.b: *S* can immediately at *T* bring about *e* directly relative to *T* and *T'* =df. there are events *f* and *g*
such that:
(i) *S* is free at *T* to will *f* at *T* in order that *g*
may occur; and
(ii) if *S* were to will *f* at *T* in order that *g* might
occur, then
(a) [*S* wills *f* in order that *g* may occur] would
contribute causally relative to *T* and *T'* to *f*, and
(b) *f* would constitute *e* at *T'*.

Now, this definition is restricted to "can *immediately,*" but, using the
water-drinking case as a cue, we may, I think, properly say that a
person can (in general) bring about an event *e* directly just in case
there is some event *f* which he can immediately bring about directly
and, if *e* is distinct from *f*, then, if he were to bring about *f* directly,
this would put him "one step closer" to being in such a position that
he could *immediately* bring about *e* directly. More precisely, where 1
is less than or equal to *i* and *i* is less than or equal to *n*:

D.11.10:   *S* can at *T* bring about *e* directly relative to *T'* and
T* =df. there are events *f1*,...,*fn*, a time *T'''*, and
times *T1*,...,*Tn* such that:

    (i) T is not later than T''';

    (ii) T'' is not later than $T1$, and..., and $Tn\text{-}1$ is not later than Tn ;

    (iii) $Tn\text{-}1$ is identical with T';

    (iv) Tn is identical with T^*;

    (v) fn is identical with e ;

    (vi) S can immediately at T''' bring about $f1$ directly relative to T''' and $T1$; and

    (vii) if $f1$ is distinct from fn, then for any event fi and for any time Ti, if S were to bring about fi directly relative to $Ti\text{-}1$ and Ti, then S could immediately at Ti bring about $fi+1$ directly relative to Ti and $Ti+1$.[3][7]

Of course, this definition deals only with the direct bringing about of an event, and not with action in general. However, given D.11.10, and keeping D.4.8 in mind, we may say the following:

D.11.11: S can at T bring about e indirectly relative to T' and T^* =df. there are an event f and a time T''' such that:

    (i) S can at T bring about f directly relative to T' and T'''; and

    (ii) if S were to bring about f directly relative to T' and T''', then f would contribute causally relative to T''' and T^* to e.

And, keeping D.4.10 in mind we may also say the following:

D.11.12: S can at T bring about e synthetically relative to T' and T^* =df. there are events $f1,...,fn$ and a time T''' such that:

    (i) for any event f, if f is identical with $f1$, or..., or f is identical with fn, then there are times T^{**} and T^{***} such that

       (a) T' is not later than T^{**}, T^{**} is not later than T^{***}, and T^{***} is not earlier than T''' and not later than T^*, and

       (b) either

(1) S can at T bring about f directly relative to T^{**} and T^{***}, or

(2) S can at T bring about f indirectly relative to T^{**} and T^{***}; and

(ii) if, for some time T^{**} not earlier than T' and not later than T^*, S were to bring about $f1$ either directly or indirectly relative to T' and T^{**}, and..., and if, for some time T^{**} not earlier than T' and not later than T^*, S were to bring about fn either directly or indirectly relative to T^{**} and T^*, then e would be composed relative to T''' and T^* of $f1,...,fn$.

With D.11.10 through D.11.12 given, definitions of the remaining two relevant phrases follow easily. These are, first:

D.11.13: S can at T bring about e actively relative to T' and T^* =df. either

(i) S can at T bring about e directly relative to T' and T^*; or

(ii) S can at T bring about e indirectly relative to T' and T^*; or

(iii) S can at T bring about e synthetically relative to T' and T^*.

(Compare D.4.11.) And second:

D.11.14: S can at T act relative to T' and T^* =df. there is an event e such that S can at T bring about e actively relative to T' and T^*.

(Compare D.4.12.) Definitions of such phrases as "S can at T act successfully relative to T' and T^*," "S can at T act intentionally relative to T' and T^*," and so on, may be given along the lines of D.11.9.b through D.11.14 and in accordance with the definitions of Chapter 6. I shall not give these definitions here.

Now consider the following principle:

(11)   Necessarily, if S brings about e actively relative
            to T and T', then S can at T bring about e actively
            relative to T and T'.

Is this a theorem of the present libertarian account? No, it is not.
Should it be? No, it should not. For S may bring about e actively
relative to T and T' and there may be a sufficient causal condition
relative to some time T^* and T of his so doing, in which case, according to the sense of "can" in D.11.9.b through D.11.14, S cannot
at T bring about e actively relative to T and T', since his willing at
T is not free. But if we call the sense of "can" given in D.11.9.a
"can*" and imagine this sense of "can" to be elaborated by means
of definitions analogous to D.11.10 through D.11.14, we may note
that the following *are* theorems of the present account:

T.11.1:   Necessarily, if S can at T bring about e actively
            relative to T' and T^*, then S can* at T bring
            about e actively relative to T' and T^*.

T.11.2:   Necessarily, if S brings about e actively relative
            to T and T', then S can* at T bring about e ac-
            tively relative to T and T'.

Given T.11.2, we may say that there is indeed a sense of "can" according to which the common philosophical dictum "'Does' implies
'Can'" is true. How interesting this sense of "can" is, however, is
another matter.[38] More important for our purposes is to note the
following theorem:

T.11.3:   Necessarily, if S freely$_1$ brings about e actively
            relative to T and T', then S can at T bring about e
            actively relative to T and T'.

But, where "S can do otherwise than bring about e " is understood
to mean roughly that S can bring about some event f *incompatible*
with e (and not merely that S can bring about some event f other
than e, which is all too easily achieved on the present finely-grained
account of events), it does *not* follow from the present account that

S can do otherwise if he acts freely$_1$. But we can invoke a new concept − that of "freedom$_2$" − and say:

D.11.15: S freely$_2$ brings about e actively relative to T and T' =df.
   (i) S freely$_1$ brings about e actively relative to T and T'; and
   (ii) there is an event f such that
    (a) S can at T bring about f actively relative to T and T', and
    (b) S cannot at T bring about $[e$ and $f]$ actively relative to T and T'.

And then we can obviously say that freedom$_2$ of action implies that one can do otherwise. In addition, definitions of "being free to do" (as opposed to "freely doing") could be drawn up on the basis of the foregoing. For instance, it might be said (roughly) that S is free$_1$ to bring about e just in case S can bring about e, and that S is free$_2$ to bring about e just in case S can bring about e and can also do otherwise. But I shall forgo presenting these definitions in detail here.

The account of "can" just presented makes use of subjunctive conditionals. This is unfortunate, for the truth conditions of such conditionals are notoriously controversial. I have successfully avoided such conditionals hitherto, but I know of no way to avoid such use in the definition of "can." Still, this is perhaps not too serious; the account of "can" is, I think, fairly intelligible despite such use. Perhaps a more serious question is: is "real" strict freedom of action freedom$_1$ or freedom$_2$? Well, it may be neither, of course; and, if Frankfurt is right, it seems not to be freedom$_2$. On the other hand, if Frankfurt is wrong, it seems legitimate to say that the question is misguided and that there just are two important senses of strict freedom of action − freedom$_1$ and freedom$_2$ − where only one was initially suspected.

Finally, use to which the foregoing analysis of freedom of action may be put may be illustrated with respect to two important concepts, namely, the concepts of the provision of opportunity and of a person. I mentioned the concept of the provision of opportunity in Section 3.1 of Chapter 3 when discussing Chisholm's use of the concept of event-causal contribution. It was noted that Chisholm regards it possible that an event should contribute causally to a free action, whereas my use of the concept of event-causal contribution (see A.3.2 and the assumptions and definitions of this chapter) rules out this possibility. I would rather say that, in such a case, the event in question provides the agent with an opportunity to act freely. It was noted also in Section 3.3 of Chapter 3 that an analysis of the concept of willing broadly (see D.3.6) rests on an analysis of the concept of the provision of opportunity. Given what has been said in this chapter, this analysis may now be provided. We may, I think, say, roughly, that an event e provides a person with the opportunity to bring about an event f just in case e contributes causally to its being the case that he can bring about f. Or more precisely:

D.11.16: e provides S, relative to T and T', with the opportunity to bring about f actively relative to T^* and $T'' =$ df.
   (i) e occurs at T ; and
   (ii) e contributes causally relative to T and T' to [S can bring about f actively relative to T^* and T''].

We could then say, roughly, that an event e provides an opportunity for f's occurrence just in case there is a person S such that e provides S with the opportunity to bring about f actively; and we could also say that a person S provides an opportunity for f's occurrence just in case there are a person S^* and an event e such that S's bringing about e actively provides S^* with the opportunity to bring about f actively. D.11.16, moreover, may serve as the basis of the analysis of such concepts as willing for a purpose, acting for a purpose, and so on. I shall provide no such analysis here, however, for it is very complicated. But, roughly, I think that we can say that a person wills an event e for the purpose of an event f just in case he wills e and he intends either that his so willing should contribute causally to f (see D.3.7), or that his so willing should (in some sense) "just be" f,[39] or that his so willing should provide the opportunity for f's occurrence. A similar statement may be made concerning acting for a purpose by substituting "brings about actively" and its cognates for "wills" and its cognates. From this an analysis of the concept of a means, a mere means, an end, an end-in-itself, and so on, could perhaps be generated. But these are matters that I shall not discuss here.

With regard to the concept of a person, it will be remembered that in Chapter 1 I did not include this concept in my list of unanalyzed concepts but referred the reader to this chapter for its analysis. Here it is:

D.11.17: S is a person at T =df.
    (i) S is an individual thing that exists at T ; and
    (ii) there are an event e and times T' and T^* such that it is physically possible that S can at T bring about e actively relative to T' and T^*.

That is, roughly: a person is an individual thing such that it is physically possible that it can act. At the end of the next chapter I shall address the charge that this definition introduces circularity into the theory that has just been presented.[40]

Notes

1   The roughness that I am here overlooking concerns: the lack of mention of times; the lack of explication of certain key terms such as "morally responsible," "free," and "can"; the fact that "a" ranges only over actions, and yet one may be morally responsible for states of affairs that are not actions; and so on.

2   Frankfurt (1969).

3   But see Zimmerman (1982) for a detailed investigation of this issue.

4   Zimmerman (1982), pp.250-1.

5   Note that, in keeping with the discussion of action from Chapter 4 onward, I here suppress all mention of the *determinate*

events to which causal contribution is relative.

6   The labels "soft determinism" and "hard determinism" derive
     from William James (1884), p.149. For a sample of soft de-
     terminists, see note 8 to this chapter. Hard determinism – a
     less popular position than soft determinism – has been advo-
     cated by (among others): Spinoza (1677); Edwards (1958);
     Hospers (1958).

7   Unger (1977) has even argued that, if determinism is true, not
     only would *free* action be impossible, but *all* action would be
     impossible. This is clearly false. Unger's argument founders
     on an equivocation on "cause" – but I shall not try to show this
     here.

8   See, among others: Hobbes (1651), p.159; Locke (1689), p.149;
     Hume (1777), p.104; Mill (1874), p.168ff.; G.E. Moore (1912),
     Chapter 6; Stevenson (1938), p.138; Schlick (1939), pp.62-3;
     Ayer (1954), p.283; Nowell-Smith (1954b), p.275.

9   Lehrer (1966a, pp.195-7; 1976, pp.248-250); Chisholm (1967,
     p.311; 1976, p.57). The argument has been challenged: see
     Aune (1967a). I believe this sort of argument to be effective
     also against the more sophisticated "hierarchical" compatibilist
     accounts that have recently appeared. See: Dworkin (1970),
     Frankfurt (1971), Neely (1974), Watson (1975). For criticism
     of these accounts see: Thalberg (1978, 1979), Slote (1980).

10   Lehrer (1976).

11   Zimmerman (1981a). Lehrer's paper is also discussed in Tichy
     and Oddie (1983).

12   Perhaps many libertarians and soft determinists have been
     somewhat at cross purposes here, in so far as the latter have
     often not drawn a distinction between strict and broad senses of
     "freedom" (or of "can," and so on) and seem often to be preoc-
     cupied with giving an account of those elements which (from a
     libertarian point of view) serve to distinguish broadly free from
     strictly free action rather than to distinguish strictly free from

strictly unfree action.

13 An interesting question to ponder in this regard is the following. It seems that one lacks broad freedom of action just in
case one is compelled or coerced to do what one does. If so, is it
the case that being broadly unfree implies being strictly free; or
can one lack *both* types of freedom at once?

14 Of course, there is a type of causation-by-agents which has
much to do with, indeed is reducible to, the concept of causal
contribution, as was explained at the end of Section 3.1 of
Chapter 3; but this type of agent-causation is to be clearly distinguished from that concept which I here call agent-effectuation. (This point is complicated somewhat by Chisholm's
definition D.II.10 in Chisholm (1976). See note 11 to Chapter
3 above.)

15 Aristotle, *Metaphysics* 1031a 24-34.

16 As Taylor (1967, p.57) notes, it is the concept of an efficient
cause that underlies both the modern concept of agent-causation and the modern concept of event-causation.

17 Aristotle, *Metaphysics* 1013a 29-32, 1013b 23-25.

18 Reid (1788), p.11. For a recent discussion of Reid's view of
agency, see Madden (1982).

19 Reid (1788), p.37.

20 Reid (1788), pp.259, 265.

21 Reid (1788), especially pp.265, 335.

22 Kant (1781/7), A532/B560 - A558/B586. To my knowledge,
Kant is the only prominent philosopher in modern times to insist on the need for this distinction and yet to hold a version
(albeit exotic) of compatibilism. (Reid's advocacy of the Principle of Sufficient Reason (see below) seems not to be compatibilist in nature, since, in advocating it, he seems to be concerned

primarily, not with event-causation, but with agent-causation.)

23　Kant (1781/7), A541/B569.

24　Campbell (1967), pp.36-7.

25　Campbell (1951, pp.131-5; 1957, pp.156-7; 1967, pp.48-9).

26　Taylor (1958, pp.227-8; 1966, pp.9, 10, 13, 21-2, 60-1, 109-112).

27　Chisholm (1966, pp.17-21; 1976, pp.69-70, 73-6). In this connection, see note 58 to Chapter 10.

28　By "*S* directly effectuates *e* at *T* " is meant: [*S* directly effectuates *e*] occurs at *T*.

29　Compare Chisholm (1971a), assumption (A3).

30　By "*S* decides *f*" I mean: either *S* decides$_1$ *f* or *S* decides$_2$ *f*. See D.9.1 and D.9.2.

31　Compare Chisholm (1971a), assumption (A4). Again, all mention is suppressed of the *determinate events* to which the causal contribution, and hence the indirect effectuation, is relative.

32　*Cf.* Rowe (1982), pp.364-5.

33　I have not assumed – see Section 3.3 of Chapter 3 – that any event *e* is such that it is metaphysically impossible for someone to will *e*. If there is any such state of affairs, however, D.11.2 must be supplemented with the clause: "and it is metaphysically possible that *S* will *e* at *T'* in order that *f* may occur." For, D.11.2, as it stands, implies that, if it is metaphysically impossible that *S* will *e* at *T'* in order that *f* may occur, then, for any time *T*, *S* is free at *T* to will *e* at *T'* in order that *f* may occur. This is, I think, an undesirable implication, if some events are such that they are metaphysically impossible to will, and it ought to be blocked in the manner just indicated. My remarks in this note are prompted by a criticism by Corrado

(1980, p.179) of a definition of Chisholm's which is similar to D.11.2.

34 Note that in this connection the classic compatibilists such as Hobbes and Hume make explicit use of the concept of willing. See note 8 to this chapter.

35 That three distinct designations of times should be made does not imply that three distinct times should be designated.

36 See note 9 to this chapter.

37 This treatment of "can" owes its inspiration in part to Chisholm's treatment of the subject in Chisholm (1976), pp.62-4. The reason for mentioning a time T''' which is possibly distinct from T is that it can sometimes occur that I can now do something later, *not* because I can *now* (at T) do something *now* (perhaps I cannot), but because it *will* be the case that I can immediately at some time T''' do something at T''' which will enable me to do something later... (and so on).

38 Indeed, given the rejection of D.11.9.a, it is debatable whether it is appropriate even to call the concept captured in D.11.9.a by the name of "can."

Note, however, this interesting disanalogy between action and omission. Given D.8.3, the dictum "'Omits' implies 'Can'" *is* true, in the full-blown sense of "can." Thus all omission necessarily involves an element of freedom, while not all action does.

For another, recent account of the relation between "Does" and "Can," see Tichy and Oddie (1983), pp.143-6.

39 If [S wills e] is caused, then this sense of "just be" is the same as that of "constitute" (see D.4.6). If [S wills e] is uncaused, however, some other sense must be given.

40 The account of free human action presented in this chapter has much in common with, though also much not in common with, Chisholm's account of free human action in Chisholm (1976), pp.61-4 – an account which I shall not go into in detail here.

The important common aspects are: the account presented here is both indeterministic (see D.11.2) and "constitutionally iffy" (see D.11.9 through D.11.14), as is Chisholm's.

Chapter 12
OBJECTIONS

The libertarian account of freedom of action presented in the last chapter inherits certain of the features of the theory of action presented in Part II. Perhaps some of these features are objectionable; but I have already tried in Chapter 10 to answer some of the main objections that might be raised, and I shall not repeat myself here. But the libertarian account also has certain features that it does not inherit from the theory that precedes it, and perhaps some of these features are objectionable too. Certainly there is one such feature which has, for many reasons, been objected to by many in the past. This is the account's reliance on the concept of effectuation. I propose now to investigate this matter more closely.

Some philosophers have claimed that libertarianism is necessarily false, and their claim has apparently been based either on the contention that there can be no such relation as effectuation or on the contention that, if there is such a relation, it can never be exemplified.[1] In the former case, the reasoning seems, in outline, to be as follows: necessarily, any causal relation, when exemplified, relates events to events; effectuation is claimed to be an exemplifiable causal relation that, when exemplified, relates persons (and not events) to events; therefore, there can be no such relation as effectuation. In the latter case, the reasoning seems to run as follows: necessarily, any causal relation, when exemplified, relates events to events; effectuation is claimed to be a causal relation that, if it were exemplified, would relate persons (and not events) to events; therefore, effectuation cannot be exemplified. To my mind, each premise of each argument is quite dubious; certainly, each premise is debatable. No doubt many of the arguments that are presented in the literature to prove libertarianism necessarily false are more complex than either of the arguments just given, but I think that in many cases the basic structure of these arguments is as just depicted. If this is correct, these attempts to show libertarianism necessarily false are surely unsuccessful.

But perhaps there is another way to try to prove libertarianism necessarily false, and this is to charge that A.11.3 is incoherent.

A.11.3 was said to be part of the "linchpin" of libertarianism; yet it is obvious that it gives rise to an infinite regress of effectuation. More precisely, if S effectuates e, then, on A.11.3, S effectuates [S effectuates e], for *all e*. Hence, S effectuates [S effectuates [S effectuates e]], and so on *ad infinitum*. Is this objectionable? It seems to me not, although this is debatable. We should note that not all infinite regresses are "vicious." After all, there seems to be nothing objectionable about the claim that, for all propositions p, if p is true then it is true that p is true; nor does there seem to be anything objectionable about the claim that, for all propositions p, if p is necessarily true, then it is necessarily true that p is necessarily true. Yet both claims give rise to infinite regresses. So the question is: is the infinite regress to which A.11.3 gives rise "vicious" or "virtuous"? I see no reason to doubt that it is the latter.[2]

Other objections to libertarianism do not seek to show it *necessarily* false, but just false. One such objection is the following. If libertarianism is true, then, given its use of the concept of effectuation, there must be "indeterminacies" in the neural activity of agents – presumably at those points in the neural apparatus where brain activity "corresponds" with decisions. But there is no evidence of such indeterminacies; on the contrary, the evidence is that neural activity is "deterministic." It seems to me that there are two main ways to respond to this objection. The first is to challenge the claim that the evidence really does point in the direction that the objector contends. This is a difficult issue. First, just what the evidence is – and I do not know just what it is – must be ascertained; but then – and this seems just as difficult – the evidence must be interpreted from the perspective of one who is trying to resolve the present issue. Until both of these things are done – and I know of no study in which they have been done – it seems to me that the libertarian may legitimately stand his ground. On the other hand, suppose that this were done and determinism (at least with respect to human action) were shown to be probably true. In this case, the libertarian must give up his position. But note that the libertarian's position is an amalgam of two distinct positions, that of incompatibilism and that of the belief that humans act freely. He need not give up both; that is, he would still have a choice between hard and soft determinism – and, if he chose the former, he could still affirm the accuracy of the analyses of the last chapter – and so the soft determinist would not necessarily have won the day.[3]

Another objection, akin to the foregoing, may be raised from an epistemological perspective. The libertarian account, it may be pointed out, is premised on the following "chain of implication":

(1)   *S* is morally responsible for *a.*

(2)   Either *S* does (or did) *a* freely, or there is an action *b* such that *S* did *b* freely and *a* is (or was) a consequence of *b.*

(3)   Either *S* 's doing *a* is (or was) not (event-)caused, or there is an action *b* such that *S* 's doing *b* was not (event-)caused and *a* is (or was) a consequence of *b.*[4]

Thus, on the libertarian account, if one is justified in believing (of a particular *S* and *a*) that (1) is true, one is justified in believing that (2) is true, and hence that (3) also is true. But, the objector may say, one is often justified in believing that (1) is true, but no one is justified in believing that (3) is true. The response to this is simple. The objection is based on this principle: if *p* implies *q* and *S* is justified in believing *p*, then *S* is justified in believing *q*. But this principle is false, even when modified to rule out the cases where *q* is necessarily true. At the very least, it seems that *S* must also *justifiably believe* that *p* implies *q* if he is to be justified in believing *q* on the basis of *p*'s implication of *q* ; but, if so, the objection seems to run aground.

Donald Davidson has given the following objection:

> One is [in trouble] if one supposes [as libertarians urge] that agent-causation does *not* introduce an event in addition to the primitive action. For then what more have we said when we say the agent caused the action than when we say he was the agent of the action? The concept of *cause* seems to play no role. We may fail to detect the vacuity of this suggestion because causality does...enter

> conspicuously into accounts of agency; but where
> it does it is the garden-variety [*i.e*, event-type] of
> causality, which sheds no light on the relation
> between the agent and his...actions.[5]

This objection may be pertinent to some accounts of effectuation (it applies to Taylor's, I think), but it is not pertinent to the one given in Chapter 11. For it is based on the understanding that, according to libertarianism, *whenever* a person acts, he effectuates his action. This is not something implied by the account given in the last chapter. According to this account, it is only when one acts freely that one (directly) effectuates one's willing and thereby (indirectly) effectuates the issues internal to one's actions. Hence there is a distinction, on this account, between being the agent of an act and "agent-causing" that act.

Another objection to the sort of account of effectuation furnished in the last chapter is to be found in Taylor's writings.[6] As recorded in Chapter 10, Taylor regards the doctrine of volitions as "quite fantastic"[7] and indefensible, and one of his arguments for this view runs roughly in this rhetorical fashion: if the concept of effectuation is found to be indispensable and I am to be said to be able to effectuate my volitions, why not simply say that I effectuate my actions and do away with the concept of volition altogether? The proper response to this is threefold: first, without the sort of account given in the last chapter and presented in terms of the effectuation of volitions, it is difficult to see how one can distinguish free action from unfree action; secondly, the sort of account given in the last chapter allows for a related account of free decision and free choice when no action ensues (for a decision may be a decision$_1$ and a choice a choice$_1$ – see Chapter 9), whereas it is again difficult to see how such an account could be given on the basis that Taylor provides; and thirdly, without such an account as that given in the last chapter, it seems that Davidson's objection, just cited, will in fact be pertinent.

But it should be explicitly noted here that the account of freedom of action given in the last chapter is fairly unusual in so far as it invokes *both* the concept of volition *and* that of effectuation. Traditionally, it seems, there has been a tendency to think that, if an account invokes one of these concepts, it can and should reject the other. (Reid's account is an exception here.) Furthermore, according to the account, effectuation is exemplified when and only when one acts freely. In this respect, the account opposes the accounts of Reid, Taylor, and Chisholm, which are less restrictive than it and according to which *all* action is effectuated by the agent.[8] Only Campbell, amongst the prominent modern agent-causation theorists, seems to be in agreement with this aspect of the account in Chapter 11; but Campbell's account is in fact far *more* restrictive than this account, in that he believes that one acts freely (and is then and only then the agent-cause of one's actions) only in those comparatively rare cases of moral temptation where one acts in accordance with one's perception of duty *and* in opposition to one's strongest desires.[9]

Another problem concerns the so-called Principle of Sufficient Reason. Many appear to be fond of this principle. Is the libertarian account of the last chapter inconsistent with its truth? That, of course, depends upon how the principle is interpreted. Roughly, the principle seems to be that every event has a cause. But what type of cause? Now Reid, who seems to have thought that *every* causal chain may be traced to an agent-cause, claims this principle to be self-evidently true and asserts that his theory is consistent with its being true.[10] Others may interpret this principle to concern event-causes only, in which case it seems to be the same as determinism, in the sense of "determinism" that I gave earlier. In this case, the "libertarian" account of freedom – *as presented* – is still not inconsistent with the principle's being true; for no claim is made *in* that account that determinism is false. What is the case, according to the account, is that it is impossible that determinism be true *and* some action be freely performed. That is, the account is explicitly committed only to incompatibilism, and not to libertarianism.[11] Still, it must be admitted that the "spirit" of the account – the rationale for its presentation at all – *is* libertarian; that is, it is predicated, albeit tacitly, on the assumption that determinism is false. So it should be acknowledged that the spirit, if not the letter, of the account *is* inconsistent with the Principle of Sufficient Reason, so understood. Is this a mark against the account? In the absence of any independent evidence in favor of the principle, so understood, I cannot see that it is. Another possible interpretation of the principle is that, according to it, every event has *either* an event-cause *or* an agent-cause. The account is certainly not inconsistent with this interpretation; indeed, some action may be freely performed *and* the principle be true, on this interpretation. I think that people are sometimes inclined to believe that every event has a cause because they believe that no event occurs or can occur in a totally "isolated" manner. Note, however, that even if it were the case that some event occurs without being either event-caused or agent-caused, this intuition may yet be accommodated. It may be that the principle that such people are groping for is that every event has an *effect*. This principle may of course be true even if indeterminism is also true.

In connection with the issue concerning there being a "sufficient reason" for the occurrence of each event one should mention the matter of the predictability of actions, which is often thought to be a function of their being caused to occur. It has been claimed that all actions are predictable in principle, but that undetermined events would not be predictable; hence no actions can be undetermined. The typical libertarian response to this objection is that it is not true that *all* actions are predictable in principle. Campbell, for instance, agrees that very many actions indeed are predictable in principle, but he maintains that there are a rare few, namely those freely performed in situations where temptation is overcome, which simply are not predictable even in principle.[1][2] I am not sure how to understand the concept of being predictable in principle, but, if I understand it at all, I think that Campbell is surely right to reject the contention that *all* actions are predictable in principle. Why on earth should we think this to be true? Cannot people sometimes act on a whim, and freely so? If so, the libertarian might plausibly deny that all action is predictable, even "in principle." But a more telling point is surely that the causes of an event need not be known in order for there to be a basis of predicting its occurrence. Prediction may be based on a statistical inference, where events occur, or at least are taken to occur, *randomly*. Thus, if prediction of an event's occurrence is often and properly based independently of any knowledge of its causes (if it has any), it would seem that whether or not it has any causes is irrelevant to the prediction.[1][3]

Some have objected to the concept of effectuation in some such manner as this:

> If we say that John moved his hand at time *t*, we may indeed add that he caused his hand to move at that time. But to say this is not to say that he was the irreducible cause of his hand's motion; if he were, then, since he existed yesterday, his hand should have moved the same way yesterday too. After all, if *A* is the irreducible cause of *B*, then whenever we have *A*, we should have *B* as well.[1][4]

The objection seems persuasive. After all, if a person *S* is sufficient for his willing as he does (which the libertarian account apparently says is true in cases of free action), what is there to stop him always willing in this way? *Why now* rather than ten minutes ago? But I would suggest that the persuasiveness of this objection lies in part in the confusion of (event-)causation with effectuation (and hence the advisability of divorcing the latter concept from that of causation). It may be that, if *A* is the irreducible *event*-cause of *B*, then, whenever *A* occurs, so does *B*. (Presumably, by "irreducible event-cause" is meant something very close to what I have called a sufficient causal condition – see D.3.2.) But what reason is there for believing, and what grounds for asserting, that, if *S effectuates e*, then *e* should occur at every moment that *S* exists? None that I can see; indeed, there is good reason not to accept this.[1][5] Perhaps part of the point of the objection is this: actions, like all events, are open to explanation; yet no explanation for (free) actions is forthcoming if all that can be said is that the agent effectuates his volitions. Perhaps, if *all* that could be said in the case of free actions is that the agent effectuates his volitions, then there would be no explanation forthcoming; and perhaps, then, the objector would have a point (although I see no reason to believe that *all* actions are open to explanation, even "in principle"). But, in most cases of free action, this is emphatically *not* all that can be said. We need to distinguish two types of explanation: rational explanation and causal explanation. I shall not by any means attempt to given an adequate account of either type of explanation here, but the distinction should be familiar enough.[1][6] When one gives a causal explanation of an event, one cites *causes* of the occurrence of that event; when one gives a rational explanation of an event (typically an action), one cites *reasons* for the occurrence of that event. Now, there are some who maintain that reasons are a type of (event-)cause, and that rational explanation is a species of causal explanation.[17] I do not share this view. Causal explanation is typically "backward-looking" and concerns what has preceded the event which is to be explained; rational explanation is typically "forward-looking" and concerns the goals and purposes that the agent has in virtue of which he decides to act as he does. (Of course, this is acknowledged by those who believe rational explanation to be a species of causal explanation; but whether or not they *successfully* accommodate this fact in their accounts of explanation is another matter.) Roughly, we may say that, according to the libertarian account given in the last chapter, all decisions which occur freely but as a result of deliberation (see D.9.3) are in principle open to rational explanation but not to causal explanation.[18] For those decisions which are impetuously but freely arrived at there is no explanation, rational or causal. (Of course, there are a number of terms which, in a fuller treatment of this issue, ought to be accounted for here, to wit, "as a result of," "explainable in principle," "rational explanation," and "causal explanation.") Those *issues* which are freely and deliberately brought about are, according to this extension of the account, in principle open to *both* types of explanation; the rational explanation will concern the reasons for the agent's decision or decisions, the causal explanation will concern how the decision or decisions contributed causally to the issue. Those decisions which are not freely arrived at, whether deliberate or impetuous, are presumably open in principle to causal explanation, unless they occur totally spontaneously; if deliberate, they are open to rational explanation also. Now all of this is certainly rough as it stands, but its statement serves two main purposes: first, it provides further reason to reject the "Why now?" type of argument, just considered, against the concept of effectuation; secondly, it provides a brief introductory account of another area in which the libertarian account of freedom of action may profitably be employed.

But, even if all of the foregoing objections to the concept of effectuation have been adequately answered for present purposes (certainly they have not been *conclusively* rebutted, for each objection raises points which deserve fuller treatment than that which I have been able to provide here), there is one objection to that concept which seems to me especially telling – much more telling than any of the preceding objections[19] — and that is simply that the concept of effectuation is extremely *obscure*. Indeed, it seems to some (when confronted, for instance, with libertarian attempts to prove the second premise of the argument cited at the beginning of the last chapter false) that the concept of effectuation is nothing more than a *deus ex machina* and that it purchases the immunity of libertarianism to standard objections concerning the "randomness" of un-(event-)caused actions only at the price of unintelligibility. Strangely enough, it seems that proponents of libertarianism are themselves more prone to consider this objection (at least in writing[20]) than opponents of libertarianism are to advance it, although at least three prominent critics of the doctrine have very recently reiterated it.[21] Campbell's response to the charge that the concept of effectuation is unintelligible is that we are all aware, from an "introspective" point of view, of the phenomenon of effectuation:

> [I]ntrospection makes it...clear that I am certain that it is *I* who choose; that the act is no "accident," but is genuinely *my* act.[22]

Hence, according to Campbell, the concept is not unintelligible, even if there is no suitable account of it forthcoming from an "external" viewpoint. Taylor's response is similar:

> Now this idea [of causation by agents] strikes many as quite incomprehensible. And indeed in a way it is... Yet it should be noted that it is mysterious or incomprehensible *only* in the sense that it is not what a man having any familiarity with physical science or the general history of speculative thought would be led to expect. In another sense it is strange indeed to speak of some perfectly familiar thing...as being in any sense mysterious.[23]

For his part, Chisholm considers the objection in the guise of the question "What is the difference between saying, of an event *A*, that *A* just happened and saying that someone caused *A* to happen?," and he responds to the objection in this way:

The only answer, I think, can be this: that the
difference between the man's causing *A*, on the
one hand, and the event *A* just happening, on the
other, lies in the fact that, in the first but not the
second, the event *A* *was* caused and was caused
by the man.[24]

Chisholm acknowledges that this answer "may not entirely satisfy,"[25] but he claims that there is an analogous problem with the
concept of event-causation.[26] How is one to answer the question
"What is the difference between saying, of two events *A* and *B*, that
B happened and then *A* happened, and saying that *B*'s happening
caused A's happening?" The only answer that one can give to this
question, he contends, is that, in the second case but not the first, *B*
did cause *A*. According to Chisholm, then, the concept of agent-
causation may not be clear, but that of event-causation is no clearer.

Chisholm overstates his point, I think. It is possible to give a
fuller characterization (see A.3.1 through A.3.6) of the concept of
event-causal contribution than that which is provided when one
merely notes that an event *e* contributes causally to an event *f* only
if *e* precedes *f*. (Indeed, if what I say in Section 3.1 of Chapter 3 is
true, then it is in fact not true that such temporal priority is a necessary condition of such causation.) But, perhaps an effort could be
made to retain the spirit of Chisholm's point by pointing out that
the assumptions given in the last chapter (namely, A.11.1 through
A.11.4) succeed in partially characterizing the concept of effectuation to an extent similar to that in which A.3.1 through A.3.6 succeed in partially characterizing the concept of causal contribution.
Hence, it might be claimed, there still appears little justification for
claiming the latter concept to be any clearer than the former.[27]
But this is a little disingenuous. Ever since Hume, the fact that
causal contribution involves the notion of *nomic* regularity (a fact
implicitly acknowledged by invoking the notion of physical necessity
in A.3.2) has been asserted and this notion has been investigated.
While no attempt has been made in this book to elucidate this notion, it must be admitted that others have made such attempts and
have perhaps met with some success.

Moreover, while I believe that both Campbell and Taylor are right in contending that we are all thoroughly familiar with the fact that we are often "in control of" what we do, they seem not to have supplied any reason for accepting that it is *effectuation* that affords such control. Indeed – and this is perhaps the most telling point of all – they have not supplied any *explanation* of how effectuation *could* or *would* afford such control. Campbell talks of introspection in this connection, but, as many have pointed out, one thing that is assuredly not a datum of such introspection is that our free decisions are not event-caused.[28] But even this most telling of objections shows only, I think, that the libertarian must give a better account of the key concept of effectuation if his account is to be persuasive. It does *not* point up anything radically wrong or incoherent in the libertarian enterprise. After all, if I cannot introspect the absence of an event-cause of my decision, nor (it seems) can I introspect the presence of such a cause.[29] The issue is thus deadlocked, but the challenge to the libertarian is clear: "Say what you *mean* by '*S* directly effectuates *e*'!" Unfortunately, beyond the rather paltry characterization of the concept of effectuation provided in A.11.1 through A.11.4, I do not know how to meet this challenge. Hence I must once again stress that the account of freedom of action given in the last chapter is tentative.

I shall complete this chapter by considering objections to D.11.17, in which the concept of a person is analyzed. First, it might be objected that the definition is circular; for it is given in terms of other definitions in which the concept of a person is invoked. Formally, this is correct. But the damage could easily be repaired by substituting "individual thing" for "person" in all of those previous definitions. Such substitution would not adversely affect those definitions. Secondly, it might be objected that a person may be born in this world and then die before it is even physically possible that he or she be able to bring about an event actively. But it seems to me (now donning the libertarian cap with bravado) that, if it is true that something of this nature concerning a human being could happen, it is then simply the case that the human being is not in fact a person (in one important sense of that word). This gives rise to the third and final objection, however, which is that it is possible, given D.11.17, that *no* human being be a person. For determinism may yet be true; but the concept of "can," according to

D.11.9.b through D.11.14, involves an element of indeterminism in its invocation of the concept of an agent's being free to will an event (see D.11.2). This is indeed so. If some find this objectionable, they may always substitute "can*" (see D.11.9.a, T.11.1 and T.11.2 of Chapter 11) for "can" in D.11.17. But this seems to me an inadvisable move. I believe that determinism is false. Moreover, I believe that people often act freely. D.11.17, indeed the whole libertarian account of freedom of action provided in the last chapter, is presented, albeit tentatively, because I believe that human beings can indeed sometimes act freely, that they can indeed achieve personhood. In other, more traditional terms: I believe that the foregoing incompatibilist account of free human action, when coupled with the claim that determinism is false, allows, as no compatibilist theory does, for the fact that human beings are blessed with a certain degree of dignity, the dignity of being, at least in part, in control of their own destiny.[30]

Notes

1   For example, see: Broad (1952), pp.214-7; Whittier (1965), p.300; Ehman (1967), pp.141-2.

2   *Cf.* Rowe (1982), p.368.

3   See again the remarks made toward the end of the last paragraph of Chapter 11, Section 11.1.

4   (1) and (2) are the same as (6) and (7'), respectively, in Chapter 11.

5   Davidson (1971), p.52.

6   Taylor (1966), p.113; see also pp.60-1, 74, 116-7.

7   Taylor (1966), p.49.

8   See once again Section 10.3 of Chapter 10, where I argue that the position that I adopt in the account of Chapter 11 is the sort of position that Chisholm *should* have adopted. In this connection, see also Ranken (1967), in which the author argues that a theory of agent-causation implies that every action, that is performed, is performed freely. Whether or not this is true of other theories involving the concept of effectuation, it is clearly not true of the one presented in the last chapter. In fact, it is also clearly not true of Taylor's; for Taylor explicitly addresses himself to this question and does not commit himself on the issue of the truth or falsity of determinism (see Taylor (1966), pp.112-5, 130-3). What is unclear on Taylor's account is how determinism might be true.

9   See Campbell (1951, pp.130-1; 1957, pp.148-153, 167-8; 1967, pp.46-7).

10   Reid (1788), pp.31, 267-8.

11   Again, see the remarks made toward the end of the last paragraph of Chapter 11, Section 11.1.

12   Campbell (1951, pp.130-2; 1967, pp.46-7).

13   *Cf.* Lucas (1970), pp.30-2.

14   The quotation is from Aune (1977), pp.5-6. See also Broad (1952), p.215; Rowe (1982), p.371; Madden (1982), p.338.

15   *Cf.* Donagan (1979), p.219.

16   For a provocative account of the distinction between rational and causal explanation, see Taylor (1966), Chapters 10 and 14; for a comment on this account, see Thalberg (1976), pp.233-5. I mention the concept of rational explanation briefly at the end of Section 6.1 of Chapter 6, where I discuss G.E.M.Anscombe's and Bruce Aune's approach to the topic of intentional action.

17   Recent proponents of this view are Davidson (1963) and Goldman (1970, Chapter 3, Section 6, and Chapter 5). Amongst

the opponents of this view are: Reid (1788, p.283ff., and Essay 3), Urmson (1952), Alston (1967, especially p.408), and Donnellan (1967, especially p.86).

18 The explanation may have to include an account of the logic of practical reasoning. For a recent treatment of this issue, see Aune (1977), Chapter 4.

19 This is not to deny that some of the preceding objections are more telling than others.

20 See Campbell (1951), pp.132-4; Taylor (1966), p.262; Chisholm (1966), pp.20-1.

21 Goldman (1970), pp.83-4; Thalberg (1976), p.216; Rowe (1982), pp.364, 371.

22 Campbell (1951), p.133.

23 Taylor (1966), p.262.

24 Chisholm (1966), p.21; the italicization of "*A* " has been added.

25 Chisholm (1966), p.21.

26 Chisholm (1966), pp.21-2.

27 Of course, this argument is a two-edged sword that could be used against a proponent of the account given in the last chapter. In response to it someone might say "So much the worse for the concept of event-causal contribution!" rather than "So much the better for the concept of direct effectuation!"

28 *Cf.* Nowell-Smith (1954a, pp.322-3; 1954b, pp.280-1).

29 See Talbott (1979), p.253ff.

30 Human beings are also cursed with the responsibility of living up to their potential – but why end this book on a negative note?

Appendix
LIST OF ASSUMPTIONS, DEFINITIONS, AND THEOREMS

Material in this appendix is presented in the same order as that in which it appears in the foregoing chapters. All assumptions and theorems listed here are ones advocated in the foregoing chapters. All definitions listed here are also ones so advocated, except where there is an explicit note to the contrary.

In what follows, "x" ranges over everything; "s," "t," "u," "v," and "w" range over and only over states of affairs; "p" ranges over and only over propositions; "e," "f," "g," and "h" range over and only over events; "d" (often with a superscript) ranges over and only over determinate events; "i" (except in D.6.1.f), "j," "m," and "n" range over and only over numbers; "S" ranges over and only over persons; "F," "G," and "H" range over and only over properties and relations; "X" and "Y" range over and only over sets; "P" (often with a sub- or superscript) ranges over and only over places; and "T" (often with a sub- or superscript) ranges over and only over times.

From Chapter 1:

D.1.1: s occurs at T =df. s exemplifies occurrence at T.

D.1.2: x exists at T =df. [x exists] occurs at T.

D.1.3: S accepts p at T =df. [S accepts p] occurs at T.

A.1.1:   Necessarily, for any property or relation F, there are states of affairs s and t such that, for any time T, s occurs at T if and only if F is exemplified at *T* and *t* occurs at *T* if and only if *F* is not exemplified at *T*.

A.1.2:   Necessarily, for any state of affairs *s*, there is a state of affairs *t* such that, for any time *T*, *s* occurs at *T* if and only if *t* does not occur at *T*.

A.1.3:   Necessarily, for any distinct states of affairs *s* and *t*, there is a state of affairs *u* such that, for any times *T* and *T'*, *u* occurs at *T* and *T'* if and only if *s* occurs at *T* and *t* occurs at *T'*.

A.1.4:   Necessarily, for any property or relation *F*, there is a property or relation *G* such that, for any time *T*, *F* is exemplified at *T* if and only if *G* is not exemplified at *T*.

A.1.5:   Necessarily, for any distinct properties or relations *F* and *G*, there is a property or relation *H* such that, for any times *T* and *T'*, *H* is exemplified at *T* and *T'* if and only if *F* is exemplified at *T* and *G* is exemplified at *T'*.

D.1.4:   *s* involves *t* =df. Necessarily, for any time *T*, whoever considers *s* at *T* also considers *t* at *T*.

D.1.5:   *s* properly involves *t* =df. *s* involves *t* and *t* does not involve *s*.

D.1.6:   *s* explicitly denies *t* =df. *s* contradicts *t* and also properly involves only *t* and what *t* involves.

D.1.7: s is the negation of t =df. either s explicitly denies t or t explicitly denies s.

D.1.8: s strictly implies t =df. Necessarily, for any time T, if s occurs at T, then t occurs at T.

D.1.9: s entails t =df.
  (i) s strictly implies t ; and
  (ii) necessarily, for any time T, whoever accepts that s occurs at T accepts that t occurs at T.

D.1.10: F entails G =df. for any thing x and any time T, [x exemplifies F at T] entails [x exemplifies G at T].

A.1.6: Necessarily, for any state of affairs s and any state of affairs t, s is identical with t if and only if s entails t and t entails s.

A.1.7: Necessarily, for any property or relation F and any property or relation G, F is identical with G if and only if F entails G and G entails F.

A.1.8: Necessarily, for any individual thing x and any individual thing y, x is identical with y if and only if, necessarily, for any place P, x exists in P if and only if y exists in P.

A.1.9: Necessarily, for any set X and any set Y, X is identical with Y if and only if, necessarily, for any thing x, x is a member of X if and only if x is a member of Y.

A.1.10:   Necessarily, for any time T and any time T', T is
           identical with T' if and only if, necessarily, for
           any thing x, x exists at T if and only if x exists at
           T'.

A.1.11:   Necessarily, for any place P and any place P', P
           is identical with P' if and only if, necessarily, for
           any thing x, x exists in P if and only if x exists in
           P'.

D.1.11: u is the conjunction of s and t = df.
             (i) u entails s ;
             (ii) u entails t ;
             (iii) s does not entail t ;
             (iv) t does not entail s ;
             (v) for any state of affairs v, if v entails both s
           and t, then v entails u.

D.1.12: p is a proposition = df.
             (i) p is a state of affairs; and
             (ii) it is impossible that there be a time T and a
           time T' such that p occurs at T and does not occur
           at T'.

D.1.13: F involves G = df. for any time T, [F is exem-
           plified at T] involves [G is exemplified at T].

D.1.14: F properly involves G = df. F involves G and G
           does not involve F.

D.1.15: F is negative = df. there is a property G such
           that:
             (i) F properly involves G ; and

(ii) necessarily, for any time T, F is exemplified at T if and only if G is not exemplified at T.

D.1.16: F is conjunctive =df. there are properties G and H such that:
  (i) F properly involves both G and H ;
  (ii) G does not entail H ;
  (iii) H does not entail G ; and
  (iv) necessarily, for any time T, F is exemplified at T if and only if both G and H are exemplified at T.

D.1.17: F is disjunctive =df. there are properties G and H such that:
  (i) F properly involves both G and H ;
  (ii) G does not entail H ;
  (iii) H does not entail G ; and
  (iv) necessarily, for any time T, F is exemplified at T if and only if either G or H is exemplified at T.

D.1.18: F is conditional =df. there are properties G and H such that:
  (i) F properly involves both G and H ;
  (ii) G does not entail H ;
  (iii) H does not entail G ; and
  (iv) necessarily, for any time T, F is exemplified at T if and only if either
    (a) G is exemplified at T only if H is exemplified at T, or
    (b) H is exemplified at T only if G is exemplified at T.

D.1.19: F is simple =df. F is neither negative, nor conjunctive, nor disjunctive, nor conditional.

D.1.20: F is universalizable $=$df. it is possible that, for some time T, everything that exists at T has F at T.

D.1.21: F is essential $=$df. necessarily, for any thing x and any time T, if x exists at T and has F at T, then there is no time T' such that x exists at T' and does not have F at T'.

D.1.22: F is a reflection of G $=$df.
(i) F is distinct from G ; and
(ii) necessarily, for any thing x and any time T, if x exemplifies F at T, then there is a time T' distinct from T such that x exemplifies G at T'.

D.1.23: F is reflective $=$df. there is a property G such that F is a reflection of G.

D.1.24: F is emergent $=$df. necessarily, for any thing x and any time T, if x exemplifies F at T, then there is a time T' earlier than T such that x does not exemplify F at T'.

D.1.25: e is an event $=$df. e is a state of affairs such that:
(i) e is not a proposition; and
(ii) there is a property F such that
(a) necessarily, for any state of affairs s, s entails e if and only if s entails [there is something which is F],
(b) necessarily, for any thing x and any time T, if x exemplifies F at T, then x is an individual thing,
(c) for any time T, it is possible that nothing exemplifies F at T, and
(d) there is a property G such that

(1) *F* entails *G*,
(2) *G* is simple,
(3) *G* is not universalizable,
(4) *G* is not essential, and
(5) either *G* is not reflective or *G* is emergent.

D.1.26: *s* entails *F* =df. necessarily, for any person *S* and any times *T* and *T'*:
(i) if *s* occurs at *T*, then *F* is exemplified at *T* ; and
(ii) if *S* accepts [*s* occurs at *T*] at *T'*, then *S* accepts [*F* is exemplified at *T*] at *T'*.

D.1.27: *Y* is a proper subset of *X* =df.
(i) every member of *Y* is a member of *X* ; and
(ii) some member of *X* is not a member of *Y*.

D.1.28: *X* concretizes *s* at *T* =df.
(i) *X* is a set;
(ii) *s* occurs at *T* ;
(iii) for every property *F*, if *s* entails *F* and it is not possible that something other than an individual thing exemplify *F*, then some member of *X* has *F* at *T* ; and
(iv) there is no proper subset *Y* of *X* such that, for every property *F* which *s* entails and which it is not possible for something other than an individual thing to exemplify, some member of *Y* has *F* at *T*.

D.1.29: *s* takes place at *T* in *P1*,...,*Pn* =df. there is a set *X* such that:
(i) *X* concretizes *s* at *T* ; and

(ii) for every place P, if P is identical with $P1$, or..., or P is identical with Pn, then some member of X exists in P at T.

D.1.30: $f1,...,fn$ are combination-fractions of e =df. $f1,...,fn$ and e are events such that:

(i) necessarily, for any times $T1,...,Tn$, if $f1,...,fn$ occur at $T1,...,Tn$, then e occurs at $T1,...,Tn$; and

(ii) if X is the set whose members are $f1,...,fn$, then

(a) there is no proper subset of X whose members are such that, necessarily, for any times $T'1,...,T'm$, if these members occur at $T'1,...,T'm$, then e occurs at $T'1,...,T'm$,

(b) necessarily, for any time T, if e occurs at T, then some member of X occurs at T, and

(c) necessarily, if $f1$ is distinct from fn, then, for any event fi that is a member of X and is distinct from fn, fi occurs at a time earlier than that at which $fi+1$ occurs.

D.1.31: e is a measure-event =df. there are events $f1,...,fn$ that are combination-fractions of e.

D.1.32: e is completed at T =df. e is an event and T a time such that: either

(i) (a) e is not a measure-event, and

(b) there is a time T' such that

(1) T is just prior to T',

(2) e occurs at T, and

(3) e does not occur at T'; or

(ii) (a) e is a measure-event, and

(b) for any events $f1,...fn$, if $f1,...,fn$ are combination-fractions of e, then, for any fi, if fi is identical with $f1$ or...or fi is identical with fn, there is a time T' such that

> (1) T' is earlier than or identical with T,
>
> and
>
> (2) fi occurs at T'.

D.1.33: d is a determinate event $=$ df.
(i) there are no events e and f such that d is the conjunction of e and f; and
(ii) for all events e distinct from d, either
(a) there is some event f such that e is the conjunction of d and f, or
(b) e does not entail d.

The next definition applies only to *determinate* events.

D.1.34: e occurs exactly n times $=$ df. there are exactly n times $T1,...,Tn$ such that e is completed at $T1$ and, ..., and e is completed at Tn.

From Chapter 3:

D.3.1: e contributes causally* relative to T and T' and to d and d' to s $=$ df.
(i) e is an event;
(ii) s is a state of affairs which is not a proposition; and
(iii) there is an event f distinct from s such that
(a) e contributes causally relative to T and T' and to d and d' to f, and
(b) it is causally necessary, given that f occurs at T', that s occur at T'.

T.3.1: Necessarily, if e contributes causally* relative to T and T' and to d and d' to s, then there is an event f distinct from s such that e contributes causally relative to T and T' and to d and d' to f.

A.3.1:   It is not necessarily the case that, if *e* contributes
           causally relative to *T* and *T'* and to *d* and *d'* to *s*,
           then there is an event *f* distinct from *s* such that *e*
           contributes causally relative to *T* and *T'* and to *d*
           and *d'* to *f*.

D.3.2:   *s* is a sufficient causal condition relative to *T* and
           T' and to *d* and *d'* of *t* =df. *s* and *t* are states of
           affairs which are not propositions and are such
           that:
               (i) *s* occurs at *T* ;
               (ii) *T* is not later than *T'*; and
               (iii) it is physically necessary, but not metaphy-
           sically necessary, that, if *s* occurs at *T*, then *t* oc-
           curs at *T'*.

D.3.3:   It is causally necessary that *t* occur at *T'* =df.
           there are a state of affairs *s*, a time *T*, and de-
           terminate events *d* and *d'* such that *s* is a
           sufficient causal condition relative to *T* and *T'* and
           to *d* and *d'* of *t.*

D.3.4:   It is causally necessary, given that *s* occurs at *T*,
           that *t* occur at *T'* =df. either
               (i) there are determinate events *d* and *d'* such
           that *s* is a sufficient causal condition relative to *T*
           and *T'* and to *d* and *d'* of *t* ; or
               (ii) there are a state of affairs *u*, a time *T**, and
           determinate events *d**, *d*, and *d'* such that:
                   (a) *u* is a sufficient causal condition relative to
           T* and *T* and to *d** and *d* of *s* ; and
                   (b) *u* is a sufficient causal condition relative to
           T* and *T'* and to *d** and *d'* of *t.*

A.3.2: Necessarily, if e contributes causally relative to T and T' and to d and d' to f, then there are an event g, a time T^*, and a determinate event d^* such that
(i) T is not later than T^*, and
(ii) g is a sufficient causal condition relative to T^* and T' and to d^* and d' of f.

A.3.3: It is not possible that, for some event e, some time T, and some determinate event d, e contribute causally relative to T and T and to d and d to e.

A.3.4: It is not possible that, for some events e and f, some times T and T', and some determinate events d and d', both e contribute causally relative to T and T' and to d and d' to f and f contribute causally relative to T' and T and to d' and d to e.

A.3.5: Necessarily, for any events e, f, and g, any times T, T', and T^*, and any determinate events d, d', and d^*, if e contributes causally relative to T and T' and to d and d' to f and f contributes causally relative to T' and T^* and to d' and d^* to g, then e contributes causally relative to T and T^* and to d and d^* to g.

D.3.5: e contributes causally relative to T and T^* and to d and d^* to g via f =df. there are a time T' and a determinate event d' such that:
(i) e contributes causally relative to T and T' and to d and d' to f; and
(ii) f contributes causally relative to T' and T^* and to d' and d^* to g.

A.3.6:   Necessarily, for any events e and f, any times T and T', and any determinate events d and d', if e contributes causally relative to T and T' and to d and d' to f, then [e occurs at T] does not strictly imply [f occurs at T'].

A.3.7:   Necessarily, if S intends e at T and S is rational, then S accepts [there is a time T' not earlier than T such that e may well occur at T'] at T.

A.3.8:   Necessarily, if S intends e at T and S is rational, then it is physically possible that, for some time T' not earlier than T, e occur at T'.

A.3.9:   Necessarily, if S wills p at T, then S intends p at T.

D.3.6: S broadly wills e at T =df. either
    (i) S wills e at T ; or
    (ii) there is an event f such that S wills f at T for the purpose of e.

D.3.7: S wills e at T in order that f may occur =df.
    (i) S wills e at T ; and
    (ii) S intends at T that, for some time T' and some determinate events d and d', [S wills e] should contribute causally relative to T and T' and to d and d' to f.

D.3.8: S directly wills e at T =df. S wills e at T.

D.3.9: S indirectly wills e at T =df. there is an event f distinct from e such that S wills f at T in order that e may occur.

A.3.10:   Necessarily, if S wills e at T, then S intends at T that, for some time T' very close to T and some determinate events d and d', [S wills e] should contribute causally relative to T and T' and to d and d' to e.

T.3.2:   Necessarily, S wills e at T if and only if S wills e at T in order that e may occur.

T.3.3:   Necessarily, if S wills e at T in order that f may occur, then S intends e at T.

A.3.11:   Necessarily, if S wills e at T in order that f may occur, then S intends f at T.

A.3.12:   Necessarily, if S wills e at T in order that f may occur, then S intends at T that, for some time T' and some determinate events d and d', [S wills e in order that f may occur] should contribute causally relative to T and T' and to d and d' to f.

From Chapter 4:

The next definition is rejected in the text.

D.4.1: S acts at T =df. there is an event e such that S wills e at T.

A.4.1:   Necessarily, S brings about e relative to T and T'
and to d and d' only if there is an event f such
that:
(i) S wills f at T ; and
(ii) [S wills f] contributes causally relative to T
and T' and to d and d' to e.

D.4.2: S brings about e unrestrictedly relative to T and
T' =df. there is an event f such that:
(i) S wills f at T ; and
(ii) [S wills f] contributes causally relative to T
and T' to e.

The next definition is rejected in the text.

D.4.3.a: S acts relative to T and T' =df. there is an event
e such that S brings about e unrestrictedly relative to T and T'.

D.4.4: S brings about e restrictedly relative to T and T'
=df.
(i) S wills e at T ; and
(ii) [S wills e] contributes causally relative to T
and T' to e.

D.4.5: S accomplishes e relative to T and T' =df. there
is an event f such that:
(i) S wills f at T in order that e may occur; and
(ii) [S wills f in order that e may occur] contributes causally relative to T and T' to e.

D.4.6: e constitutes f at T =df.
(i) e occurs at T ;
(ii) f occurs at T ;

(iii) there are an event g and a time T' such that g contributes causally relative to T' and T to e; and

(iv) for any event g and any time T', if g contributes causally relative to T' and T to e, then g contributes causally relative to T' and T to f.

T.4.1:   Necessarily, if e occurs at T and there are an event f and a time T' such that f contributes causally relative to T' and T to e, then e constitutes e at T.

D.4.7: S brings about e directly relative to T and T' =df. there are events f and g such that:
    (i) S wills f at T in order that g may occur;
    (ii) [S wills f in order that g may occur] contributes causally relative to T and T' to f; and
    (iii) f constitutes e at T'.

The next definition is rejected in the text.

D.4.3.b: S acts relative to T and T' =df. there is an event e such that S brings about e directly relative to T and T'.

D.4.8: S brings about e indirectly relative to T and T' =df. there are an event f and a time T^* such that:
    (i) S brings about f directly relative to T and T^*; and
    (ii) f contributes causally relative to T^* and T' to e.

T.4.2:   Necessarily, if S brings about e indirectly relative to T and T', then there are an event f and a time

T^* such that S brings about f directly relative to T and T^*.

D.4.9: e is composed relative to $T1$ and Tn of $f1,...,fn$
           $=$df.
           (i) e and $f1,...,fn$ are events; and
           (ii) $f1$ constitutes e at $T1$ and,...,and fn constitutes e at Tn.

D.4.10: S brings about e synthetically relative to T and T'
           $=$df. there are events $f1,...,fn$ and a time T''' such
           that:
           (i) e is composed relative to T''' and T' of
           $f1,...,fn$; and
           (ii) for any event f, if f is identical with $f1$ or...or
           f is identical with fn, then there are times T^* and
           T^{**} such that:
               (a) T is not later than T^*, T^* is not later than
           T^{**}, and T^{**} is not earlier than T''' and not later
           than T', and
               (b) either
                   (1) S brings about f directly relative to T^*
           and T^{**}, or
                   (2) S brings about f indirectly relative to
           T^* and T^{**}.

D.4.11: S brings about e actively relative to T and T' $=$df.
           either
           (i) S brings about e directly relative to T and T';
           or
           (ii) S brings about e indirectly relative to T and
           T'; or
           (iii) S brings about e synthetically relative to T
           and T'.

D.4.3.c: *S* acts relative to *T* and *T'* =df. there is an event
e such that *S* brings about *e* actively relative to *T*
and *T'*.

From Chapter 5:

D.5.1: *e* is a direct action of *S* 's =df. there is an event *f*
such that *e* is [*S* brings about *f* directly].

D.5.2: *e* is an indirect action of *S* 's =df. there is an
event *f* such that *e* is [*S* brings about *f* indirectly].

D.5.3: *e* is a synthetic action of *S* 's =df. there is an
event *f* such that *e* is [*S* brings about *f* syntheti-
cally].

D.5.4: *e* is an action of *S* 's =df. either
(i) *e* is a direct action of *S* 's; or
(ii) *e* is an indirect action of *S* 's; or
(iii) *e* is a synthetic action of *S* 's.

D.5.5: *e* is a direct issue of an action of *S* 's at *T'* =df.
there is a time *T* such that *S* brings about *e* directly relative to *T* and *T'*.

D.5.6: *e* is an indirect issue of an action of *S* 's at *T'*
=df. there is a time *T* such that *S* brings about *e*
indirectly relative to *T* and *T'*.

D.5.7:   *e* is a synthetic issue of an action of *S*'s at *T'*
=df. there is a time *T* such that *S* brings about *e*
synthetically relative to *T* and *T'*.

D.5.8:   *e* is an issue of an action of *S*'s at *T'* =df. either
     (i) *e* is a direct issue of an action of *S*'s at *T'*; or
     (ii) *e* is an indirect issue of an action of *S*'s at *T'*;
or
     (iii) *e* is a synthetic issue of an action of *S*'s at
T'.

From Chapter 6:

The next two definitions are rejected in the text.

D.6.1.a: *S* intentionally brings about *e* directly relative to
T and *T'* =df.
     (i) *S* intends *e* at *T* ; and
     (ii) *S* brings about *e* directly relative to *T* and *T'*.

D.6.1.b: *S* intentionally brings about *e* directly relative to
T and *T'* =df. there is an event *f* such that:
     (i) *S* wills *f* at *T* in order that *e* may occur;
     (ii) [*S* wills *f* in order that *e* may occur] contrib-
utes causally relative to *T* and *T'* to *f*; and
     (iii) *f* constitutes *e* at *T'*.

D.6.2:   *S* successfully brings about *e* directly relative to *T*
and *T'* =df. there is an event *f* such that:
     (i) *S* wills *f* at *T* in order that *e* may occur;
     (ii) [*S* wills *f* in order that *e* may occur] contrib-
utes causally relative to *T* and *T'* to *f*; and
     (iii) *f* constitutes e at *T'*.

The next four definitions are rejected in the text.

D.6.1.c: *S* intentionally brings about *e* directly relative to
T and *T'* =df. there is an event *f* such that:
(i) *S* wills *f* at *T* in order that *e* may occur;
(ii) [*S* wills *f* in order that *e* may occur] contributes causally relative to *T* and *T'* to *f*;
(iii) *f* constitutes *e* at *T'*; and
(iv) for any event *g*, if *S* also wills *g* at *T* in order
that *e* may occur, then [*S* wills *g* in order that *e*
may occur] contributes causally relative to *T* and
T' to *g*.

D.6.1.d: *S* intentionally brings about *e* directly relative to
T and *T'* =df. there is an event *f* such that:
(i) *S* wills *f* at *T* in order that *e* may occur;
(ii) [*S* wills *f* in order that *e* may occur] contributes causally relative to *T* and *T'* to *f* in a manner
which does not surprise *S* ; and
(iii) *f* constitutes *e* at *T'*.

D.6.1.e: *S* intentionally brings about *e* directly relative to
T and *T'* =df. there is a rational explanation of
[*S* brings about *e* directly relative to *T* and *T'*].

D.6.1.f: *S* intentionally brings about *e* directly relative to
T and *T'* =df. there are an intention *i* and a time
T* such that [*S* has *i* at *T**] rationally explains [*S*
brings about *e* directly relative to *T* and *T'*].

D.6.3:   *e* comes about at *T'*, as a result of *f* occurring at
T, as *S* intends at *T'''* =df.
(i) there are events *g1*,...,*gn* such that
(a) *S* intends at *T'''* that, for some time *T**, *f*
should contribute causally relative to *T* and *T** to
e either via *g1* or...or via *gn*, and

(b) f (in fact) contributes causally relative to T and T' to e either via $g1$ or...or via gn ; and
    (ii) there is no event g such that
    (a) S accepts at T''' that, for any time T^*, if f contributes causally relative to T and T^* to e, then f does not contribute causally relative to T and T^* to e via g, and
    (b) f (nevertheless) contributes causally relative to T and T^* to e via g.

D.6.1.g: S intentionally brings about e directly relative to T and T' =df. there is an event f such that:
    (i) S wills f at T in order that e may occur;
    (ii) [S wills f in order that e may occur] contributes causally relative to T and T' to f;
    (iii) f constitutes e at T'; and
    (iv) e comes about at T', as a result of [S wills f in order that e may occur] occurring at T, as S intends at T.

T.6.1:   Necessarily, if S intentionally brings about e directly relative to T and T', then S successfully brings about e directly relative to T and T'.

D.6.4: S intentionally brings about e indirectly relative to T and T' =df. there are an event f and a time T^* such that:
    (i) S intentionally brings about f directly relative to T and T^*; and
    (ii) e comes about at T', as a result of f occurring at T^*, as S intends at T.

D.6.5: S intentionally brings about e synthetically relative to T and T' =df. there are events $f1,...,fn$ and a time T''' such that:

    (i) e is composed relative to T''' and T' of $f1,...,fn$;

    (ii) for any event f, if f is identical with $f1$ or...or f is identical with fn, then there are times T^* and T^{**} such that

      (a) T is not later than T^*, T^* is not later than T^{**}, and T^{**} is not earlier than T''' and not later than T', and

      (b) either

        (1) S intentionally brings about f directly relative to T^* and T^{**}, or

        (2) S intentionally brings about f indirectly relative to T^* and T^{**}; and

    (iii) S intends at T that, for some time T^*, e should be composed relative to T''' and T^* of $f1,...,fn$.

D.6.6: S intentionally brings about e actively relative to T and T' =df. either

    (i) S intentionally brings about e directly relative to T and T'; or

    (ii) S intentionally brings about e indirectly relative to T and T'; or

    (iii) S intentionally brings about e synthetically relative to T and T'.

D.6.7: S acts intentionally relative to T and T' =df. there is an event e such that S intentionally brings about e actively relative to T and T'.

T.6.2:   Necessarily, if S acts relative to T and T', then there is an event e such that S intends e at T.

T.6.3:   Necessarily, if S acts relative to T and T', then there are an event e and a time T^* such that S

successfully brings about e directly relative to T and T^*.

D.6.8: S acts deliberately relative to T and $T' =$ df. there are events e and f such that:
(i) there are times $T1$, $T2$, ..., Tn such that
    (a) Tn is just prior to T,
    (b) $T1$ is not later than $T2$, and..., and Tn-1 is not later than Tn, and
    (c) S considers [S wills e in order that f may occur] at $T1$, and..., and at Tn ; and
(ii) S intentionally brings about f actively relative to T and T'.

D.6.9: S acts impetuously relative to T and $T' =$ df.
(i) S acts relative to T and T'; and
(ii) S does not act deliberately relative to T and T'.

D.6.10: S acts voluntarily$_1$ relative to T and $T' =$ df. S acts intentionally relative to T and T'.

D.6.11: S acts voluntarily$_2$ relative to T and $T' =$ df. S acts either intentionally or believingly relative to T and T'.

D.6.12: S acts voluntarily$_3$ relative to T and $T' =$ df.
(i) S acts voluntarily$_1$ relative to T and T'; and
(ii) [S acts] is uncoerced at T.

D.6.13: S acts voluntarily$_4$ relative to T and $T' =$ df.
(i) S acts voluntarily$_2$ relative to T and T'; and
(ii) [S acts] is uncoerced at T.

From Chapter 7:

D.7.1:   S brings about f directly relative to T and T' by
          bringing about e directly relative to T and T' =df.
          (i) S brings about e directly relative to T and T';
          (ii) S brings about f directly relative to T and T';
          and
          (iii) e constitutes f at T'.

D.7.2:   S brings about f indirectly relative to T and T' by
          bringing about e directly relative to T and T*
          =df.
          (i) S brings about e directly relative to T and T*;
          and
          (ii) e contributes causally relative to T* and T' to
          f.

D.7.3:   S brings about f indirectly relative to T and T' by
          bringing about e indirectly relative to T and T*
          =df.
          (i) S brings about e indirectly relative to T and
          T*; and
          (ii) either
              (a) e contributes causally relative to T* and
          T' to f, or
              (b) (1) T* is identical with T', and
                  (2) e constitutes f at T*.

D.7.4:   S intentionally brings about f unrestrictedly rela-
          tive to T and T' =df. there is an event e such
          that:
          (i) S wills e at T ; and
          (ii) f comes about at T', as a result of [S wills e]
          occurring at T, as S intends at T.

The next definition is rejected in the text.

D.7.5.a: *S* brings about *f* unrestrictedly relative to *T* and
T' by bringing about *e* directly relative to *T* and
T* =df. there are events *g* and *h* such that:
  (i) *S* wills *g* at *T* in order that *h* may occur;
  (ii) [*S* wills *g* in order that *h* may occur] contributes causally relative to *T* and *T** to *g* via *f* at *T'*;
and
  (iii) *g* constitutes *e* at *T**.

D.7.6: *f* is a side-effect of [*S* brings about *e* directly relative to *T* and *T**] =df. there is a time *T'* such
that *S* brings about *f* unrestrictedly relative to *T*
and *T'* by bringing about *e* directly relative to *T*
and *T**.

D.7.5.b.: *S* brings about *f* unrestrictedly relative to *T* and
T' by bringing about *e* directly relative to *T* and
T* =df. there are events *g* and *h* such that:
  (i) *S* wills *g* at *T* in order that *h* may occur;
  (ii) either
    (a) [*S* wills *g* in order that *h* may occur] con-
tributes causally relative to *T* and *T** to *g* via *f* at
T', or
    (b) (1) *T** is identical with *T'*,
      (2) [*S* wills *g* in order that *h* may occur]
contributes causally relative to *T* and *T** to both *f*
and *g*, and
      (3) *f* constitutes *e* at *T**; and
  (iii) *g* constitutes *e* at *T**.

D.7.7: *S* brings about *f* synthetically relative to *T* and *T'*
by bringing about *e* directly relative to *T** and
T** =df.
  (i) *S* brings about *f* synthetically relative to *T*
and *T'*;

(ii) S brings about e directly relative to T^* and T^{**}; and

(iii) there are events $g1,...,gn$ and a time T''' such that

(a) f is composed relative to T''' and T' of $g1,...,gn,$

(b) e is identical with $g1$ or...or with gn, and

(c) T is not later than T^*, T^* is not later than T^{**}, and T^{**} is not earlier than T''' and not later than T'.

D.7.8: S brings about e basically relative to T and T' = df.

(i) S brings about e directly relative to T and T'; and

(ii) there is no event f distinct from e such that S brings about e directly relative to T and T' by bringing about f directly relative to T and T'.

T.7.1:   Necessarily, if S brings about e actively relative to T and T', then there are an event f and a time T^* such that S brings about f basically relative to T and T^*.

T.7.2:   Necessarily, if S brings about e basically relative to T and T', then S successfully brings about e directly relative to T and T'.

D.7.9: e is a basic action of S's relative to T and T' = df. there is an event f such that:

(i) e is [S brings about f directly]; and

(ii) S brings about f basically relative to T and T'.

D.7.10:   *e* is a basic issue of an action of *S*'s at T' =df.
there is a time *T* such that *S* brings about *e* basically relative to *T* and T'.

From Chapter 8:

D.8.1:   *S* intentionally omits at *T* to bring about *e* actively relative to *T* and T' =df. there are an event *f* and a time T^* such that:

(i) *S* can at *T* bring about *e* actively relative to *T* and T';

(ii) *S* can at *T* bring about *f* actively relative to *T* and T^*;

(iii) *S* cannot at *T* both bring about *e* actively relative to *T* and T' and bring about *f* actively relative to *T* and T^*;

(iv) *S* considers at *T* each of the propositions contained in (i) - (iii);

(v) *S* accepts at *T* each of the propositions contained in (i) - (iii);

(vi) *S* intends at *T* [*S* does not bring about *e* actively relative to *T* and T']; and

(vii) *S* intentionally brings about *f* actively relative to *T* and T^*.

D.8.2:   *S* omits at *T* to bring about *e* actively relative to *T* and T' =df.

(i) *S* can at *T* bring about *e* actively relative to *T* and T'; and

(ii) *S* does not bring about *e* actively relative to *T* and T'.

D.8.3:   *S* omits at *T* to bring about *e* actively relative to T' and T^* =df.

(i) S can at T bring about e actively relative to T' and T^*; and

(ii) S does not bring about e actively relative to T' and T^*.

D.8.4: S intentionally omits at T to bring about e actively relative to T' and T^* =df. there are events $f1,...,fn$, times $T''1,...,T''n$, and times $T^{**}1,...,T^{**}n$ such that:

(i) S can at T bring about e actively relative to T' and T^*;

(ii) S can at T bring about $f1$ actively relative to $T''1$ and $T^{**}1$, and..., and S can at T bring about fn actively relative to $T''n$ and $T^{**}n$;

(iii) S cannot at T both bring about e actively relative to T' and T^*, and bring about $f1$ actively relative to $T''1$ and $T^{**}1$, and..., and bring about fn actively relative to $T''n$ and $T^{**}n$;

(iv) S considers at T each of the propositions contained in (i) - (iii);

(v) S accepts at T each of the propositions contained in (i) - (iii);

(vi) S intends at T [S does not bring about e actively relative to T' and T^*]; and

(vii) S intentionally brings about $f1$ actively relative to $T''1$ and $T^{**}1$, and..., and S intentionally brings about fn actively relative to $T''n$ and $T^{**}n$.

D.8.5: S prevents# e relative to T and T' =df. there are an event f and a time T^* such that:

(i) S brings about f actively relative to T and T^*;

(ii) it is not possible# that e occur at T' and f occur at T^*; and

(iii) it is possible# that e occur at T'.

D.8.6: S lets# at T e happen at T' =df. there are an
event f and times T''' and T^* such that:
(i) S omits at T to bring about f actively relative
to T''' and T^*;
(ii) it is not possible# that e occur at T' and f occur at T^*; and
(iii) e occurs at T'.

D.8.7: S intentionally prevents# e relative to T and T'
=df. there are an event f and a time T^* such
that:
(i) S intentionally brings about f actively relative
to T and T^*;
(ii) it is not possible# that e occur at T' and f occur at T^*;
(iii) it is possible# that e occur at T';
(iv) S considers at T each of the propositions
contained in (ii) and (iii);
(v) S accepts at T each of the propositions contained in (ii) and (iii); and
(vi) S intends at T that e not occur at T'.

D.8.8: S intentionally lets# at T e happen at T' =df.
there are an event f and times T''' and T^* such
that:
(i) S intentionally omits at T to bring about f
actively relative to T''' and T^*;
(ii) it is not possible# that e occur at T' and f occur at T^*;
(iii) it is possible# that e occur at T';
(iv) S considers at T each of the propositions
contained in (ii) and (iii);
(v) S accepts at T each of the propositions contained in (ii) and (iii);
(vi) S intends at T that e occur at T'; and
(vii) e occurs at T'.

D.8.9:   *S* merely lets# at *T e* happen at *T'* =df.
        (i) *S* lets# at *T e* happen at *T'*; and
        (ii) there is no time T^* such that *S* brings about
e actively relative to T^* and *T'*.

From Chapter 9:

D.9.1:   *S* decides$_1$ *e* at *T* =df.
        (i) *S* intends *e* at *T* ; and
        (ii) there is a time *T'* such that
           (a) *T'* is just prior to *T*, and
           (b) *S* does not intend *e* at *T'*.

D.9.2:   *S* decides$_2$ *e* at *T* =df. there is an event *f* such
that *S* wills *f* at *T* in order that *e* may occur.

In the next definition, 1 is less than or equal to *i* and *i* is less than
or equal to *n*.

D.9.3:   *S* deliberately decides$_1$ *e* at *T* =df. there are
times *T1, T2, ..., Tn* such that:
        (i) *Tn* is just prior to *T* ;
        (ii) *T1* is not later than *T2*, and..., and *Tn-1* is
not later than *Tn* ;
        (iii) for any time *Ti*, either *S* considers [*S* de-
cides$_1$ *e*] at *Ti* or *S* considers [*S* does not decide$_1$
e] at *Ti* ;
        (iv) there is a time *Ti* such that *S* considers [*S*
decides$_1$ *e*] at *Ti* ; and
        (v) *S* decides$_1$ *e* at *T*.

D.9.4:   *e* is an alternative to *f* for *S* at *T* =df. there are
times *T'*, T^*, *T''*, and T^{**} such that:

(i) S can at T bring about e actively relative to T' and T^*;

(ii) S can at T bring about f actively relative to T''' and T^{**}; and

(iii) S cannot at T both bring about e actively relative to T' and T^* and bring about f actively relative to T''' and T^{**}.

In the next definition, 1 is less than or equal to i and i is less than or equal to n.

D.9.5: S chooses$_1$ e at T =df. there are an event f and times $T1$, $T2$, ..., Tn such that:

(i) Tn is just prior to T ;

(ii) $T1$ is not later than $T2$, and..., and $Tn\text{-}1$ is not later than Tn ;

(iii) S accepts [e is an alternative to f for S at T] at $T1$, and..., and at Tn ;

(iv) for any time Ti, either S considers [S decides$_1$ e and does not decide$_1$ f] at Ti or S considers [S decides$_1$ f and does not decide$_1$ e] at Ti ;

(v) there is a time Ti such that S considers [S decides$_1$ e] at Ti ;

(vi) there is a time Ti such that S considers [S decides$_1$ f] at Ti; and

(vii) S decides$_1$ e at T.

T.9.1:   Necessarily, if S chooses$_1$ e at T, then S deliberately decides$_1$ e at T.

D.9.6: S makes an attempt at T that e occur =df. there is an event f such that S wills f at T in order that e may occur.

T.9.2:   Necessarily, if S chooses$_1$ e at T, then S decides$_1$ e at T.

T.9.3:   Necessarily, if S decides$_1$ e at T, then S intends e at T.

T.9.4:   Necessarily, if S chooses$_2$ e at T, then S decides$_2$ e at T.

T.9.5:   Necessarily, S decides$_2$ e at T if and only if there is an event f such that S wills f at T in order that e may occur.

T.9.6:   Necessarily, S decides$_2$ e at T if and only if S makes an attempt at T that e occur.

From Chapter 11:

A.11.1:   Necessarily, if S directly effectuates e at T, then
           (i) S is a person and S exists at T, and
           (ii) e is an event and e occurs at T.

A.11.2:   Necessarily, if S directly effectuates e at T, then there is no event f which strictly implies e and which is such that, for some time T' not later than T, there is a sufficient causal condition relative to T' and T of f.

A.11.3:   Necessarily, if S directly effectuates e at T, then S directly effectuates [S directly effectuates e] at T.

In the next definition, "S decides f" means the same as "either S decides$_1$ f or S decides$_2$ f."

A.11.4: Necessarily, if S directly effectuates e at T and there is no event f such that e strictly implies [S directly effectuates f], then there is an event f such that e strictly implies [S decides f].

D.11.1: S indirectly effectuates e relative to T and T' =df. there is an event f such that:
(i) S directly effectuates f at T; and
(ii) f contributes causally relative to T and T' to e.

D.11.2: S is free at T to will e at T' in order that f may occur =df. for any time T^* not later than T:
(i) there is no sufficient causal condition relative to T^* and T' of [S wills e in order that f may occur]; and
(ii) there is no event g such that
(a) it is physically necessary that, if g occurs at T', then S does not will e at T' in order that f may occur, and
(b) there is a sufficient causal condition relative to T^* and T' of g.

D.11.3: S freely wills e at T in order that f may occur =df. S directly effectuates [S wills e in order that f may occur] at T.

D.11.4: S freely$_1$ brings about e directly relative to T and T' =df. there are events f and g such that:
(i) S freely wills f at T in order that g may occur:
(ii) [S wills f in order that g may occur] contributes causally relative to T and T' to f; and
(iii) f constitutes e at T'.

D.11.5:   *S* freely$_1$ brings about *e* indirectly relative to *T* and *T'* =df. there are an event *f* and a time *T** such that:

(i) *S* freely$_1$ brings about *f* directly relative to *T* and *T**; and

(ii) *f* contributes causally relative to *T** and *T'* to *e*.

D.11.6:   *S* freely$_1$ brings about *e* synthetically relative to *T* and *T'* =df. there are events *f1,...,fn* and a time *T'''* such that:

(i) (as in clause (i) of D.4.10); and

(ii) (preamble as in clause (ii) of D.4.10)

    (a) (as in subclause (a) of clause (ii) of D.4.10), and

    (b) either

      (1) *S* freely$_1$ brings about *f* directly relative to *T** and *T***, or

      (2) *S* freely$_1$ brings about *f* indirectly relative to *T** and *T***.

D.11.7:   *S* freely$_1$ brings about *e* actively relative to *T* and *T'* =df. either

(i) *S* freely$_1$ brings about *e* directly relative to *T* and *T'*; or

(ii) *S* freely$_1$ brings about *e* indirectly relative to *T* and *T'*; or

(iii) *S* freely$_1$ brings about *e* synthetically relative to *T* and *T'*.

D.11.8:   *S* freely$_1$ acts relative to *T* and *T'* =df. there is an event *e* such that *S* freely$_1$ brings about *e* actively relative to *T* and *T'*.

The next definition is rejected in the text.

D.11.9.a: *S* can immediately at *T* bring about *e* directly
relative to *T* and *T'* =df. there are events *f* and *g*
such that, if *S* were to will *f* at *T* in order that *g*
might occur, then
(i) [*S* wills *f* in order that *g* may occur] would
contribute causally relative to *T* and *T'* to *f*, and
(ii) *f* would constitute *e* at *T'*.

D.11.9.b: *S* can immediately at *T* bring about *e* directly relative to *T* and *T'* =df. there are events *f* and *g*
such that:
(i) *S* is free at *T* to will *f* at *T* in order that *g*
may occur; and
(ii) if *S* were to will *f* at *T* in order that *g* might
occur, then
(a) [*S* wills *f* in order that *g* may occur] would
contribute causally relative to *T* and *T'* to *f*, and
(b) *f* would constitute *e* at *T'*.

In the next definition, 1 is less than or equal to *i* and *i* is less than
or equal to *n.*

D.11.10: *S* can at *T* bring about *e* directly relative to *T'* and
T* =df. there are events *f1*,...,*fn*, a time *T'''*, and
times *T1*,...,*Tn* such that:
(i) *T* is not later than *T'''*;
(ii) *T'''* is not later than *T1*, and..., and *Tn-1* is
not later than *Tn* ;
(iii) *Tn-1* is identical with *T'*;
(iv) *Tn* is identical with *T**;
(v) *fn* is identical with *e* ;
(vi) *S* can immediately at *T'''* bring about *f1* directly relative to *T'''* and *T1*; and
(vii) if *f1* is distinct from *fn*, then for any event *fi*
and for any time *Ti*, if *S* were to bring about *fi*
directly relative to *Ti-1* and *Ti*, then *S* could immediately at *Ti* bring about *fi+1* directly relative
to *Ti* and *Ti+1*.

D.11.11: S can at T bring about e indirectly relative to T' and T^* =df. there are an event f and a time T''' such that:
(i) S can at T bring about f directly relative to T' and T'''; and
(ii) if S were to bring about f directly relative to T' and T''', then f would contribute causally relative to T''' and T^* to e.

D.11.12: S can at T bring about e synthetically relative to T' and T^* =df. there are events $f1,...,fn$ and a time T'' such that:
(i) for any event f, if f is identical with $f1$, or..., or f is identical with fn, then there are times T^{**} and T^{***} such that
(a) T' is not later than T^{**}, T^{**} is not later than T^{***}, and T^{***} is not earlier than T''' and not later than T^*, and
(b) either
(1) S can at T bring about f directly relative to T^{**} and T^{***}, or
(2) S can at T bring about f indirectly relative to T^{**} and T^{***}; and
(ii) if, for some time T^{**} not earlier than T' and not later than T^*, S were to bring about $f1$ either directly or indirectly relative to T' and T^{**}, and..., and if, for some time T^{**} not earlier than T' and not later than T^*, S were to bring about fn either directly or indirectly relative to T^{**} and T^*, then e would be composed relative to T''' and T^* of $f1,...,fn$.

D.11.13: S can at T bring about e actively relative to T' and T^* =df. either
(i) S can at T bring about e directly relative to T' and T^*; or

(ii) S can at T bring about e indirectly relative to T' and T^*; or

(iii) S can at T bring about e synthetically relative to T' and T^*.

D.11.14: S can at T act relative to T' and T^* = df. there is an event e such that S can at T bring about e actively relative to T' and T^*.

In the next two theorems, "can*" is to be understood as that sense of "can" analyzed in terms of D.11.9.a and elaborated in terms of definitions analogous to D.11.10 through D.11.14.

T.11.1:   Necessarily, if S can at T bring about e actively relative to T' and T^*, then S can* at T bring about e actively relative to T' and T^*.

T.11.2:   Necessarily, if S brings about e actively relative to T and T', then S can* at T bring about e actively relative to T and T'.

T.11.3:   Necessarily, if S freely$_1$ brings about e actively relative to T and T', then S can at T bring about e actively relative to T and T'.

D.11.15: S freely$_2$ brings about e actively relative to T and T' = df.

(i) S freely$_1$ brings about e actively relative to T and T'; and

(ii) there is an event f such that

(a) S can at T bring about f actively relative to T and T', and

(b) S cannot at T bring about $[e$ and $f]$ actively relative to T and T'.

D.11.16: *e* provides *S*, relative to *T* and *T'*, with the opportunity to bring about *f* actively relative to *T** and *T''* = df.
(i) *e* occurs at *T* ; and
(ii) *e* contributes causally relative to *T* and *T'* to [*S* can bring about *f* actively relative to *T** and *T''*].

D.11.17: *S* is a person at *T* = df.
(i) *S* is an individual thing that exists at *T* ; and
(ii) there are an event *e* and times *T'* and *T** such that it is physically possible that *S* can at *T* bring about *e* actively relative to *T'* and *T**.

BIBLIOGRAPHY

This bibliography is restricted to those items to which reference is made in the preface and in the main body of the text.

Alston, William P. (1967). "Motives and Motivation." *The Encyclopedia of Philosophy*, V: 399-409.

Anscombe, G.E.M. (1963). "The Two Kinds of Error in Action." *The Journal of Philosophy*, LX: 393-401.

Anscombe, G.E.M. (1969). *Intention*. Ithaca: Cornell University Press.

Anscombe, G.E.M. (1979). "Under a Description." *Noûs*, XIII: 219-233.

Aristotle. *Metaphysics*. In *The Basic Works of Aristotle*, edited by Richard McKeon. New York: Random House, Inc., 1941.

Audi, Robert (1973). "Intending." *The Journal of Philosophy*, LXX: 387-403.

Aune, Bruce (1967a). "Hypotheticals and 'Can': Another Look." *Analysis*, XXVII: 191-5.

Aune, Bruce (1967b). "Intention." *The Encyclopedia of Philosophy*, IV: 198-201.

Aune, Bruce (1971). "Comments" on Chisholm (1971a) in Binkley, *et al.* (1971): 69-75.

Aune, Bruce (1977). *Reason and Action*. Dordrecht: D. Reidel Publishing Co.

Austin, J.L. (1956). "A Plea for Excuses." In White (1968): 19-42.

Austin, J.L. (1966). "Three Ways of Spilling Ink." *The Philosophical Review*, LXXV: 427-440.

Ayer, Alfred J. (1954). "Freedom and Necessity." In his *Philosophical Papers*. London: Macmillan: 271-284.

Bach, Kent (1978). "A Representational Theory of Action." *Philosophical Studies*, XXXIV: 361-379.

Bach, Kent (1980). "Actions Are Not Events." *Mind*, LXXXIX: 114-120.

Baier, Annette C. (1970). "Act and Intent." *The Journal of Philosophy*, LXVII: 648-658.

Baier, Annette C. (1971). "The Search for Basic Actions." *American Philosophical Quarterly*, VIII: 161-170.

Baier, Annette C. (1976). "Intention, Practical Knowledge and Representation." In Brand and Walton (1976): 27-43.

Baier, Annette C. (1977). "The Intentionality of Intentions." *The Review of Metaphysics*, XXX: 389-414.

Baier, Kurt (1965). "Action and Agent." *The Monist*, XLIX: 183-195.

Beardsley, Monroe C. (1975). "Actions and Events: The Problem of Individuation." *American Philosophical Quarterly*, XII: 263-276.

Beardsley, Monroe C. (1980). "Motives and Intentions." In Bradie and Brand (1980): 71-9.

Berofsky, Bernard (ed.) (1966). *Free Will and Determinism*. New York: Harper and Row, Inc.

Binkley, R. (1965). "A Theory of Practical Reason." *The Philosophical Review*, LXXIV: 423-448.

Binkley, Robert *et al.* (ed.) (1971). *Agent, Action and Reason.* Toronto: University of Toronto Press.

Boër, Steven E. and Lycan, William E. (1980). "Who, Me?" *The Philosophical Review,* LXXXIX: 427-466.

Bradie, Michael and Brand, Myles (ed.) (1980). *Action and Responsibility.* Bowling Green: Bowling Green State University Press.

Braithwaite, R.B. (1932). "The Nature of Believing." In Griffiths (1967): 28-40.

Brand, Myles (ed.) (1970). *The Nature of Human Action.* Glenview: Scott, Foresman and Co.

Brand, Myles (1971). "The Language of Not Doing." *American Philosophical Quarterly,* VIII: 45-53.

Brand, Myles (1976). "Particulars, Events, and Actions." In Brand and Walton (1976): 133-157.

Brand, Myles (1979). "The Fundamental Question in Action Theory." *Noûs,* XIII: 131-151.

Brand, Myles and Walton, Douglas (ed.) (1976). *Action Theory.* Dordrecht: D. Reidel Publishing Co.

Bratman, Michael (1979). "Simple Intentions." *Philosophical Studies,* XXXVI: 245-259.

Broad, C.D. (1952). *Ethics and the History of Philosophy.* London: Routledge and Kegan Paul, Ltd.

Butler, Ronald J. (1978). "Report on *Analysis* Problem No. 16." *Analysis,* XXXVIII: 113-4.

Campbell, C.A. (1951). "Is 'Freewill' a Pseudo-Problem?" In Berofsky (1966): 112-135.

Campbell, C.A. (1957). *On Selfhood and Godhood.* London: George Allen and Unwin, Ltd.

Campbell, C.A. (1967). *In Defence of Free Will.* London: George Allen and Unwin, Ltd.

Castañeda, Hector-Neri (1975). *Thinking and Doing: The Philosophical Foundation of Institutions.* Dordrecht: D. Reidel Publishing Co.

Castañeda, Hector-Neri (1979). "Intensionality and Identity in Human Action and Philosophical Method." *Noûs,* XIII: 235-260.

Chisholm, Roderick M. (1958). "Responsibility and Avoidability." In Hook (1958): 157-9.

Chisholm, Roderick M. (1964). "The Descriptive Element in the Concept of Action." *The Journal of Philosophy,* LXI: 613-625.

Chisholm, Roderick M. (1966). "Freedom and Action." In Lehrer (1966): 11-44.

Chisholm, Roderick M. (1967). "He Could Have Done Otherwise." *The Journal of Philosophy,* LXIV: 409-417.

Chisholm, Roderick M. (1970a). "Events and Propositions." *Noûs,* IV: 15-24.

Chisholm, Roderick M. (1970b). "The Structure of Intention." *The Journal of Philosophy,* LXVII: 633-647.

Chisholm, Roderick M. (1971a). "On the Logic of Intentional Action." In Binkley, *et al.* (1971): 38-69.

Chisholm, Roderick M. (1971b). "States of Affairs Again." *Noûs,* V: 179-189.

Chisholm, Roderick M. (1976). *Person and Object.* La Salle: Open Court Publishing Co.

Chisholm, Roderick M. (1977). *Theory of Knowledge,* second edition. Englewood Cliffs: Prentice-Hall, Inc.

Chisholm, Roderick M. (1979). "Objects and Persons: Revisions and Replies." In Sosa (1979): 317-388.

Chisholm, Roderick M. (1981). *The First Person.* Minneapolis: University of Minnesota Press.

Copp, David (1979). "Collective Actions and Secondary Actions." *American Philosophical Quarterly,* XVI: 177-186.

Corrado, Michael (1979). "The Logic of Intentional Action." *Philosophical Research Archives,* V.

Corrado, Michael (1980). "The Power to Act." *Philosophical Studies,* XXXVII: 177-185.

Corrado, Michael (1983). "Trying." *American Philosophical Quarterly,* XX: 195-205.

Danto, Arthur C. (1963). "What We Can Do." *The Journal of Philosophy,* LX: 435-445.

Danto, Arthur C. (1965). "Basic Actions." In White (1968): 43-58.

Danto, Arthur C. (1966). "Freedom and Forbearance." In Lehrer (1966): 45-63.

Danto, Arthur C. (1973). *Analytical Philosophy of Action.* Cambridge: Cambridge University Press.

D'Arcy, Eric (1963). *Human Acts: An Essay in Their Moral Evaluation.* Oxford: at the Clarendon Press.

Davidson, Donald (1963). "Actions, Reasons and Causes." In Davidson (1980): 3-19.

Davidson, Donald (1967). "The Logical Form of Action Sentences." In Davidson (1980): 105-148.

Davidson, Donald (1969). "The Individuation of Events" (with Criticism, Comment, and Defence). In Davidson (1980): 163-180.

Davidson, Donald (1970). "Events as Particulars." In Davidson (1980): 181-7.

Davidson, Donald (1971). "Agency." In Davidson (1980): 43-61.

Davidson, Donald (1973). "Freedom to Act." In Davidson (1980): 63-81.

Davidson, Donald (1978). "Intending." In Davidson (1980): 83-102.

Davidson, Donald (1980). *Essays on Actions and Events.* Oxford: at the Clarendon Press.

Davies, Kim (1981). "Killing People Intentionally, by Chance." *Analysis*, XLI: 156-9.

Davies, Kim (1982). "Intentionality: Spontaneous Ascription and Deep Intuition." *Analysis*, XLII: 169-171.

Davis, Lawrence H. (1979). *Theory of Action.* Englewood Cliffs: Prentice-Hall, Inc.

Davis, Lawrence H. (1980). "Wayward Causal Chains." In Bradie and Brand (1980): 55-65.

Donagan, Alan (1979). "Chisholm's Theory of Agency." In Sosa (1979): 215-229.

Donnellan, Keith S. (1967). "Reasons and Causes." *The Encyclopedia of Philosophy*, VII: 85-8.

Dretske, Fred I. (1977). "Referring to Events." *Midwest Studies in Philosophy*, II: 90-9.

Dworkin, Gerald (1970). "Acting Freely." *Noûs*, IV: 367-383.

Edwards, Paul (1958). "Hard and Soft Determinism." In Hook (1958); 117-125.

Ehman, Robert R. (1967). "Causality and Agency." *Ratio*, IX: 140-154.

Evans, J.L. (1955). "Choice." *The Philosophical Quarterly*, V: 303-315.

Farrell, Robert (1981). "Metaphysical Necessity Is Not Logical Necessity." *Philosophical Studies*, XXXIX: 141-154.

Feinberg, Joel (1965). "Action and Responsibility." In White (1968): 95-119.

Fitzgerald, P.J. (1961). "Voluntary and Involuntary Acts." In White (1968): 120-143.

Foley, Richard (1977). "Deliberate Action." *The Philosophical Review*, LXXXVI: 58-69.

Frankfurt, Harry G. (1969). "Alternate Possibilities and Moral Responsibility." *The Journal of Philosophy*, LXVI: 829-839.

Frankfurt, Harry G. (1971). "Freedom of the Will and the Concept of a Person." *The Journal of Philosophy*, LXVIII: 5-20.

Frankfurt, Harry G. (1978). "The Problem of Action." *American Philosophical Quarterly*, XV: 157-162.

Glasgow, W.D. (1957). "On Choosing." *Analysis*, XVII: 135-9.

Goldberg, Bruce (1965). "Can a Desire Be a Cause?" *Analysis*, XXV: 70-2.

Goldman, Alvin I. (1970). *A Theory of Human Action*. Princeton: Princeton University Press.

Goldman. Alvin I. (1976). "The Volitional Theory Revisited." In Brand and Walton (1976): 67-84.

Gordon, Lorenne M. (1966). "The Range of Application of 'Voluntary', 'Not Voluntary', and 'Involuntary'." *Analysis*, XXVI: 149-152.

Gorr, Michael (1979). "Omissions." *Tulane Studies in Philosophy*, XXVIII: 93-102.

Gorr, Michael and Horgan, Terence (1982). "Intentional and Unintentional Actions." *Philosophical Studies*, LXI: 251-262.

Green, O.H. (1979). "Refraining and Responsibility." *Tulane Studies in Philosophy*, XXVIII: 103-113.

Grice, H.P. (1971). "Intention and Uncertainty." *Proceedings of the British Academy*, LVII: 263-279.

Griffiths, A. Phillips (ed.) (1967). *Knowledge and Belief.* Oxford: Oxford University Press.

Grimm, Robert (1977). "Eventual Change and Action Identity." *American Philosophical Quarterly*, XIV: 221-9.

Grimm, Robert (1980). "Purposive Actions." *Philosophical Studies*, XXXVIII: 235-259.

Gruner, Rolf (1976). "On the Actions of Social Groups." *Inquiry*, XIX: 443-454.

Hacker, P.M.S. (1982). "Events, Ontology and Grammar." *Philosophy*, LVII: 477-486.

Harman, Gilbert (1976). "Practical Reasoning." *The Review of Metaphysics*, XXIX: 431-463.

Hart, H.L.A. (1968). "Acts of Will and Responsibility." Reprinted in his *Punishment and Responsibility*. Oxford: at the Clarendon Press: 90-112.

Hilpinen, Risto (ed.) (1981). *New Studies in Deontic Logic.* Dordrecht: D. Reidel Publishing Co.

Hobbes, Thomas (1651). *Leviathan*. Edited by Michael Oakeshott. New York: Collier Books, 1962.

Hook, Sidney (ed.) (1958). *Determinism and Freedom in the Age of Modern Science*. London: Collier-Macmillan, Ltd.

Horgan, Terence E. (1978). "The Case Against Events." *The Philosophical Review*, LXXXVII: 28-47.

Hornsby, Jennifer (1980). *Actions*. London: Routledge and Kegan Paul, Ltd.

Hospers, John (1958). "What Means This Freedom?" In Hook (1958): 126-142.

Hume, David (1777). *An Inquiry Concerning Human Understanding*. Edited by Charles W. Hendel. Indianapolis: the Bobbs-Merrill Co., Inc., 1955.

Husak, Douglas N. (1980). "Omissions, Causation and Liability." *The Philosophical Quarterly*, XXX: 318-326.

James, William (1884). "The Dilemma of Determinism." In his *Essays on Faith and Morals*. Cleveland: World Publishing, 1962.

Kant, Immanuel (1781/7). *Critique of Pure Reason*. Translated by Norman Kemp Smith. New York: St. Martin's Press, 1929.

Kenny, Anthony (1966). "Intention and Purpose." *The Journal of Philosophy*, LXIII: 642-651.

Kim, Jaegwon (1973). "Causation, Nomic Subsumption, and the Concept of an Event." *The Journal of Philosophy*, LXX: 217-236.

Kim, Jaegwon (1976). "Events as Property Exemplifications." In Brand and Walton (1976): 159-177.

Kim, Jaegwon (1977). "Causation, Emphasis, and Events." *Midwest Studies in Philosophy*, II: 100-3.

Kim, Jaegwon (1979). "States of Affairs, Events, and Propositions." In Sosa (1979): 147-162.

Kleinig, John (1976). "Good Samaritanism." *Philosophy and Public Affairs*, V: 382-407.

Kraemer, Eric Russert (1978). "Intentional Action, Chance and Control." *Analysis*, XXXVIII: 116-7.

Lambert, Karel (ed.) (1969). *The Logical Way of Doing Things*. New Haven: Yale University Press.

Lehrer, Keith (1966a). "An Empirical Disproof of Determinism?" In Lehrer (1966b): 175-202.

Lehrer, Keith (ed.) (1966b). *Freedom and Determinism*. New York: Random House, Inc.

Lehrer, Keith (1976). "'Can' in Theory and Practice: A Possible Worlds Analysis." In Brand and Walton (1976): 241-270.

Locke, John (1689). *An Essay Concerning Human Understanding*. Edited by Maurice Cranston. New York: Collier Books, 1965.

Lombard, Lawrence Brian (1974). "A Note on Level-Generation and the Time of a Killing." *Philosophical Studies*, XXVI: 151-2.

Londey, David (1978). "On the Actions of Teams." *Inquiry*, XXI: 213-221.

Lowe, E.J. (1978). "Neither Intentional Nor Unintentional." *Analysis*, XXXVIII: 117-8.

Lowe, E.J. (1980). "Peacocke and Kraemer on Butler's Problem." *Analysis*, XL: 113-8.

Lowe, E.J. (1982). "Intentionality and Intuition: A Reply to Davies." *Analysis*, XLII: 85.

Lucas, J.R. (1970). *The Freedom of the Will*. Oxford: at the Clarendon Press.

Mack, Eric (1980). "Bad Samaritanism and the Causation of Harm." *Philosophy and Public Affairs*, IX: 230-259.

Mackie, John L. (1965). "Causes and Conditions." *American Philosophical Quarterly*, I: 245-264.

Mackie, John L. (1977). *Ethics: Inventing Right and Wrong*. Harmondsworth: Penguin Books, Ltd.

Madden, Edward H. (1982). "Commonsense and Agency Theory." *The Review of Metaphysics*, XXXVI: 319-341.

McCann, Hugh (1975). "Trying, Paralysis, and Volition." *The Review of Metaphysics*, XXVIII: 423-442.

Meiland, J.W. (1963). "Are There Unintentional Actions?" *The Philosophical Review*, LXXII: 377-381.

Melden, A.I. (1961). *Free Action*. London: Routledge and Kegan Paul, Ltd.

Mill, John Stuart (1874). "The Freedom of the Will." In Berofsky (1966): 159-174.

Moore, George Edward (1912). *Ethics*. Oxford: Oxford University Press.

Moore, George Edward (1953). *Some Main Problems of Philosophy*. London: George Allen and Unwin, Ltd.

Moore, Robert E. (1979). "Refraining." *Philosophical Studies*, XXXVI: 407-424.

Neely, Wright (1974). "Freedom and Desire." *The Philosophical Review*, LXXXIII: 32-54.

Nichols, Kenneth E. (1973). *The Concept of Choice*. Doctoral dissertation, University of Massachusetts at Amherst.

Nowell-Smith, P.H. (1954a). "Determinists and Libertarians." *Mind*, LXIII: 317-337.

Nowell-Smith, P.H. (1954b). *Ethics*. Harmondsworth: Penguin Books, Ltd.

Nowell-Smith, P.H. (1958). "Choosing, Deciding and Doing." *Analysis*, XVIII: 63-9.

Nowell-Smith, P.H. (1960). "Ifs and Cans." In Berofsky (1966): 322-339.

O'Shaughnessy, Brian (1973). "Trying (as the Mental Pineal Gland)." *The Journal of Philosophy*, LXX: 365-386.

Pollock, John L. (1979). "Chisholm on States of Affairs." In Sosa (1979): 163-175.

Prichard, H.A. (1949). "Acting, Willing, Desiring." In White (1968): 59-69.

Ranken, Nani L. (1967). "The 'Unmoved' Agent and the Ground of Responsibility." *The Journal of Philosophy*, LXIV: 403-8.

Reid, Thomas (1788). *Essays on the Active Powers of the Human Mind*. Cambridge, Mass.: The M.I.T. Press, 1969.

Rescher, Nicholas (1970). "On the Characterization of Actions." In Brand (1970): 247-254.

Richard, Mark (1981). "Temporalism and Eternalism." *Philosophical Studies*, XXXIX: 1-13.

Roberts, Joy H. (1979). "Activities and Performances Considered as Objects and Events." *Philosophical Studies*, XXXV: 171-185.

Ross, David (1978). "He Loads the Gun, Not the Dice." *Analysis*, XXXVIII: 114-5.

Ross, Glenn (1982). "Knowledge and Intentional Action." *Philosophical Studies*, XLI: 263-6.

Rowe, William L. (1982). "Two Criticisms of the Agency Theory." *Philosophical Studies*, XLII: 363-378.

Russell, Bertrand (1959). *The Problems of Philosophy*. London: Oxford University Press.

Ryckman, Tom (1978). "Kim on Chisholm's Reduction of Events and Propositions to States of Affairs." Xeroxed.

Ryle, Gilbert (1949). *The Concept of Mind*. New York: Barnes and Noble.

Schlick, Moritz (1939). "When Is a Man Responsible?" In Berofsky (1966): 54-63.

Sellars, Wilfrid (1966a). "Thought and Action." In Lehrer (1966b): 105-139.

Sellars, Wilfrid (1966b). "Fatalism and Determinism." In Lehrer (1966b): 141-174.

Sellars, Wilfrid (1969). "Metaphysics and the Concept of a Person." In Lambert (1969): 219-252.

Sellars, Wilfrid (1976). "Volitions Re-Affirmed." In Brand and Walton (1976): 47-66.

Slote, Michael A. (1980). "Understanding Free Will." *The Journal of Philosophy*, LXXVII: 136-151.

Sosa, Ernest (ed.) (1979). *Essays on the Philosophy of Roderick M. Chisholm.* Amsterdam: Editions Rodopi N.V.

Spinoza, Benedict de (1677). *The Ethics.* Translated by R.H.M. Elwes. Garden City: Doubleday and Co., Inc., 1960.

Steinbock, Bonnie (ed.) (1980). *Killing and Letting Die.* Englewood Cliffs: Prentice-Hall, Inc.

Stevenson, Charles L. (1938). "Ethical Judgments and Avoidability." In his *Facts and Values.* New Haven: Yale University Press: 138-152.

Stiffler, Eric (1981). "Butler's Problem Again." *Analysis,* XLI: 216-8.

Stoutland, Frederick (1968). "Basic Actions and Causality." *The Journal of Philosophy,* LXV: 467-475.

Talbott, Thomas B. (1979). "Indeterminism and Chance Occurrences." *The Personalist,* LX: 253-261.

Taylor, Richard (1958). "Determinism and the Theory of Agency." In Hook (1958): 224-230.

Taylor, Richard (1966). *Action and Purpose.* Englewood Cliffs: Prentice-Hall, Inc.

Taylor, Richard (1967). "Causation." *The Encyclopedia of Philosophy,* II: 56-66.

Thalberg, Irving (1962). "Intending the Impossible." *Australasian Journal of Philosophy,* XL: 49-56.

Thalberg, Irving (1971). "Singling Out Actions, Their Properties and Components." *The Journal of Philosophy,* LXVIII: 781-6.

Thalberg, Irving (1976). "How Does Agent Causality Work?" In Brand and Walton (1976): 213-238.

Thalberg, Irving (1978). "Hierarchical Analyses of Unfree Action." *Canadian Journal of Philosophy*, VIII: 211-226.

Thalberg, Irving (1979). "Socialization and Autonomous Behavior." *Tulane Studies in Philosophy*, XXVIII: 21-37.

Thomson, Judith Jarvis (1971). "The Time of a Killing." *The Journal of Philosophy*, LXVIII: 115-132.

Thomson, Judith Jarvis (1977). *Acts and Other Events*. Ithaca: Cornell University Press.

Tichy, Pavel and Oddie, Graham (1983). "Ability and Freedom." *American Philosophical Quarterly*, XX: 135-147.

Unger, Peter (1977). "Impotence and Causal Determinism." *Philosophical Studies*, XXXI: 289-305.

Urmson, J.O. (1952). "Motives and Causes." In White (1968): 153-165.

Walton, Douglas N. (1979). "Relatedness in Intensional Action Chains." *Philosophical Studies*, XXXVI: 175-223.

Walton, Douglas N. (1980). "Omitting, Refraining and Letting Happen." *American Philosophical Quarterly*, XVII: 319-326.

Ware, Robert (1973). "Acts and Action." *The Journal of Philosophy*, LXX: 403-418.

Watson, Gary (1975). "Free Agency." *The Journal of Philosophy*, LXXII: 205-220.

Weinryb, Elazar (1980). "Omissions and Responsibility." *The Philosophical Quarterly*, XXX: 1-18.

White, Alan R. (ed.) (1968). *The Philosophy of Action*. Oxford: Oxford University Press.

Whittier, Duane H. (1965). "Causality and the Self." *The Monist,* XLIX: 290-303.

Wierenga, Edward R. (1974). *Three Theories of Events.* Doctoral dissertation, University of Massachusetts at Amherst.

Wittgenstein, Ludwig (1953). *Philosophical Investigations.* Translated by G.E.M. Anscombe. New York: The Macmillan Co.

Wolterstorff, Nicholas (1979). "Can Ontology Do Without Events?" In Sosa (1979): 177-201.

Wright, Georg Henrik von (1963). *Norm and Action: A Logical Enquiry.* London: Routledge and Kegan Paul, Ltd.

Wright, Georg Henrik von (1971). *Explanation and Understanding.* Ithaca: Cornell University Press.

Wright, Georg Henrik von (1981). "On the Logic of Norms and Actions." In Hilpinen (1981): 3-35.

Wright, Larry (1974). "Emergency Behavior." *Inquiry,* XVII: 43-7.

Zimmerman, Michael J. (1981a). "'Can,' Compatibilism, and Possible Worlds." *Canadian Journal of Philosophy,* XI: 679-691.

Zimmerman, Michael J. (1981b). "Taking Some of the Mystery Out of Omissions." *Southern Journal of Philosophy,* XIX: 541-554.

Zimmerman, Michael J. (1982). "Moral Responsibility, Freedom, and Alternate Possibilities." *Pacific Philosophical Quarterly,* LXIII: 243-254.

INDEX